LOG OF THE LIBERATORS

LOG OF
THE LIBERATORS

An Illustrated History of the B-24

STEVE BIRDSALL

Color Illustrations by John Preston

1973

DOUBLEDAY & COMPANY, INC., *Garden City, New York*

Unless credited otherwise, all photographs in this book are from the files of the United States Air Force, Navy, Army, and Marine Corps.

ISBN: 0-385-03870-4
Library of Congress Catalog Card Number 74-173267

FOR SANDRA

Foreword

There were nearly eighteen and a half thousand Liberators built between 1939 and 1945, and between 1939 and 1970 they have been flown by the air forces of Australia, Canada, China, Czechoslovakia, England, Germany, Holland, India, Poland, South Africa, South America, and the United States. Their elongated sisters, the Privateers, added France to that list.

From the blackened skies above Ploesti to the smoky skies above an Oregon forest fire is a long way, in miles and years . . . too long. This book is a combat log of the Consolidated B-24 and it soon became obvious that even then only some of the units and men involved with the aircraft could be covered in these pages. My choice has been arbitrary. Often information proved elusive in specific areas, but over-all the choice of material has been broad. Some individual squadrons and groups have been singled out as exemplary of their contemporaries, and again the choice was quite arbitrary.

I have not dwelt on the intricacies of B-24 production, deciding the differences between riveting rituals at San Diego and Willow Run should be secondary to the story of what the Liberator accomplished; neither have foreign air forces or "non-combatant" units using the machines been given their full due.

While many fascinating sidelights of the Liberator story have been mentioned in passing, I have tried to be a good historian and stick to the basic story, keeping it as easy to understand as possible. The B-24 was flown in combat by the Army Air Forces in all theaters, so my breakdown of the story has been geographical, and it is my hope that any Liberator veteran will be able to quickly trace the chain of events he was a part of all those years ago.

The selection of the several hundred photographs was made the same way as the selection of material for the text, and I have tried to show, at least once, a Liberator from every Army Air Force bomb group. I am particularly pleased to be able to include, for the first time, the names of some of the

often forgotten combat photographers who took some of the most memorable
and chilling photographs of World War II. Similarly, some of the talented
individuals who decorated the noses of the bombers and gave them a person-
ality which their serial numbers never could, appear here with some of their
most impressive work.

The large, flat fin and rudder assembly of the Liberator was ideal for
identification markings, and most of the combat groups in the larger air forces
used them for that purpose. Accordingly, I have included as much information
on group and squadron markings as possible, usually in the captions to
pertinent photographs.

John Preston's paintings of some of the major models of the Liberator, along
with some of the friends or foes they might have met, set a new standard
in this field of art, and I am very proud to present them here.

One area which I may seem to have overlooked is the perpetual comparison
of the Liberator to the more glorious Boeing Flying Fortress, but during the
course of years of research into both types I have reached the conclusion that
if you flew the B-17 she was the best, if you flew the Liberator, she was. Each
type was ideal or less then ideal for the many kinds of missions they flew,
and there seems little need to rake over the coals again. After all, this is a
log of the Liberators.

Steve Birdsall, Sydney, Australia

CONTENTS

LOG OF THE LIBERATORS

I

Blood and Sand

From the air she looked like a great dead bird, swatted down and cruelly left, crushed and broken. One engine had been ripped completely from her left wing and the three remaining propellers were bent and scored into a mockery of flight.

On the nose, weathered into a faint outline, was the name *Lady Be Good,*

Reported "lost over the Mediterranean" in April 1943, the Liberandos' Lady Be Good was found here, sixteen years later. Although abandoned she had made a creditable crash landing on the hard desert floor.

and in front of that the number 64, painted in the gently stylized fashion of the Ninth Air Force's 376th Bomb Group. Corroded guns on either side of the crimped nose discouraged the approach of strangers and the shiny ammunition belts still hung gracefully from the breeches. But not a living soul had boarded *Lady Be Good* in sixteen years.

Lady Be Good had soared from the 376th's dusty Soluch runway on April 4, 1943, and headed out for Naples Harbor. The dusky pink, sandblasted Liberator was one of twenty-five aircraft cleaving the desert heat, their engines straining.

Thirty miles from the target, near Sorrento, *Lady Be Good* was leading three other aircraft, the four being the remnants of the second section of thirteen aircraft; a sandstorm during takeoff and oxygen failures had whittled down the force. It was almost dark and Naples city was a forbidden target, so the Liberators decided to abort. One of the four ran out of fuel and landed on Malta, two made it back to Soluch in Libya, and the *Lady Be Good* kept on flying.

As the hands on his watch met at the glowing number twelve Lieutenant William Hatton, the pilot, broke radio silence to call Benghazi. They gave him the inbound bearing he wanted and *Lady Be Good's* virgin crew settled down again, their first mission seemingly all but complete. They were on a direct line from Naples to Benghazi . . . no problems. Hatton did not know that his aircraft had already crossed the coast without anyone on board realizing it, and he did not know that he was now grinding away from Benghazi on a direct line from Naples, over his base, and into the Libyan Sand Sea.

As the fuel gauges relentlessly fell away Hatton ordered the crew to bail out, following them into the silky darkness. While her airmen drifted silently down the *Lady Be Good* droned ahead.

* * * *

An oil prospecting team first found the *Lady Be Good* 350 miles south of Benghazi twisted and broken. That was November 1958. The pilot of their survey C-47 reported the sighting, but as expected it failed to arouse any interest . . . this had been a battleground fifteen years ago and the desert was still littered with the decaying monuments. Still, it was a landmark in a blank wasteland and the pilot recorded the position on maps which would be passed on to a ground exploration team coming into the area. The ground team found *Lady Be Good* a year later; they became the first men to step inside her ovenlike fuselage in sixteen years. There was still brackish water, a flask of coffee, the navigator's log . . . and thumbing through the yellow-edged,

The ammo belt still undulated into the breech of the left waist gun, and a flask contained drinkable coffee. . .

The last faint pages from the diary of co-pilot Robert Toner of the Lady Be Good.

SUNDAY, APR. 4, 1943

Naples — 28 planes — things pretty well mixed up — got lost returning, out of gas, jumped, landed in desert at 2:00 in morning, no one badly hurt, can't find John, all others present.

MONDAY 5

Start walking N.W., still no John. a few rations, 1/2 canteen of water, 1 cap full per day. Sun fairly warm good breeze from N.W. Nite very cold no sleep. Rested & walked.

TUESDAY 6

Rested at 11:30 sun very warm no breeze, spent p.m. in hell, no planes, etc. rested until 5:00 p.m. walked & rested all nite, 15 min. on, 5 off.

WEDNESDAY, APR. 7, 1943

Same routine, every one getting weak, can't get very far, prayers all the time, again p.m. very warm, hell. Can't sleep. every one sore from ground.

THURSDAY 8

Hit Sand Dunes, very miserable, good wind but continues blowing of sand, every one very weak, thought Sam & Moore were all done. La Motte eyes are gone, every one else's eyes are bad. Still going N.W.

FRIDAY 9

Shelly, Rip, moore separate & try to go for help, rest of us all very weak, eyes bad, not any travel, still very weak, nites are about 35°, good N. wind, no shade. 1 parachute left.

brittle pages they came to the last penciled entries about *Naples, April 4, 1943.*

The explorers walked around the aircraft, looking in uneasy silence at the broken aircraft. There was something out of tune about *Lady Be Good* . . . no bullet holes, no damage other than that which would have been caused in the crash. It was just as if the crew had been plucked from their airplane. Extensive searches using helicopters and ground transport revealed marker triangles still pointing the way north, the path of the B-24's crew, but twenty-five miles from the Sand Sea the traces came to an abrupt halt. After four months the searchers gave up.

Then in February 1960 the oil prospectors stumbled onto another piece of the puzzle, when co-pilot Robert Toner's diary was discovered. In sparse detail it revealed that eight of the crew had linked up with each other, and on the morning of Monday, April 5, they headed out, with one flask of water, some food, and their parachute canopies for shelter. They had no knowledge that their aircraft had fluttered to earth in one piece perhaps 25 miles to the south; they were more concerned with their fruitless search for bombardier John Woravka.

As night came they grew unbearably cold and were unable to sleep, so they decided to keep moving, plodding along until midmorning of Tuesday, April 6. With Wednesday's fierce heat they began to realize they would not be able to keep moving much longer. They had rationed their water to a capful each per day, but half was gone already.

The next day they came to the Libyan Sand Sea, 70 miles from the forgotten spot where they had formed their forlorn little party. Billows of sand blew into their crusted eyes and their legs, aching unbearably, seemed to turn to jelly. They subsided into the soft, gritty sand, each man screaming inside.

By Friday, April 9, only gunner Guy Shelley, engineer Rip Ripslinger, and radioman Vernon Moore had the strength to carry on. Through cracked and stinging lips they tried to smile reassurance that they would get help and come back for the other five.

The stranded group waited through the night and prayed. With dawn their burning eyes searched the empty sky for a friendly plane, and in their ears they willed a distant hum of engines which somehow never came closer. Toner's diary entry, scrawled and spare, was his last: *Monday, April 11, 1943: No help yet, very cold nite.*

*   *   *   *

The little cluster of five bodies was found on an undulation in the dunes and the prospectors fanned out to find the rest, but without success. It was months later when two more bodies came to light. Ripslinger had fallen,

This C-47 from Wheelus Air Force Base *have made a normal landing on the desert* *confirmed that Hatton and his crew could* *floor, had they known where they were.*

twenty miles from the others; Shelley had pressed on another seven miles. Moore's body was never found, but it is not likely that he lasted as long as the other two. With the finding of the crushed body of the bombardier and his unopened parachute, and the crew's second canteen of water, the mystery of the *Lady Be Good* was solved. Had the crew been aware of what their situation was, and had they been equipped with adequate maps, or had they found the wreck of their aircraft, they would probably have survived. The will to live which carried them as far as it did makes this almost certain. But that was not to be, and after sixteen years the elusive "further information" always mentioned in the Adjutant General's numbing telegram to next of kin was forthcoming.

June 1942: Harry Halverson's Buccaneering B-24s

Tobruk, cut off and under siege, was expected to fall within days. The water supply, stores, and excellent harbor of this Mediterranean port were a valuable prize which the British intended to hold and which Rommel's Afrika Korps, with equal resolve, intended to capture. British tanks and Australian infantry had captured the city months before, but Lieutenant General Sir Claude Auchinleck knew now that their tenure was coming to an end unless something could be done. By the end of June the British had pulled back 300 miles from Tobruk to set up a new resistance at El Alamein, and there hung the fate of Egypt. General Lewis Brereton had been summoned from India to the Middle East with "such heavy bombers as were available" and that month Colonel Harry A. Halverson had arrived from the states with his twenty-three B-24D Liberators, known simply and secretly as "Halpro"; this was an air task force optimistically gathered to bomb Tokyo from China.

This élite force had been gathered together from various Army Air Force units and sent to Fort Myers in Florida for training. Two dozen brand-new B-24Ds were earmarked for them and sent to Mobile for modification, where Halpro's assistant engineering officer, Lieutenant Scotty Royce, supervised the removal of the useless belly turret, the fitting of twin waist guns on mounts he designed, and the addition of two fixed forward-firing machine guns in the nose. Fired by a button on the pilot's yoke, these were of limited effect, but the Halpro people expected their streams of tracer would have a worthwhile deterrent value during head-on attacks. Bomb-bay fuel tanks were installed, along with a cross-feed fuel system, and after about a month the Liberators were ready to meet their new crews.

At Fort Myers one Liberator was washed out due to the common problem of nose wheel shimmy, but the rest finally staged to West Palm Beach to begin the great adventure. By early June, Halpro* was intact at Fayid, an airport on the Great Bitter Lake near the Suez Canal.

Late in the evening of June 11 thirteen aircraft left Fayid and proceeded individually to Ploesti in Romania, where twelve of them bombed through solid cloud cover. Only seven of them made it to Iraq as planned, including the optimistically named *Jap Trap,* landed wheels up in the desert by Mark Mooty. *Babe the Big Blue Ox* and another turned up at Alepo in Syria; *Brooklyn Rambler, Town Hall, Blue Goose,* and *Little Eva* were interned in Turkey. There were negligible results from the mission, and no serious casualties, but Halpro was sorely depleted.

The little band moved from Fayid to Lydda, near Tel Aviv, and on an early mission *Ball of Fire* was shot down over the Delta by a watchful Spitfire . . . the crew had been improperly briefed and knew neither the colors of the day nor the places where it was permissible to cross the Suez Canal. With the gradual depletion of the force, maintenance in Halpro was a challenging job. There were no spare parts and even less facilities, but they got a mobile machine shop from the British, along with fifty Australian mechanics and some Greek aircraft workers. The latter were able to keep Halpro in bomb doors, a priority item; since aircraft had been bringing their bombs back after the doors had failed to function, Royce removed the interlock between the

* For details of the Halpro B-24os see appendix.

When Halverson's wandering B-24s hit Ploe-sti the long-range bomber strength in the Middle East was limited to those aircraft and five more Liberators of the Royal Air Force's 160 Squadron. The British LB-30s had been head- *ing for India but were temporarily detained, as was a detachment of similarly bound 159 Squadron, which had the distinction of flying the first Liberator bombing mission of the war. This aircraft flew with both squadrons.*

Halpro's Edna Elizabeth *managed to hold on longer than most of her contemporaries, but* *after a nosewheel transplant from* Hellsapop-pin *failed she was consigned to the boneyard.*

Captain Candy Sanders lifts Halpro's Malicious *into the air. The old B-24D was ditched in the Mediterranean after a later mission.*

door lock switches and the bomb release apparatus. Scotty Royce got tired of watching B-24s landing with the last three or four feet of their bomb doors swinging in the breeze, but the bomb door production line soon produced enough.

Then one day a brand-new B-24D appeared, fresh and complete in every way. The pilots viewed her with ill-concealed lust, but the aircraft came with the strict instruction that she was not to be flown in combat . . . she was for spare parts only. Royce puzzled over this stroke of genius and solved the problem by doing some midnight painting . . . the following morning the new ship bore the number of the very worst Halpro aircraft.

Halpro had originally been held in the Middle East for a single mission to Ploesti, but the survivors were still in the desert when the 376th Bomb Group landed its pink Liberators at Lydda in October. Halpro was absorbed into the new group and gave them a core of experience.

July 1942: The Pyramiders Come to the Holy Land

Late in the month Colonel Hugo Rush and the first of his 98th Bomb Group had arrived and set up at Ramat David, 35 miles east of Haifa in Palestine. On the first day of August this group, the Pyramiders, attacked a convoy 90 miles north of Benghazi sinking one of the five 10,000-ton tankers which supplied the bulk of Rommel's fuel and oil. This aerial might, such as it was, was directed against Rommel's supply lines and communications over the weeks and months that followed. By September the combined onslaught by land, sea, and air had crushed the German's chances of capturing Egypt. The wheel had turned full circle and the Italians and Germans, on the defensive, were kept under pressure. Montgomery's Eighth Army was building for its offensive in late October, and the heavies were again pressed into destruction of communications.

The battle of El Alamein began to the thunder of a night-long artillery barrage lasting into the dawn of October 23. By November 4 the Germans were retreating, with British armor snapping at their heels.

Brereton received authority to activate the Ninth Air Force in November, with Brigadier General Patrick W. Timberlake commanding the Ninth Bomber Command, the 98th and 376th Bomb Groups. On November 22 they roared in on Tripoli, the first Americans to wage war against that city since the U. S. Marines landed there in the early nineteenth century. Into the new year the Ninth continued their necessarily minor missions. Rommel's last offensive came out of the dawn on March 6 of the following year; it failed and he was recalled to Berlin. The Ninth's next job would be the pre-invasion softening of Sicily.

In April 1943 London pressed for another attack on the Ploesti oil fields, but Brereton was not in favor of bleeding his bomber strength to the detriment of the Tunisian battle and the upcoming Sicilian operations. So he told them that he was sure they could do it, but not at that time.

Rest and recreation, Pyramiders style, in September 1942. On the left is Lieutenant William Elliott, soon to be pilot of the Northern Star, *and on his left Lieutenant Roger Huff, navigator on* The Squaw. *On the right is Lieutenant Gomer Wolf, co-pilot of* Snow White.

Early in December 1942 the 93rd Bomb Group was ordered from England to North Africa for ten days to add their weight to the disruption of Axis supply ports. The crews had left muddy England with great expectations, but at their North African base they found . . . mud. Three missions were called off after rain made taxiying impossible, and when a mission was finally forced through on December 12, Geronimo's nose wheel collapsed and she buried herself in the muck. The mission was called off. A change in weather hardened the ground and left the B-24 high and dry. The 93rd moved on to Gambut Main under Ninth Air Force command, from where they attacked ports and supported the British Eighth Army. After twenty-two missions and eighty-one days the Traveling Circus went back to England, but they would fly with the Ninth again.

The new commander of Ninth Bomber Command, Brigadier General Uzal G. Ent, led seventy B-24s against the aerodrome at Bari, Italy, and destroyed over fifty planes on the ground, a force being built up to bolster Tunisia. A little over two weeks later Axis resistance in North Africa ended. It was time for Husky, the invasion of Sicily, and the heavies attacked Reggio di Calabria on May 6, the terminus of the San Giovanni-Messina ferry line to Sicily.

Brereton learned early in June that three Eighth Air Force groups would join his Ninth Air Force for the oilfields attack and before the end of the month Colonel Addison Baker's 93rd Bomb Group was in the Middle East, along with Colonel Leon Johnson's 44th, and the 389th followed in July.

Brereton held a conference about Tidal Wave, (the code name for Ploesti), on July 6, with General Ent and his staff and the five group commanders who would fly the mission: Colonel John Kane of the 98th Pyramiders, Keith Compton of the 376th Liberandos, Leon Johnson of the 44th Eight Balls, Addison Baker of the 93rd Traveling Circus, and Jack Wood of the brand-new 389th Sky Scorpions.

Brereton announced that he had decided on a low-level daylight attack, and proceeded to explain the decision: "I feel the surprise element will weigh heavily in our favor. It is necessary to insure the heaviest possible damage in the first attack. Because of the long distance involved, over two thousand miles, and the danger of bad weather, I feel that our formations might get

Dan Story's Blonde Bomber II *landed on enemy held Sicily after a mission to Naples on February 20, 1943. That day the Pyramiders had taken off into a weather front which stretched from their North African base to within sight of the target. Flying out into heavy flak and some fighter attacks, the few B-24s which had found their way to the area soon slipped back under the cloak of the weath-er, but not before* Blonde Bomber II *had received engine damage. Searching in darkness for Malta, the crew was deceived by a runway illuminated by the Germans, who shot up the colors of the day. The B-24 landed at Pachino and took some hits from small arms fire. Bombardier Ed Griffin blasted his bombsight into uselessness with a .45, and the crew surrendered. (Alberto Salvati)*

Suzy Q, (*tail marking "S"*), *the Eight Balls'* *led her group for the first attack on Rome, and* *grand old lady, to the right over England. She* *carried Leon Johnson to Ploesti on August 1.*

dispersed and not hit the target so effectively from a high altitude as they would in a low-level attack. After receiving the target folders I studied them for two weeks before making up my mind on the low-level attack." He invited no discussion—the decision was his and he had made it.

*   *   *   *

The first air attack on Rome in history was made on July 19, 1943, when the Liberators were assigned the Littoria marshaling yards, which carried all the rail traffic from Germany and northern Italy to the southern areas. Every precaution had been taken to protect the religious shrines of the city—target maps were checked by bright red squares with the instruction "Must Not Be Harmed," and bombardiers were ordered to bring back their loads rather than drop them on doubtful areas. Crewmen of the Catholic faith were allowed to skip the mission, but nobody is known to have accepted this rather incongruous offer.

Captain Bill Cameron led the Eight Balls in the battered old *Suzy Q,* one of the last survivors of the original 44th Bomb Group . . . as was Captain

Back from Rome Ripper the First, *one of the last survivors of the original twenty-three Halpro aircraft, suffers nose wheel failure.*

Nose wheel shimmy was such a problem in the early B-24s that all Halpro aircraft carried a spare nose wheel when they left Florida.

Beside the Ploesti command aircraft, Teggie Ann, *Brereton talks Tidal Wave with Uzal Ent, and Keith Compton of the Liberandos.*

Cameron. The crews approaching the city strained to see this target which had been spared so long, and with no flak and no fighter interception the planes droned unmolested to their appointed places.

A few minutes after noon the Eight Balls's first bombs whistled down on the railroad yard, followed by a shower of explosives and incendiaries which turned the yards into blazing wreckage. Only one bomb strayed outside the appointed limits, but the Liberators left the almost clear skies and flew off into an intense barrage of condemnation from the press and public, which was stilled only by the release of official reports on the bombing accuracy.

August 1943: Ploesti, the Flight into Hell

Meanwhile, the planning of Tidal Wave was going on under a cloak of utmost secrecy as huge B-24s scraped their bellies along the desert, indicating to all but the blind that a very low level attack was in the offing. Frequent mock attacks were made on a scale Ploesti built in the desert and the die was being cast.

Four days before the mission Brereton rode above the five Tidal Wave groups in General Ent's Liberator and wrote this in his diary: *The final test for the Ploesti raid was a pronounced success. I was with General Ent and the senior intelligence and operations officers of the Bomber Command, observing overhead in a Liberator, when all five groups, loaded with 100-lb delayed action bombs, went through a dress rehearsal for Tidal Wave. Almost two hundred Liberators, skimming low over the desert wastes in tight formation, executed their last practice flight. They reached the target on split-second schedule and bombed with deadly accuracy, destroying the desert Ploesti.*

The day before the mission Brereton visited his groups and talked to the combat crews. He had built seven forces from the five units; Compton would command thirty Liberandos hitting White I, the Romana Americana refinery; Baker would lead twenty-one Circus Liberators to White II, Concordia Vega; Major Ramsey Potts would lead the balance of the Circus, fifteen aircraft, against White III, the Standard Petrol Block and Unirea-Spiranza; Kane would lead his forty-six Pyramiders against White IV, Unirea-Orion and Astra Romana. The Eight Balls, like the Circus, were split into two forces. Leon Johnson would lead eighteen against White V, Colombia Aquila, while James Posey, Johnson's deputy would lead another eighteen to attack Blue I, Creditul Minier Brazi. The fledgling Sky Scorpions would be taken to Red I, Steaua Romana at Campina, by Jack Wood.

Brereton left delighted with the thoroughness of the training of the force, and looked to August 1 with optimism; he had told the Eight Balls and Pyramiders that "we expect our losses to be 50 percent, but even though we should lose everything we've sent, but hit the target, it will be worth it." Brereton had intended to go in the command aircraft, but an order from Arnold in Washington grounded him and Ent took his place beside K. K. Compton in the Liberandos' *Teggie Ann.*

Along the 40 miles of coast that housed the Ninth Air Force's heavy bombers the dust boiled up as nearly two hundred Liberators, each loaded with over three thousand gallons of gasoline and more than four thousand pounds of bullets and bombs, moved in prehistoric procession toward their takeoff points.

As the restrained B-24s thundered in the clouds of grit, thickly coated fuel trucks moved around topping off tanks with the few gallons which could mean the difference between life and death. At 7 A.M. that desert morning the lead plane of Tidal Wave, Brian Flavelle's *Wongo Wongo!,* carrying the mission navigator, pounded down the runway at Berka Two. The dust grew thicker

Ploesti, and the crews gather around their air-craft. John Palm and his crew talk by the ill-fated Brewery Wagon, *and third in line* *stands Flavelle's* Wongo Wongo! *which will crash into the sea and become the Liberandos' first Tidal Wave loss.*

Ploesti, and Colonel K. K. Compton and Brigadier General Uzal G. Ent run up the engines on the command ship, Teggie Ann.

as the minutes passed and one boxcar after another joined the formations at two thousand feet, still shaking the dust from their heels.

Kickapoo, a Sky Scorpions plane loaned to the Pyramiders to fill a hole in their force, had an engine failure on takeoff and the pilot banked and plowed through the dust to land again. His wing struck a concrete telephone pole and the ship tumbled and burst into flames. Two survivors, badly burned, got out. Bill Cameron in the 44th's *Buzzin' Bear* looked back at the boiling black and white smoke and murmured, "My God, what a way to start a mission." Bill Dabney, his co-pilot, did not answer, but Cameron could read his eyes.

As the phalanx formed up behind *Wongo Wongo!* it became possible to count heads. The Liberandos had twenty-nine aircraft up front, a pinkish force spotted every now and then by an olive drab misfit like *Brewery Wagon.* Following them were thirty-nine mottled green B-24s from the Traveling Circus,

Ploesti, and the Liberandos take to the air from Berka Two.

Colonel Leon Johnson, commander of the Eight Balls and leading them to Ploesti in Suzy Q.

The Squaw *of Killer Kane's Pyramiders* *Ninth Air Force veterans like* Chug-a-Lug,
managed to survive Ploesti and scores of other Blue Streak *and the last of Halpro,* Wash's
missions, earning herself a trip home with other Tub.

forty-seven Pyramiders, and after them Leon Johnson's thirty-seven Eight
Balls. Trailing the field were the freshly painted Sky Scorpions, twenty-six
of them. Tidal Wave had 178 airborne.

Stretched out over five miles of sky in their stepped up three-plane vees,
they proceeded in silence to Corfu. Before they were two hours out mechanical
unpredictables began taking their toll; seven worn Pyramiders were forced
to turn back, cutting Kane's force considerably, and three more from the
other groups fell out.

The force spread out as it encountered light haze and the instruction to
retain visual contact of five hundred yards between groups had to be disregarded; the three Eight Air Force groups, taught to fly the tight combat
box, began to draw away from Killer Kane's battered, slower Pyramiders.
Before they were three hours out the distance between the Circus (the second
group), and Kane's Pyramiders (the third), had widened to the extent that
they were hardly in sight of one another at all. Up front the Liberandos could
not see Kane, and the Eight Balls and Sky Scorpions were reluctantly holding
back with Kane, Leon Johnson chewing his mustache.

Nearing landfall at the German island of Corfu *Wongo Wongo!* the Tidal

Wave leader, began to go out of control. Undulating wildly and scattering the aircraft around her she rose up, slid over onto her back and plummeted straight down into the sea. One of Flavelle's wingmen dropped down to the smoking, churning hole in the blue water that marked *Wongo Wongo!*'s grave. but there was nothing left. He could not get his overloaded Liberator back up in the formation and turned back, carrying in his aircraft the deputy lead navigator. Lieutenant John Palm's *Brewery Wagon* slipped forward into the lead slot and his navigator, William Wright, was now drawing Tidal Wave across the map.

The Liberandos and the Circus turned inland, the other three groups lost from their sight. Compton was tempted to break radio silence to reassure his people, but disciplined himself, little knowing that the Luftwaffe was well

Snow White *was the flag ship of the 343rd Squadron, whose aircraft all bore characters from the Walt Disney movie. Killer Kane led* the Pyramiders to Ploesti in Grumpy, *re-named* Hail Columbia *for the occasion.*

aware of a "large force of Liberators" which they now knew was not going to Wiener Neustadt in Austria . . . Ploesti was a possibility.

At the Greek border the B-24s faced another obstacle in the Pindus Range, which demanded an 11,000-foot altitude to clear it safely, and the horizon was full of cumulus clouds towering to 17,000 feet. Compton again found himself with a vexing decision to make. Beside him General Ent's face was equally lined by concern. Collision was a terrible possibility if the planes continued on through that solid front of clouds—Compton could set his aircraft circling, then when he had gathered the formation into a huge wheeling mass, *Teggie Ann* and her two wing ships could peel off, spread out and bore into the white mountain. The others would follow in their appointed threesomes. Once through the cloud, they would repeat their circle and reform and set course again. Compton was happy and unhappy with that plan. He would beat the obstacles of the elements, but he would lose fuel and time. So he decided to climb up to the cloud tops and go through in the formation he had. The Liberandos and Circus leveled off at 16,000 feet and the crews put on their oxygen masks.

Behind, Killer Kane's Pyramiders and their vanguard of Scorpion and Eight Ball Liberators came upon the clouds. Many of Kane's aircraft were not equipped with oxygen for this low level mission, and their commander decided to employ the tactic Compton had disregarded. The three groups formed their huge circle and began churning through the cloud in threes and while the aircraft droned around Compton's two groups were getting farther and farther away.

The leading Liberators were picked up by German radar near Sofia as the Liberandos and Circus rolled across the Yugoslavian mountains, while somewhere a mile below and 60 miles behind the rest of Tidal Wave followed. Compton crossed the Yugoslav-Bulgarian border unaware of the excitement he was causing around the radarscopes below. A brisk tail wind was helping his planes along, but Kane's force was not in its path, and the distance separating them was becoming even greater.

Compton began a slithering descent down the mountains to allow Kane to catch up, but they spent several extra minutes and still the others did not appear behind them.

In the last planes of the Sky Scorpions the crews had seen two Bulgarian fighters come in for a look at them, but Kane, and Compton, could not be warned. Not knowing the mission had been discovered long before, the crews greeted the prospects with foreboding. Leon Johnson's crew on *Suzy Q* had also seen the intruders, and he was the sole group commander aware of their discovery, but he decided to observe radio silence.

Compton's planes were down the mountains and leveling off to streak across the Danube basin to the three initial points northwest of Ploesti. Compton, after months in the desert, could not believe his eyes. Beneath his plane lay a carpet of green, and the Liberandos' dull pink aircraft were suddenly out of place. Flying too low to be picked up on radar, they churned across the Danube and Compton led them over flat ground to their first Initial Point, Pitesti.

In Ploesti the air raid sirens whined; the Liberators had been in the air seven and one half hours, and *Teggie Ann* was now twenty minutes away from Ploesti. Watching the rivers and towns streaking past, Compton knew his force would go into Ploesti alone. Behind and just through the last of the mountains, Kane poured on the coal in *Hail Columbia* and raced across the plain.

Compton was past Pitesti, the first Initial Point, and was now in the foothills of the Transylvanian Alps. The B-24s slipped lower and spread out. The bomb-bay doors began to creak up the sides of the planes, and the bellies of the Liberators grinned with black, ugly mouths. *Teggie Ann* was slightly behind *Brewery Wagon* and, as they hummed over Targoviste, Compton slid *Teggie Ann* to the lead and took up the bomb run heading. Everyone followed except Palm in *Brewery Wagon* . . . he flew on over Targoviste, alone.

Radio silence was broken by urgent cries: "Wrong turn, wrong turn!" Targoviste was only the second Initial Point, and all those behind *Teggie Ann* were caught up in the error. Compton kept going, heading not for Ploesti but for Bucharest, and over the heaviest flak concentration in Europe.

The Liberandos struck a tremendous salvo from short-fused 88-mm guns. A mile behind, Lieutenant Norman Appold, a daring pilot who had originally been Halpro's first replacement, saw it all. His top turret gunner was a Royal Air Force gunnery expert by the name of George Barwell, an errant squadron leader who should not have been with the Americans at all. He began directing Appold this way and that to give himself clear shots at the gunners sighting on the huge bomber roaring along at two hundred miles an hour within fifty feet of them. Appold credits Barwell with killing the crews of six guns in their path.

The German fighters which had been waiting were thrown off by the error and were forty miles away, one tiny piece of luck for the Liberators. All manner of German aircraft were appearing before them like startled birds, but they were getting out of the way, not in it. A few Liberators were being attacked by Romanian fighters from the rear, and the tail gunner of the Circus's *Joisey Bounce* became the first loss of the Ploesti battle.

The Circus had followed Compton into the wrong turn, then Baker turned his lead aircraft, *Hell's Wench*, 90 degrees left and streaked off for the smokestacks of Ploesti. Ramsey Potts, leading the second collection of Circus ships, followed. The force attacking the White targets was now down to one group, with another heading for Bucharest and two more trailing miles behind.

Whipping a wake through the corn fields and wheat stacks the Circus closed up, fifty feet from the ground. Coming in from this unfamiliar heading, the Ploesti before them and the model desert Ploesti did not meld as they should have. Baker's target, White II, was across the city, but the Circus was going to bomb as soon as a target passed beneath them.

The flak batteries were pounding at them, sending a stream of hot metal toward the thin-skinned Liberators. The gunners answered back, and .50-calibers rained about the batteries. The Liberators got as low as twenty feet, floundering in each other's prop wash but holding desperately to their bomb run. During the five-minute run to the target guns appeared from everywhere beneath them. The air between and around the twenty-two Liberators was alive with whining shells ranging from .50-calibers to 105-mm. The noise was incredible, a crescendo of unrelieved force. The aircraft were full of the smell of cordite as the Circus raced through the gauntlet at 245 miles an hour, a torrent of metal bouncing off and through their aircraft. In the last Circus aircraft the crew saw the Liberandos turning from Bucharest to follow them, but a few seconds later they turned east, not wishing to be caught in the maelstrom that was tearing the Liberators of the Traveling Circus to pieces.

In the planes to the rear of the Circus the pilots watched pieces of junk stream past them, clunking off their aircraft and denting the metal. Swirls of smoke from wounded bombers encased them, and inside the aircraft the wounded were sweating out the moments until aid could be given them. Only the dead were free. A B-24 called *Euroclydon,* probably the most cultured name ever given to a Liberator, trailed a 200-foot sheet of flame, paused while four men managed to get out, and crashed at the edge of a village. The co-pilot of *Tarfu* was emptying a submachine gun through his cockpit window as the lead plane, *Hell's Wench,* slammed into a barrage balloon cable, snapping it. A direct hit in the nose by an 88-mm shell almost stopped *Hell's Wench* dead in the air, then more shells hit around the wings and cockpit. The wing tanks caught fire a few minutes before bombs away.

Baker decided to jettison his bombs to stay in the air, because he and his co-pilot, John Jerstad, were choosing to die. They roared on across the open fields which might have saved them and headed for the smokestacks. *Hell's Wench* took another direct hit and the right wing began to droop as the doomed aircraft surged up to three hundred feet over the target. Some of the crew bailed out before *Hell's Wench* fell over and slid back, crumpling down onto her wing. *Bomerang* and the survivors of the Circus hit Ploesti; the second wave went in as the grimy, scorched survivors of the first leaped through—*Ball of Fire, Jr.* led them out . . . *Thar She Blows* got through. At Colombia Aquila, planned target for Leon Johnson's Eight Balls, the tank

Lieutenant Colonel Addison Baker of the Flying   *sky long enough to get his force over the target.*
Circus decided to keep Hell's Wench *in the*   *It cost him his life.*

farms began to explode with devastating effect, embroiling the bombers in flame and smoke. *José Carioca,* a ball of flame, slid into a building and came out again through the other side, minus her wings. The firebrand finally imbedded itself into another refinery.

The second Circus force, led by Ramsey Potts in the *Duchess,* now had their turn. They had been briefed to attack the Standard Petrol Block and

Unirea Speranza refineries and Potts, unaware that these targets lay on his course, in the confusion veered toward the target at hand, Astro Romana, the priority target of Ploesti and Kane's goal.

Beside the *Duchess* were *Lucky* and *Joisey Bounce,* her shattered tail carrying the lifeless body of Ploesti's first American casualty. She had taken hits in the nose, and the wind whistled through her long fuselage. Then number 4 engine was knocked out and a shell blew up the control pedestal. Two flak towers laced each side as she raced between them, and number 1 engine caught fire. Somehow the pilots coaxed her through the fire and smoke and put her down in an open field . . . the survivors were dazed and under German guard as *Ready and Willing,* the last of the Circus, added her bombs to blazing Astro Romana and sped from the target.

There were fifteen Traveling Circus Liberators left after the target, ten of them damaged, when fifty Messerschmitts jumped them. Somehow the battered Liberators waded through it until the fighters left them for the other Liberators heading for the refineries.

* * *

In *Brewery Wagon,* Palm's navigator was sure he was right, but how could all the others be wrong? The Liberandos had broken away to the southeast but Palm believed in his man and tried to save the day by leading them on, only to be left all alone. Over a hill and across an open field he saw Ploesti and headed for the nearest refinery at twenty feet. Before boarding old *Brewery Wagon* he had thrown stones at her, because she was such a bad-luck ship. A shell burst in her nose, killing navigator William Wright and the bombardier. One engine was blown to pieces and two others caught fire, almost turning the plane over into the ground as three quarters of her power ebbed or died. Palm's right leg was almost shot off. He jettisoned the bombs as a Messerschmitt came off the Circus and saw his aircraft trailing her long smoke marker. One pass was all it took. *Brewery Wagon* mashed into the ground and the survivors tumbled out.

The rest of the Liberandos continued to drone toward Bucharest. In *Teggie Ann* Compton was trying to make the best of a bad situation. He and Ent decided to attack Astro Romana rather than try to rearrange the group as briefed or search out their target from an unfamiliar route.

Nearing the target the Liberandos saw the Circus battling their way through, with planes streaking in several directions, streaming smoke and shedding pieces. Flying through the flak corridors Ent decided it was suicidal to try to hold the formation and cleared the bombers to attack targets of opportunity. The Liberandos scattered, Compton and the rest dropping on anything that looked worthy of their bomb loads.

Norm Appold held his section of Liberandos in formation, and with four planes following him headed for their briefed target, White I, but they skimmed past it and bored on unknowingly. Ent sent a code signal meaning "mission successful," but that was debatable as the Liberandos wandered around the deadly sky.

Compton's planes passed Ploesti and began climbing up the foothills east of the city. The men in *Teggie Ann* saw other Liberators coming down toward them and that had to be Kane's force. Tidal Wave was spending itself in all directions. The lead force, with Compton and Ent, was headed west; the Circus had come off the targets and was virtually blocking the streets of Ploesti as it skidded through the city, and the three other forces, left behind, were rolling in from the northwest. Appold was coming in formation from the northeast.

Appold had spotted Concordia Vega, White II, which had been assigned to the now spent Traveling Circus; yet as they headed for the smokestacks they saw green Liberators rumbling through the greasy smoke on the other side. The survivors of the Circus's second force were on a collision course but Appold put this out of his mind; the shambles seemed beyond redemption, and he cast his eyes away from the Liberators closing with his at a rate of five hundred miles an hour. Then grayish shapes appeared and disappeared through the black haze to his far right and higher. The Pyramiders, with Kane up front in *Hail Columbia,* were coming in on White IV as briefed, where Ramsey Potts and the Circus had already been. Explosions and turbulence over the target flung them around the sky, but Appold's little force managed to knock out forty percent of Concordia Vega's refining capacity. Appold lifted a bit to clear the oncoming Circus ships as Kane's higher Pyramiders loomed larger. Charging through the smoke of White V Appold dropped down, followed a damp river bed, avoided guns and radar, shot out a flak tower and got all his people home from hell.

North of Ploesti, Compton's Liberandos met the onrushing Sky Scorpions at right angles; the Scorpions knew nobody else was supposed to be near them, but weathered the storm as the Liberandos dumped their loads on the edges of Target Red I.

Now the Eight Balls and Pyramiders were crossing the city from the northwest, heading for targets which were already spewing flame and smoke. The battle had been going on for fifteen minutes as the two large forces came in abreast. On the left was Kane heading for White IV, then Leon Johnson with sixteen aircraft after White V, and on his right his deputy leader, James Posey, in Jon Diehl's ship, taking twenty-one aircraft to Blue I.

Thy Pyramiders go into the cauldron of White IV.

Johnson could only see a dense black mass over where his target was supposed to be, which turned into a field of raging fire. True to form, he decided to go on.

The Liberators had been following the rail line into Ploesti, and at that moment a flak train chose to open up on the B-24s. Riding along with them, the ambusher was pouring shells into the Eight Balls on its right and the Pyramiders on its left until the B-24 gunners finally succeeded in blowing up the locomotive.

As the smoke momentarily cleared following a huge explosion, Johnson rode *Suzy Q* into the tunnel of clear, hot air and dropped his bombs. His two wingmen got through too, and Bill Cameron in *Buzzin' Bear* took the second wave in. Cameron had flown twenty-five missions and did not have to go to Ploesti. He is one of the few who does not think of Ploesti as something apart from all other experiences—it was not the roughest mission he'd flown. *Buzzin' Bear* roared away from her bombs at seventy-five feet and into the maw of the flak that had torn the Circus to pieces. The third Eight Ball wave found the black pall had again descended; the leader, *Lil Abner,* came out of it on one good engine to belly land 40 miles from the target. The leader of the fourth wave was the sole survivor, harried by fighters as he fought his way away with one engine blazing, a two-foot hole in the fuselage and a missing vertical stabilizer. The last wave of the Eight Balls at White V were four aircraft led by *Porky II.* They had watched waves three and four go in, seen two aircraft collapse at the same time and a third point nose upward and rise a hundred feet before tumbling down on its back. Three fighters were waiting as *Porky II* cleared the target and slithered into a cornfield, blazing furiously.

Leon Johnson had lost nine of sixteen . . . but there was no time to ponder Brereton's words about losses. The combined weight of his and Baker's attacks had knocked out Colombia Aquila better than any other target at Ploesti— cold comfort for the flak-torn, smoke-stained Liberators wandering dazedly through the demented skies of Romania.

The rest of the Eight Balls were after Blue Target, the relatively isolated Creditul Minier refinery at Brazi, five miles south of Ploesti toward Bucharest. These twenty-one aircraft had had the most definitive role of all, each aircraft being assigned individual targets, individual points on individual buildings. This was the way it was supposed to be as the Eight Balls approached their untouched target. The flak was murderous, but they were not flying under the conditions Johnson and Kane were going through. The lead ship commanded by Colonel James Posey and piloted by Jon Diehl was one of five in the first wave and behind were three more. The traces of smoke pots eddied across the refinery as the B-24s closed in. A flak gun chewed off part of the lead ship's tail and killed a waist gunner as the bombardier lined up his sight and the navigator vibrated bodily as his twin guns barked at a flak tower dead ahead. He and the top turret gunner knocked out the eight guns.

Diehl pulled up to 250 feet to clear the smokestacks and the bombs dropped as he cleared the obstructions and made for ground level again. Behind him *Princess* and all the rest pinpointed their bombs without losing a single aircraft over the target and flew on into the blood bath of flak, fighters and lost Liberators on the other side.

The last aircraft off Blue Target was straggling with a badly shot-up wing. The Messerschmitts pounced and shot the aircraft to pieces. She trailed a stream of oil and large and small pieces of herself as the pilot took her up and bailed out from 3,500 feet. Another of Blue Target's force, caught at the rear of an attempt at a formation, crashed and burned . . . two aircraft lost out of twenty-one which had managed to put Creditul Minier, the most modern aviation gasoline producer in Europe, out of the war.

Kane's Pyramiders were the largest single force in Tidal Wave, with the now dubious honor of attacking the priority target . . . White IV. Kane, with thick black mustache and heavy build, slumped in the seat of *Hail Columbia*. He was tough, perhaps as tough as other people were supposed to believe. With an almost poetic core, the burly Texan has been the subject of many words. Opinions ranged wide, particularly amongst the 44th and 98th Groups, side by side at Benina Main for Ploesti. To his own men he was "the best," although one Pyramiders navigator, after a day in the *Stinger* with pilot Kane breaking formation to chase fighters, wrote in his diary a simple statement: *I hope I never ride with Colonel Kane again.*

As they bored in, the target exploded at the Pyramiders. Kane sat there in the left seat, the metal spewing from the specially filled twin .50-caliber nose guns he was firing to lessen the feeling of helplessness. He watched his tracer bullets walking along in front of the ship, almost mowing a path through the haystacks which were suddenly blooming into flak positions. It was a nightmare, unreal and incredible. A train was racing along their path, shooting them down. It was impossible. The nose guns died as the ammunition was spent, 2,400 rounds in less than two minutes. Kane saw his burning target take shape in the thick black fog ahead. *The Squaw* and the other aircraft around *Hail Columbia* bucked and shuddered as the enemy metal hit them.

Then Kane was flying through the flames of the target, the heat singeing the hair from his beefy arm as it seeped through the cockpit window. The right outboard engine took a hit and Kane feathered it. Their bombs dropped into the fires below as the raging turbulence lifted the bombers, cinders, pieces of metal and everything else that cluttered the sky above the cauldron. Then

The Sandman *trails* Chug-a-Lug *across the burning target.*

There were six direct hits on Chug-a-Lug, *one hitting the top turret and killing the engineer instantly.* (*LeRoy Morgan*)

the second wave was in, and the third, and inside the boiling black mass there was a jumble of burning airplanes, dying men, aircraft ripping themselves to pieces on balloon cables and careening into buildings in the choking, blinding smoke and irresistible turbulence. The three planes on the right wing of the third wave leader all plowed into buildings, showering flaming rubble into the sea of fire. Three of the fourth wave's right-flank aircraft were also destroyed and the survivors came out into the light to find Messerschmitts waiting for them. One ship, riding out the turbulence at 1,300 feet, was shot down.

The fifth and final wave was six aircraft when it entered the target. LeRoy Morgan, fighting *Chug-a-Lug* through the air, slammed into a balloon cable and bashed out part of a wing. He was to be the last Pyramider over the target, and *Chug-a-Lug* was equipped with an automatic camera to record the results. In the turbulence Morgan's ship slewed in front of *The Sandman*, then six flak hits slammed into her, punching over 250 holes and knocking out radio, hydraulics, and oxygen. One shell hit the upper turret, exploding in the gunner's face and killing him instantly. Another banged into the nose below Morgan's seat, exploded and wounded the navigator. It looked to Morgan as if *Chug-a-Lug* had hit a bunch of chickens as pieces of shredded insulation snowflaked around the nose.

Kane, the Pyramiders' leader, was short one engine, pouring fuel into the others to get out of the mess, and under attack by fighters. He was dragging behind the rest of his survivors and there was a sudden silence and stillness which his cluttered mind could not focus on. Then he realized his top turret was not hammering above his head, the gunner out of ammunition. The Germans put five hits into another of *Hail Columbia*'s engines, shot the tip off a prop and holed a blade on another. Kane headed for Cyprus, knowing he was out of the race back to Libya.

Three aircraft decided to join him in the dash: *Hadley's Harem* with her nose shot out and a dead bombardier and wounded navigator, Royden LeBrecht in *The Squaw*, in one piece but low on fuel, and one more. Kane began getting rid of excess weight in preparation for the 7,000-foot climb over the Balkans. Behind the struggling remnants of the Pyramiders twenty-two more lay broken and consumed by flames along their path.

The Sky Scorpions' target was at Campina and relatively isolated, eighteen miles from Ploesti. Some of the Scorpions' new Liberators carried ball turrets and Wood had organized them to attack their diamond-shaped target in three waves, one directly across, the other two from opposing oblique angles. They had left Kane and Johnson at the first Initial Point, Pitesti, to proceed to their target, but as they moved on and minutes passed, Wood feared they had missed their IP in the clouds. Working on elapsed time, he made a turn,

Chug-a-Lug's *ultimate total of 105 missions earned her a ticket home.*

LeRoy Morgan and his co-pilot receive their three-hundred-hour diplomas from Colonel John R. Kane. To Morgan the burly group commander was "the best." (LeRoy Morgan)

Julian Darlington managed to crash-land The Witch *in Yugoslavia after a running fight with Messerschmitt 109s.*

brought the force around, and turned into a valley. He breathed heavily as he saw the big plant at the mouth of it, but in his second element they weren't sure . . . and they were right. Wood had turned too soon. The Scorpions were setting up to bomb a cement factory in Târgoviste. Wood realized his error and saved the plan by doubling his twelve planes back and snaking over the next ridge, trailing the other seventeen ships behind him.

Down the ravine they saw Red I and the Scorpions closed up their formation. The ground fire opened up and the Liberator gunners returned the fire as the lead ship's delayed action bombs smashed through a boiler house and plunged through their other target. One of the Scorpions slithered off the target with wings flaming to belly in, killing everyone but the top turret gunner. In the second wave across Red I Lieutenant Lloyd Hughes, bracketing the leader and on his left wing, took flak hits in the bomb-bay tanks. A stream of misty fuel began to syphon from the aircraft's fuselage. The lead plane

Prince Charming *was caught by fighters after*
the target and went down in flames.

hit a boiler which exploded as Hughes held course, with the gas stream
growing to a gush which obscured the waist window from view. Hughes passed
into the flames and his aircraft became a torch; flames billowed from the
waist windows, the top turret and the left wing. He dropped his bombs,
crossed the target area and slowed to around 110 miles an hour, evidently
trying for a belly landing in a dry river bed. He skipped over a bridge, eased
down, and grazed the river bank with his right wing. The B-24 cartwheeled
end over end, spilling balls of fire over the area. Two gunners survived.

A B-24 called the *Vagabond King* dropped the last bombs of Tidal Wave;
shot up, she immediately lit out for Cyprus. Wood had lost six of twenty-nine
but Steaua Romana was completely destroyed. Red and Blue Targets were
out of the war.

The planned orderly return of Benghazi might have been a cause for wry
smiles in the Liberators, had their plight not been so deadly serious. Stretched

out over a hundred miles, trailing smoke and jettisoned ammo, guns, and equipment, with pieces of their flesh flaking off around flak wounds, the Liberators, pink, green, and all smoke blackened, formed a sorry parade.

In the twenty-seven minutes over Ploesti few of the Liberators had escaped without more than negligible damage, and now it was six or seven hours to Benghazi. The aircraft commanders were making their decisions . . . to Turkey, or Cyprus a little bit farther, or Yugoslavia, or perhaps Malta, southern Sicily . . . or Libya?

Most decided to head for home if they could, and the tattered, scattered remnants linked up as best they could to thread their way through the endless country along the road to home.

Two of the surviving Pyramiders were from the 343rd Squadron, which had decorated its B-24s with the Disney characters from *Snow White*. Now *The Witch* and *Prince Charming* were sailing along together, and it seemed quite possible Julian Darlington's crew would be adding another hard-earned miniature witch to the rows along the nose. They linked up with *Daisy Mae* and another Pyramider and were climbing through heavy clouds as Bulgarian fighters took a crack at them. The first and second attacks were ineffectual,

Kate Smith *of the Pyramiders undergoes a thorough overhaul in Libya. She went down in the summer of 1943.*

then six Me-109s joined in. Their leader shot out both *The Witch*'s inboard engines, and the plane lagged behind. James Gunn, in *Prince Charming*, throttled back to join his friend Darlington. As he slowed the fighters hit him, and white smoke streamed back from the B-24. As the two aircraft pulled together, flame was pouring from the *Prince*'s waist windows.

The Messerschmitts came in again and *Prince Charming* turned over and dropped down in flames, burning parachutes popping from her. The same firing pass wounded four of the crew of *The Witch* and sealed her fate. Darlington hit the bailout bell and nosed down for a crash landing. Three of his people got out on the way down and saw Darlington skid the big bomber into a wheat field below them. When the smoke pall of Ploesti fell behind the battle had been far from over. Fighters chased the fleeing bombers out to sea, pecking away at them until lack of fuel forced them to return to their bases.

Teggie Ann was the first home to Benghazi, landing at Berka Two. Appold followed soon after. *Hail Columbia* was cracked up on Cyprus. As the pieces fell into place Tidal Wave's cost amounted to fifty-three aircraft: eight were interned in Turkey, forty-five lay along the route to and from the target. Twenty-three landed in Cyprus, Sicily, or Malta. Eighty-eight had made it to Benghazi, fifty-five of them battle damaged.

The morning after Tidal Wave Ninth Bomber Command could probably have put thirty Liberators up; the problems facing Colonel Ulysses S. Nero, a volatile Italian and one of the most valuable remnants of Halpro, seemed insurmountable. He had the job of turning the tattered warriors into aircraft again . . . and within a few days. Such was the sorry lot of one Ninth Air Force engineering officer.

General Brereton's first estimate of damage came from British Intelligence and it went like this: White I not reached by attackers, White II not likely to be out of action for any time, White III no important damage, White IV immobilized for six months or more, White V out of action for at least six months, Red I reasonable expectation of very serious damage, Blue I very good work.

So Ploesti was over, at least for a while. Before the Eighth's groups could return to England, they were to undertake another major operation with the two dusty Ninth Air Force groups. This was Operation Juggler, which had originally been planned to take place on August 7, but had been dogged by bad weather. Juggler was a combined assault on Wiener Neustadt, center of Messerschmitt 109 production, to coincide with a raid by English based Flying Fortresses on Regensburg.

When the English weather failed to co-operate it was decided to send the Liberators out on their portion of the plan on August 14. In all the five

The fledgling Sky Scorpions handled their Ploesti task with expertise, and among them was The Little Gramper, a B-24D with one of the most colorful careers of them all. After flying her missions she was turned over to the 491st Bomb Group to become their formation assembly ship, so they repainted her yellow all over with red polka dots.

Liberator groups were able to put 101 bombers into the air, but the trailing
Ninth Air Force complement was forced to abandon the mission over the
Adriatic. The three Eighth Air Force groups went on. The 389th's *Little
Gramper* and all the other scarred Ploesti veterans took the Germans com-
pletely by surprise. It was a round trip of nearly 2,400 miles and the sole
loss was one B-24 which was forced to land in neutral Switzerland.

An attack on Foggia on August 16 stirred up a hornet's nest, and while
the 93rd and 389th emerged virtually unscathed the cost to the Eight Balls
was high—*Suzy Q* and *Buzzin' Bear* with their new crews, and six more . . .
these eight aircraft were the only losses. The 44th's luck seemed bad.

At the end of August the three Eighth Air Force groups were ordered back
to England, and the Liberandos and Pyramiders were transferred to the
Twelfth Air Force. General Brereton's last official act as commander of the
Middle East Ninth Air Force and its proud Liberator fliers was to pin medals
on the Ploesti heroes on the polo field of the Gezira Sporting Club.

Liberators over the Adriatic.

II

That Was the Liberator

When David R. Davis, a slight, bespectacled man with a narrow mustache and receding wavy hair, patented a "Fluid Foil" on May 25, 1931, he would never in his wildest dreams have envisaged his idea going to war on more than 19,000 four-engined aircraft. But Davis had solved a problem which had defied the others since the Wright Brothers: air resistance. Calling himself a "nut" on aviation, he had started out to be a lawyer, completed the course at Vanderbilt, then found he did not want that after all.

There is a trace of bitterness in this tale for Davis. A man who shunned the glory and regarded himself as a "little fellow trying to get along," he *gave* his wing design to Reuben Fleet of Consolidated, asking only for a royalty on foreign sales. Davis had wanted to build and fly airplanes, but poor eyesight propelled him toward the drafting board, where he proceeded to become a self-taught aerodynamics expert.

During World War I he had tried to join the Air Corps, but had ended up as an anonymous private in the infantry. Throughout the 1920s he searched for some fulfillment of his aviation dream, and while he was never poor or hungry, they were frustrating years.

Davis and Bill Henry, a young journalist, were able to persuade Donald Douglas, at the time Glenn L. Martin's chief engineer, to come west, and Douglas got his start in manufacturing airplanes from David Davis; they formed the Davis-Douglas Aircraft Corporation and Douglas's first transport, the Cloudster, was built with $30,000 from Davis, who also put up the finance for the DT torpedo plane. Before the production order for the DT came in, Davis had been to Washington, looked around, realized that the military authorities were too stubborn and set in their ways for him to get along with

Sleek and shining, the XB-24, 39-680, was the first of 18,482 Liberators. She was also the sole XB-24B, and was ultimately fitted out as a deluxe transport. (Convair)

them. So he decided to sever the partnership and left Douglas to continue, with replacement finances from a colorful Air Corps man by the name of Billy Mitchell, and Bill Henry, who talked the publisher of the Los Angeles *Times* into raising the money to keep Douglas in business while the DT project went through. Leaving everything in the hands of Douglas, Davis moved on.

Living with his unique ideas, Davis free-lanced in the aeronautical engineering field, in the late 1920s joining the Bendix Aviation Corporation where he developed the first variable pitch propellers without mechanical control. All the while he never lost his primary interest in wings; he remembers that "in the old Curtiss days, everybody had a secret wing section in his hip pocket. He guarded it with his life."

Davis had wondered what *made* the wing lift an airplane. Why did the wing curve function as it did? His conception, and his answer, was simple. The curve was a living, operating thing and he departed from the previous "cut and try" methods; the early approach had been to take a wooden board and sand it down to different shapes, testing each in a wind tunnel for efficiency until the best showed itself. A step up from this technique was established by the National Advisory Committee for Aeronautics, which developed a system of aerofoil families with known lift capabilities.

So David Davis began drafting his application for the patent: "This invention relates to the construction of foils to be driven through a fluid, and particularly concerns the profile of the foil in its front to rear section. While the invention may be applied to a foil used in any medium, it has its greatest usefulness when applied in the construction of airfoils for air vehicles." The Davis Wing first appeared on the Consolidated Model 31 seaplane, which also employed Davis symmetrical shapes on the boat hull and engine housings. The seaplane was a complete success, with a top speed of 300 miles an hour, but it was turned down by the Navy. Davis flatly states his belief that this was "because it did not use an NACA foil shape." The British did not stick to rules so rigidly . . . on the basis of Model 31's performance they bought the concept of Model 32, the Liberator, and here Davis ran aground again. He notes that "the project then moved into the Big Brass category, where none of my suggestions were heeded. Imagine leaving half of the landing gear exposed under the wing!"

The extremely narrow Davis Wing was designed for high-speed performance, and on the Liberator it was combined with Fowler Flaps which slid back and down from the trailing edge of the wing to give greater wing area for better low speed performance.

Reuben Fleet, president of Consolidated, was one of the few believers, and Davis is convinced that but for Fleet his wing would never have flown. He can be excused his cynicism when he recalls being told by the best-known experts that the wind tunnel tests of his new wing just "couldn't be so."

Davis received almost no recognition, and the Liberator, far from being built around the wing as he advised, became a pugnacious, porcupine-gunned bomber which quite incongruously had the most beautiful and graceful wing one could ever hope to see.

XB-24: The Birth of a Bomber

For the United States, World War II began with a devastating air attack and ended with a much more devastating air attack almost four years later. The Liberator was hardly fully developed when the aerial conflict began, and essentially obsolete when it ended.

In June 1938 the Joint Board of the Army and Navy had concluded that "based on the present situation it is not considered probable that the Army Air Corps will be called upon in war to perform any missions that require the use of reconnaissance and heavy bombardment planes of greater practical ferrying range, greater tactical radius, and greater carrying capacity than those of the B-17." This wonderful stop-the-clock attitude was soon shattered, and perhaps the kindest words to be said for the opponents of air power are that they were naïve, lost and confused in a field of incredibly rapid technological growth.

By the beginning of 1939 America was awakening. That other heavy bomber, the B-17 Flying Fortress, had flown enough record-breaking flights to convince even the most skeptical that four-engined bombers were not winged waste. The prewar battle had been long, and as can be seen from the grand scale of early Air Corps orders, was not quite over, but those with foresight saw what was happening in an unsettled world, and they kept up the pressure.

In January 1939, General Henry H. ("Hap") Arnold invited Consolidated to present a design study of a bomber superior to the B-17. His specification was fairly open, with certain specifics—speed of the bomber was to exceed 300 miles per hour, range was to be 3,000 miles, ceiling 35,000 feet.

On the basis of preliminary data a contract for a prototype of Model 32 was signed in March, and its Army Air Force designation would be XB-24. The deadline was the end of the year.

The range factor was the focal point for the Consolidated design team led by Isaac M. Laddon; they selected Davis's design for its high efficiency, and shoulder-mounted the wings for maximum bomb stowage and easy loading. The rest of the design was more or less conventional, except for the retraction of the main undercarriage into the wings. The aircraft had the progressive tricycle undercarriage and the designers settled on a twin rudder and fin assembly not unlike that employed on their Model 31 seaplane.

The bomb bay had room for 8,000 pounds of explosives and was divided into front and rear compartments where the bombs would be stowed vertically. The fuselage keel beam formed a catwalk through the bomb bay, and the designers came up with a unique bomb door arrangement, comprising two roller-type segments retracting up the sides of the fuselage from the central keel beam, cutting down drag appreciably when the doors were open.

The big, slab-sided fuselage was generous in space by comparison to other bombers, and this led ultimately to the Liberator's adaptability. In the Model 32 there was provision for only a few hand-held .30-caliber machine guns . . . one in the transparent nose where the navigator would work, and in hatches above, below and on each side of the fuselage additional weapons, as well as a cupola in the tail for one more gun. These were innocent days.

Consolidated brought the gleaming XB-24 in one day ahead of schedule and on December 29, 1939, test pilot William R. Wheatley took her up for the first time. The Air Corps had already placed an order for an initial test batch of seven YB-24s, and an evaluation quantity of thirty-six B-24As. The French government, embroiled in war already, had committed itself even further by ordering 120 airplanes to back up the Maginot line, and the British Government Purchasing Commission ordered 164 more in 1940.

The XB-24 was powered by 1,200 horsepower Pratt & Whitney Twin Wasps, and had a gross weight of 41,000 pounds, a wingspan of 110 feet, and was 63 feet long. The test flights were successful—the XB-24's maximum speed was 273 miles per hour, a little less than the current model of the Flying Fortress, but the range was more than had been hoped for. During 1940 the YB-24 was delivered, differing from the XB-24 only in the addition of rubber de-icing boots on the wings and tail, increased gross weight, and, for a while, airscrew spinners.

This is the Davis Wing, lending grace to the box car. (Convair)

The first production Liberators were six LB-30As, bought by the British for hard cash, and these aircraft were used on the Transatlantic Return Ferry Service between Scot- *land and Canada. The four survivors operated with British Overseas Airways Corporation for a long time. (BOAC)*

When France collapsed their order was transferred to the British, and the first Liberators to roll out at San Diego were for the Royal Air Force, paid for in cash prior to Lend-Lease arrangements. These were called LB-30As, and were built to British specifications; even the name "Liberator" was British, and the first of these, AM258, flew in January 1941, five more following soon after. From March 1941 they were used as unarmed transports on the Transatlantic Return Ferry Service between Montreal and Prestwick, Scotland, a distance of around 3,000 miles. The first aircraft made the trip on March 24, and although two crashes, grimly similar, cost forty-four lives in August, they were considered an outstanding success. The remaining four aircraft carried on, eventually carrying the civil registrations of BOAC.

The next twenty aircraft were dubbed Liberator 1s, and these were the first to see operational service. Fitted out with an array of aerials and a gun pack just forward of the bomb bays housing four 20-mm cannon, they moved in with 120 Squadron of Royal Air Force Coastal Command. It did not take long for them to prove their worth. Arriving in June 1941, their range of around 2,400 miles gave Coastal Command their Very Long Range aircraft, and enabled them to begin closing the very dangerous gaps in their sea lanes.

Boldly neutral, this B-24A was one of the pioneer aircraft on Ferry Command's North Atlantic run.

In June 1941 the Army Air Corps accepted its first B-24A, one of the nine built. These went to Air Corps Ferrying Command, newly formed under the command of Colonel Robert Olds with the express purpose of delivering aircraft to Montreal for movement to Britain, with broader powers to "maintain such special air ferry service as may be required." The first overseas pilots were among the very best the Air Corps had to offer: Lieutenant Colonel Caleb V. Haynes, Major Curtis E. LeMay, Captain Carlos Cochrane, Captain James H. Rothrock, and ten other officers and twenty-one hand-picked enlisted men.

In July Colonel Haynes crossed the North Atlantic and the following month he and LeMay pioneered the South Atlantic route. In September two other B-24As, boldly marked with the neutrality flags of the United States, took part of the Harriman mission to Moscow by way of England. One carried on from Russia through the Middle East, India, Singapore, Australia, New Guinea, Wake, and Hawaii. The other flew home via Egypt, Central Africa, the South Atlantic, and South America. In another Air Corps Ferrying

Command flight, Captain James Rothrock and his observer, Captain Elliott Roosevelt, took the first aircraft over the Greenland icecap.

Air Corps Ferrying Command Liberators flew with a crew of seven, and their original mission had been to carry diplomatic passengers and mail from Washington to Prestwick, Scotland, and back again. They boarded up their aircraft's bomb bays, put benches along the sides, and carried two unmounted .50-caliber machine guns as "baggage." Flying at around 9,000 feet they usually crossed the Atlantic in around nine hours, with all the luxury of sheepskin clothing, box lunches, and thermos coffee.

Two of the B-24As were scheduled to fly reconnaissance over Japanese installations in the Marshalls and Carolines, particularly Truk, but only one had arrived when the Japanese attacked, and this machine, 40-2370, was destroyed at Hickam Field. It was the first American aircraft lost in World War II.

LIBERATOR II: A Bomber for All Seasons

The Liberator II was unique to the Royal Air Force, her extended nose adding nearly three feet to the aircraft's length. Two Boulton-Paul four-gun .303 turrets replaced some of the hand-held guns, one being fitted in the mid-upper position, the other in the tail. The first Liberator II, AL503, crashed on June 2, 1941, killing William Wheatley, but this bad beginning hardly set a trend. The second aircraft, AL504, became Winston Churchill's personal transport, *Commando.* This aircraft carried Churchill to his first wartime meeting with Stalin in Moscow, slipping over nearly five thousand square miles of German-occupied territory in doing so. In 1944 she was modified almost to the Navy's RY-3 standard, with the extended fuselage and single tail. She was finally lost off the Azores in March 1945, soon after completing a mammoth 45,000 mile flight around the British Empire. The Liberator IIs, serialed AL503 to AL641 (with a ring-in, FP685, replacing the crashed aircraft), had the most colorful and varied careers of all Liberators. Royal Air Force Bomber Command's 159 and 160 Squadrons became the first bombing units to use the Liberator, and Liberator IIs equipped three squadrons of Coastal Command. Some, unarmed, went to the Return Ferry Service and BOAC, and later the Australian airline, Qantas. Others served with Southern Cross Airways in the Pacific.

The British were to have received 139 Liberator IIs, but the fifty-one undelivered aircraft were taken over by the United States immediately after Pearl Harbor. Three of these LB-30s (as they were called in U. S. service), joined two Flying Fortresses in the first bombing attack by American-manned Liberators, thundering over Kendari on Celebes on January 16, 1942.

In the desperate days following December 7 three of the LB-30s were sent to Alaska, five more to Hawaii, eight were used in the transport role and three were used for training; seventeen were sent to the Panama Canal area where an impending Japanese attack was feared. Carrying British radar but a Martin upper turret and other American modifications, the seventeen Liberator IIs left for the Canal Zone as part of the 6th Bomb Group and were at their stations in April 1942.

But no one ever came, and these Liberators flew the most unrewarding patrols of the war. After two long, dull years, punctuated by a series of operational accidents which accounted for ten of the aircraft, the other seven were recalled in May 1944. They were converted to the C-87 configuration and moved on to Consairway, the contract transport service operated by Consolidated for the Air Transport Command . . . and all survived the war.

B-24D: A Promise Fulfilled

The XB-24 had been reworked into the XB-24B, with self-sealing tanks,

This B-24D-5-CO flew with the Eight Balls in England.

B-24Ds equipped units of the Army Air Forces Antisubmarine Command, including the 479th and 480th Antisubmarine Groups. The 479th began operations from Saint-Eval in Cornwall on July 13, 1943, and operated smoothly under the operational control of Coastal Command. This ship is from Colonel Jack Roberts's 480th Group which had the primary mission of patrolling the Atlantic north and west from Port Lyautey in Morocco. With their hastily sprayed white bellies, adopted after the British had found this rendered the U-boat attacker invisible for the greatest period of time, the 480th had many good days among enemy submarines concentrated off the coast of Portugal to break up convoys bound for the Mediterranean. The 479th was disbanded in November 1943, and the 480th in January of the following year.

armor, and turbosuperchargers which increased the speed to 310 miles per hour, and thus the Liberator had met the initial requirements.

Nine B-24Cs resulted, equipped with the Martin upper turret and Consolidated tail turret, each housing the twin .50-caliber guns which became standard armament on USAAF bombers.

Then along came the B-24D. Consolidated built 2,415 at San Diego and 303 more at Fort Worth, with Douglas contributing ten from Tulsa, Oklahoma. The first B-24Ds retained the hand-held nose gun, a Bendix lower turret and four more guns in the other two positions. Later aircraft were fitted with a single ventral gun, fired through the camera hatch, and still later two more nose guns were added, plus two waist guns—ten machine guns in all.

Bomb load was increased to 12,800 pounds, and absolute maximum gross weight ultimately climbed to 71,200 pounds and the hand-held tunnel gun was finally replaced by the retractable Sperry ball turret.

On October 9 1942, B-24Ds joined the Eighth Air Force in an attack against Lille. From the 93rd Bomb Group, these planes and their crews, along with the following "Eight Balls," put the B-24D to the first real combat test. The tactical lessons learned were noted by 8th Bomber Command in a report entitled *The First 1100 Bombers,* and the conclusions they drew were that "the B-24D is a better bombardment airplane than the B-17F on the premise that the purpose of a bomber is to 'pick them up and drop them over there.' The B-24 picks more of them up and carries them further and faster, because of larger bomb capacity, greater range and the opportunity offered of converting greater fuel capacity into higher throttle settings. Not enough experience has been gained with the B-24 to state that it can absorb an amount of punishment from antiaircraft and fighters equal to the remarkable durability of the B-17, but there is as yet no evidence to the contrary. In spite of the absence of a satisfactory under-turret, B-24s have shown defensive fire-power against fighters comparable to the B-17s and have returned safely to base after sustaining major damage. A lone B-24 on anti-submarine patrol was attacked by six Ju-88s, shot down one for certain and one probable, dispersed the rest of the formation and returned home unscathed."

The Royal Air Force received B-24Ds with Anglicized armament as Liberator IIIs, or as Lend-Lease Liberator IIIAs with American equipment, in mid-1942. Nearly all went to Coastal Command, some being fitted with retracting chin and belly radar domes, the Leigh Light under the right wing, greater fuel capacity due to less armor, and sometimes provision for eight rockets on stub wings.

The Navy had received a quantity of B-24Ds as PB4Y-1s, and these equipped their early Liberator squadrons. VB-101 and 102 went to the Pacific, and VB-103 had flown Liberators from Argentia in Newfoundland for three months before moving to St. Eval, Cornwall, in August 1943, where they worked with Coastal Command in the Bay of Biscay for twenty-two months more. One VB-103 story which deserves a place here is that of Lieutenant C. F. Willis: on January 20, 1944, a British ship shot his Liberator to pieces before he could get out of the way, but she limped back as far as Wales. With the hydraulics out Willis managed to lower one wheel by manual crank, but the other stayed up in the wing. The pilot brought the lop-sided Liberator in perfectly on his one wheel, and narrowly averted a real tragedy.

On D-Day the Navy squadrons supported the invasion with Coastal Command, corking up the entire southern entrance to the English Channel, aircraft patrolling the area at regular thirty-minute intervals. By December

The British called this version of the B-24D the Liberator G.R.V. when converted for Coastal Command. These 120 Squadron aircraft carried the Leigh Light under the right wing, were stripped of the Martin upper turret, and carried a multitude of aerials. The third aircraft in line, FL952, is equipped with a chin radome.

The Navy received 977 Liberators, beginning with B-24Ds. This aircraft is from the second batch of forty-eight aircraft, Bureau Numbers 32288 through 32335, and she served with Fleet Air Wing Seven in the Atlantic.

1943 there had been nine Navy Liberators squadrons in the Atlantic, all making it tougher for the U-boats.

C-87: An Evil, Bastard Contraption

In other roles the B-24Ds became the first Liberator Expresses, the original C-87 being the result of a crash-landing by a B-24D early in 1942. The aircraft was repaired and flown to San Diego with fixed landing gear, where Isaac Laddon and an Army Air Force representative organized a three-week modification. Laddon recalls that "we did it mostly by waving our arms and pointing to show where we wanted equipment taken out, a deck laid, or openings cut."

The British called these aircraft Liberators C.VIIs, and they could carry twenty passengers and their crew of five—in all 280 C-87s and six C-87As were built, all at Fort Worth. Air Transport Command pilot Ernest Gann called them something else: "It was said the assembly of parts known collectively as a C-87 would never replace the aeroplane . . . they were an evil bastard contraption, nothing like the relatively efficient B-24 except in appearance . . . the C-87s would not carry enough ice to chill a highball."

Five more C-87s were built as AT-22 trainers, and later TB-24s when fitted out as B-29 gunnery trainers. The Navy called the transport Liberator the RY-2, and their C-87A and RY-1. It was as the C-87A that the Liberator's greatest aspiration was almost realized. It was in a plane called *Guess Where II,* the first aircraft built especially for the use of the President of the United States. The White House wanted long range to eliminate the security problems of frequent stopovers, and the necessity of a loading ramp for the invalid President Roosevelt presented similar problems with higher aircraft. The Liberator Express seemed to fill the requirements, so three C-87s were selected for conversion into C-87A VIP transports. All three would go to Washington, but 41-24159 would be for FDR.

Along the right side of the fuselage they placed four Pullman-style compartments, each with double seats and a removable table between. These could be made up into curtained upper and lower berths. Under the wing was another compartment with one bunk, and there were two lavatories, a galley equipped with electric stove and oven, and on the left side of the big fuselage a davenport, opposite the central compartment, which was arranged so that one section of the fuselage could be closed off from the rest of the aircraft. A C-54 fuselage tank was added for greater range, but Mr. Roosevelt never did use *Guess Where II.*

Still another B-24D became the XB-41, a bomber escort equipped with fourteen machine guns and 11,000 rounds of ammunition. Additional upper turret, chin turret, and twin waist guns were the main features. The aircraft was never tested operationally, the miserable failure of similarly conceived Fortresses voiding the project.

The B-24E, the next model, was little different from its predecessor, and one of these was modified late in 1943 as the fuel-carrying XC-109. Its purpose was to overcome the immense logistical problem involved in the Superfortress campaign soon to be launched from China. Range and capacity made the B-24 a natural choice, so metal nose and bomb-bay tanks were fitted, with a 2,900-gallon capacity, which could be pumped out in an hour. The B-24Ds and B-24Es which were modified to C-109s carried flexible bag tanks.

Vulnerability to head-on attack was not the exclusive problem of the B-24; it was one example of a lack of experience which culminated in a lot of stop-gap measures, and a lot of experimenting. The initial result in Europe was the placing of twin guns in the nose, lashed together. The recoil was tremendous, and manipulating these weapons was hard work for the gunner, but many of the pilots recall the arrangement as superior to the nose turrets. The B-24D, with its porcupine array of nose guns, was more flyable than the pug-nosed later versions, and nose turret Liberators did not arrive in Europe until the crisis was more or less past.

Lieutenant Bill Strong, pilot of a 44th Bomb Group B-24D named *Baldy and His Brood,* fitted twin waist guns to his aircraft just before the Ploesti mission, and credits the extra firepower that day with his life. Some 11th Bomb Group Liberators in the Pacific were equipped with twin waist guns, but recoil presented problems and the experiment was abandoned. VPB-108, a Privateer squadron, had a later, more successful try at field modification—Lieutenant Commander Robert Lefever installed two forward-firing 20-mm cannon in his aircraft, an idea which proved so effective it spread through the squadron. Many Seventh Air Force Liberators had a ball joint for a .30-caliber machine gun, centrally fitted in a flat circle of armor glass, in place of the astrodome forward of the cockpit. Most crewmen remember it as "useless."

In January 1943 General George C. Kenney asked for thirty-five Consolidated tail turrets, following the successful fitting of one of these turrets into the nose of a B-24D, and he also requested that the Hawaiian Air Depot make the installation on all future deliveries to the Fifth Air Force. His turrets arrived late in March, and in May he requested thirty-six more. Kenney had also decided to substitute manually operated twin fifties for the Sperry ball turret, and although this posed production problems it was agreed in September that his aircraft would differ in this regard too.

The third producer of the Liberator, Ford, began with 480 B-24Es at their

With his ship's hydraulics shot out over Bud-apest, Captain Bill Adams of the 455th Bomb Group got down safely at San Giovanni by using parachutes for brakes. Like all B-24Gs, this aircraft was built by North American Aviation at Dallas. The 430 B-24Gs were *not all alike—the first twenty-five did not have the electrically powered Emerson nose tur-ret, and although the following B-24Gs were the equivalent of the B-24H they were not re-designated.*

giant Willow Run plant. The War Production Board had asked Ford to try its assembly line techniques on aircraft, and at its peak Willow Run was operating twenty hours a day and turning out a Liberator every fifty minutes. They had a few bugs to work out . . . one early aircraft had the controls installed in reverse, but the error was exposed when the aircraft roared to the end of the runway without ever looking like she was going to fly.

In all 791 B-24Es were built, by Ford, Douglas, and Consolidated at Fort Worth. The XB-24F was a B-24D with thermal de-icing in place of the standard rubber boots, but the model never reached production. The Thermal Ice Preventative System was introduced on later B-24Js, using a system of hot air ducted along the leading edges, and such was the XB-24F's legacy.

North American began building Liberators, initially without the ball turret, as B-24Gs, and these were the first of 430 of this model, unique to the Dallas supplier.

*   *   *   *

By this time the Liberator had achieved an outstanding reputation in some areas, but the Flying Fortress was still the symbol of all that was fine and desirable in a four-engined bomber. Crews had an inbuilt preference for the Fortress, and the maligning of the Liberator was so far-reaching in its effects that one group of trainee crews at March Field in California were taken out to the flight line to watch as a pilot flew a Liberator low over the field, with his radio hooked up to a loudspeaker on the ground. The pilot was a Consolidated man, and he broadcast all his intentions, along with a little sales pitch on the old B-24. He banked and made low turns over the field with one engine off (it didn't fall straight down), then two off (it didn't fly like a rock), and finally three off. Some happier crews walked away, but they still had time to compose poems like *The Unsung Hero's Lament*. Nobody knows who wrote it, but it turned up in the 484th Bomb Group, training in Kansas prior to moving to Italy to join the Fifteenth Air Force. The poem recounted the story of a B-24 pilot who made it to the Heavenly Hall of Fame, where he was called upon to give his qualifications to be there with the likes of Julius Caesar, Ulysses S. Grant, and others. His credentials were his flights in the Liberator . . .

For there's a sort of maniac madness in the superchargers' whine,
As you hear the ice cubes tinkling in the Turbo-Balance line,
And the runways strips are narrow, but the snow banks, they were wide,
While the crash trucks say, in a mournful way, you're on your final ride.

The nose gear rocks and trembles, for it's held with bailing wire,
And the wings are filled with thermite, to make a hotter fire,
The camouflage is peeling off, it lends an added luster,
While pilot heads are filled with lead to help the load adjuster.

The bomb bay doors are rusted, and close with a ghastly shreik,
And the Plexiglas is smeared with some forgotten oil leak,
The oleo struts are twisted, and the wheels are not quite round,
And the bulkheads thin (Ford builds with tin) admit the slightest sound.

You taxi out on the runway, 'mid groans of tortured gear,
And you feel the check-rider's practiced teeth, gnawing your tender rear;
The co-pilot sitting on the right, in a liquor-laden coma,
Mingles his breath, like the kiss of death, with the put-put's foul aroma.

So it's off in the overcast yonder, though number one is missing,
And the hydraulic fluid escaping, sets up a gentle hissing,
The compass dial is spinning in a way that broods no stopping,
And row by row, the fuses blow, with an intermittent popping.

It was named the "Liberator" by a low and twisted mind . . .

(And so on, for a couple more verses.)

Master Sergeant Howard M. Hill of the 458th Bomb Group, Eighth Air Force, was crew chief of Final Approach. *She was a B-24H-15 built by Ford at their huge Willow Run* plant. *This model of the Liberator was the first to carry the nose turret, and in all 3,100 were built—1,780 by Ford, 582 by Douglas and 738 by Consolidated at Fort Worth.*

Last flight for Final Approach. *After more than a hundred missions they finally got her* over Munich on April 9, 1945. Back at Horsham St. Faith Howard Hill waited in vain.

B-24H: Beginning of the Bulldog Breed

The B-24H was the first Liberator model to be equipped with a nose turret on the production line, and 738 were built by Consolidated at Fort Worth and fitted with Emerson electric nose turrets. Ford built 1,780 B-24Hs, and Douglas built 582, both using hydraulically operated Motor Products nose turrets designed by Consolidated. As usual, quantities of these Liberators went to Royal Air Force Coastal and Bomber Commands, as Liberator VIs, where their tail turrets were replaced by the four-gun Boulton-Paul installation.

The most numerous Liberator was the B-24J, built by all five plants and differing little from its immediate predecessor. About 1,200 went to the British for varied work, and others became F-7As or F-7Bs, each with six cameras in various positions; the XF-7 had been developed from a B-24D at the Northwest Airlines Modification Center at St. Paul, Minnesota, and carried extra fuel tanks in the bomb bay, a five-window cabin behind the fuel tanks, and eleven cameras. These photo Liberators equipped a number of squadrons which were scattered throughout the Army Air Forces from the Aleutians to the Philippines.

The Navy kept calling their Liberators PB4Y-1s, but their nose turreted aircraft were re-equipped with the Erco gun position, distinctive in appearance and very much to the Navy's liking. Vice Admiral Harry E. Sears, first-tour commander of the Buccaneers squadron, recalls taking conventional B-24s from the line at San Diego, flying across the bay to North Island, and modifying them: "In the nose, which we extended about three feet, we fitted

Converted to an aerial tanker from a Ford B-24J, this C-109 flew with the Ninth Troop   *Carrier Command, supplying the swiftly moving ground forces in Europe.*

San Diego in full swing. These aircraft are the final twenty of a batch of fifty B-24J-120-COs. (Convair)

Photo Queen, *an F-7 from the 20th Combat Mapping Squadron. The rear bomb bay was sealed and contained the photographer's station with the intervalometer switch panel which enabled him to operate all the cameras, including the tri-metragon cameras in the nose.* (E. P. Stevens)

The B-24J was the most numerous model of the Liberator, and the first to be built at all five factories. The Sniffin Griffin was a B-24J-175-CO from the 494th Bomb Group. The San Diego B-24Js were distinguished by their Motor Products nose turrets, introduced due to a shortage of Emerson models. Hydraulically operated by pressure from the main wheel brake accumulators, the turret was almost identical to the Motor Products tail turret fitted to the B-24M, and carried by #057 here. Ford built 1,587, Douglas 205, North American 536, Fort Worth 1,558 and San Diego 2,792 . . . 6,678 B-24Js in all.

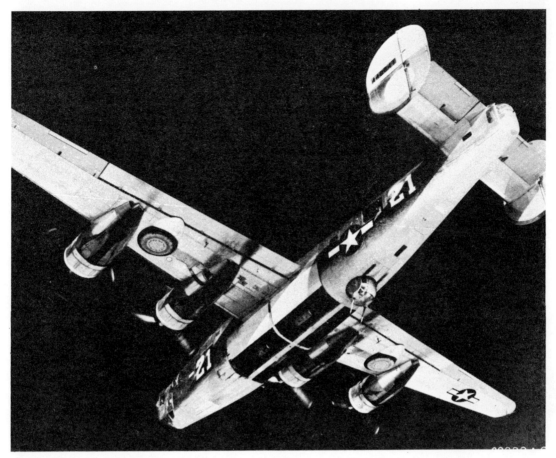

The distinctive tail position of the B-24L was designed by the Consolidated-Vultee Modification Center at Tucson, Arizona, and gave a wider field of fire and saved two hundred pounds in weight. A B-24L-10-FO, 44-49647 is a 451st Bomb Group aircraft, ready to unload on Vienna in January 1945. Consolidated built 417 B-24Ls at San Diego, and Ford built 1250 more at Willow Run.

Specially modified at Willow Run, Warm Front served with the 55th Recon Squadron (Long Range Weather); the tiny umbrellas and lightning flashes signify ten specialized missions.

an Erco ball turret. This was a dandy apparatus in which the gunner was integral with his twin .50-caliber guns and had twice the ammo supply of the other turrets . . . 800 versus 400. He also had a nice slab of armor in front of him which extended a cone of protection to the pilots as well. The longer nose added to the plane's longtitudinal stability, though it did increase our overall weight."

The B-24L, in turn, was similar to the B-24J, except for a lighter tail turret designed by the Consolidated Modification Center at Tucson, which improved handling and gave a wider field of fire. A few were modified with remote-control turrets to train future B-29 Superfortress gunners and were called RB-24Ls, or with radar they became TB-24Ls.

One bunch of B-24L-10-FOs were modified at Willow Run, retagged B-24L-11-FOs, and sent out to a special squadron with a special job. The 55th Recon Squadron (Long Range Weather), commanded by Colonel Nicholas Chavasse, was formed in September 1944 due to the problems arising from the changeableness of the weather in the Central and North Pacific near the Empire. Its effect on the B-29 strikes already was serious and this squadron was rushed into the breach. Instead of bombardiers they had weather observers on their Liberators, and weather forecasters and technicians were assigned to their organization.

The first of their kind, they were divided into three flights, each with its own area to cover, and were attached to XXI Bomber Command. Flight A arrived on Guam about the first part of January 1945, Flight B for Iwo Jima arrived in April, and Flight C, to operate from Okinawa, came in around midyear.

Their B-24s, Captain William Atwood's *Weather Witch, Beaufort Belle,* the bosomy *Warm Front* and the rest, flew three-legged missions to obtain information as the basis for forecasts. Approaching storms and typhoons were covered, the Liberators flying right into the eye of these disturbances to gather data.

Due to the emergency situation a combination of Flights A and B was sent to Iwo, flying weather missions of a different nature. These were to give Army Air Forces Pacific Ocean Area Weather Central definite information on weather for the B-29 missions and fighter strikes over the Empire. The B-24Ls normally took off at midnight and got back about 8 A.M. after flying over the various Japanese cities. The 55th's aircraft's bomb bays contained auxiliary tanks and instead of the belly turret they carried a retractable parabolic ball containing their radar.

*   *   *   *

The final B-24 model produced in quantity was the B-24M; there were 916 produced by San Diego and 1,677 by Ford, 2,593 in all. Bolivar Jr. flew with the 11th Bomb Group, although she was intended as a "replacement" for 30th's Bolivar, which crashed in California at the beginning of a bond tour.

"Ditchability" tests were conducted with this old B-24D; the Liberator had a tendency to squash, and Eight Air Force crews were hardly delighted by the fact that they had only one-tenth of the ditching survival chance of a Fortress crew. (Convair)

A war-weary B-24D, "First Sergeant" became the formation assembly ship of the Eighth Air Force's 458th Bomb Group. Her whole front area had been painted white, then red, black and yellow polka dots were added . . . but underneath she was still the old Traveling Circus plane Thar She Blows, *a veteran of Ploesti and scores of other missions.*

Last of the main Liberator line was the B-24M, equipped with a lightweight power tail turret. Later came the XB-24P, a modified B-24D, which was allocated to the Sperry Gyroscope Company for fire-control research. The XB-24Q was a B-24L with a radar-controlled tail installation of the kind used in the B-47 Stratojet. Not overshadowed by any of these was the result of discussions at Wright Field in Dayton, Ohio, that prompted the grafting of a B-17G nose onto a B-24J in June 1944. The aircraft was found to be "operationally unsuitable."

As the earlier B-24s, those that had managed to survive, grew more tired and worn, they were found less demanding roles. *Charlot the Harlot,* a white-bellied relic from 480th Antisubmarine Group, was training crews at Peterson Field in Colorado in March 1944, still proudly displaying eleven varicolored submarine stencils. Other old B-24Ds were flying booze runs to Cairo, Sydney, or anywhere else where luxuries could be bought for the men in lonely bases. Or there was Project Aphrodite, a scheme involving the sending of radio controlled, explosive-laden war wearies against secret weapon sites in the Pas-de-Calais; the Air Force was using B-17s, and the Navy shared in the project using PB4Y-1s. On August 12, 1944, Lieutenant Joseph P. Kennedy, Jr., was piloting one of the flying bombs, bound for Heligoland. As the crew were about to jump after turning control over to the mother ship a huge explosion occurred, followed by another. The blast caused damage over a five-mile area, and similar misfortunes led to the abandonment of the project.

One of the most successful retirement plans for the B-24 was used by the Eighth Air Force . . . war weary aircraft were painted up in gaudy color schemes to assist assembly of the groups over England. Stripped of armament and festooned with lights, these flare-firing Judas Goats served with most of the Second Air Division's groups, and the original B-24Ds were almost all proud old ladies from the 93rd or 44th Groups. The 93rd had *Ball of Fire,* striped in yellow, black, and white, one of their own original aircraft, and the 44th had *Lemon Drop,* again a group original, with black and yellow bands. The golden orange *Fearless Freddie* of the 446th had been the 93rd's *Eager Beaver,* and the 448th got the same group's *Hellsadroppin' II* and painted black and yellow checks all over her. Other old 93rd aircraft went to the 453rd, who received *Wham Bam* and decorated her with yellow checks, the 445th who striped *Luck Gordon* in orange and black, the 466th, who scraped down *Ready and Willing,* the last Circus plane over Ploesti, and zigzagged her metal body with red flashes, and the 458th at Horsham Saint-Faith polka-dotted the famous *Thar She Blows.*

In 1942 it had been reasoned that the Liberator would be more stable with a single fin, and in 1943 the Consolidated company had modified a B-24D as the XB-24K. It definitely did have improved stability and control, so in April 1944 it was decided that future Liberators would be minus the twin tail, and the XB-24N and seven YB-24Ns resulted before May 31, 1945, when Liberator production ceased. The B-24N orders were canceled but the Navy received 739 single-finned Liberators contracted for in May 1943; called the PB4Y-2 Privateer these aircraft were heavily modified, with seven feet added to the length, two Martin upper turrets, and twin-gun Erco waist blisters. A transport version was also built, the RY-3. The oval cowlings which distinguished regular B-24s (this was necessitated by the supercharger installation and the subsequent placing of the oil coolers on each side of the engine) were installed vertically instead of horizontally in the Privateer and 1,350-horsepower engines were used.

* * * *

Designed as a fat bellied, single tailed cargo plane for the Navy, Model 39 flew on April 5, 1945. The Navy ordered 253 as R2Y-1s, but the order was canceled and it was decided to adapt the plane as Convair's first peacetime commercial transport.

Convair and American Airlines outfitted the plane as the Liberator Liner in the summer of 1945 and used her for mutual research in air shipment of cargo. On thirty-seven flights they handled 283 tons of cargo, anything

The single-finned XB-24N was built by Consolidated, and based on a Ford modification to a B-24D which resulted in the XB-24K. The nose and tail turrets were completely new, and *although 5,168 B-24Ns were ordered from Ford only seven YB-24Ns were built before Liberator production ceased. (Convair)*

Our Baby, a PB4Y-2 Privateer from VPB-106, based at Shanghai shortly after VJ Day. (Peter Bowers)

from strawberries to magazines. Meteorologists charted temperature forecasts for various altitudes along the way so the shipper and flight captain could then choose altitudes to suit the cargo, helping produce ripen or keeping it unchanged as required.

* * * *

With war's end the armed forces had little use for the B-24, and 5,518 went to the Reconstruction Finance Corporation. Aircraft like *The Dragon and His Tail* of the 43rd Bomb Group were crimped and crumbled to manageable scrap at Kingman, Arizona, while a thousand of her sisters joined the jumble of bulldozed Liberators on Biak. They were soon forgotten junk, remembered only in faded yellow photos and fading memories.

In 1951 only one B-24 appeared on the USAF's inventory, a B-24M used by the Aero Icing Research Laboratory, an almost unbelievable fact when peak Liberator strength had been 6,043 in the Army Air Forces in September 1944. That was approximately fifteen hundred more than the highest figure for the B-17, and by that time the Liberator was liberally spread throughout foreign air forces and the Navy. Of fifty-one heavy bomb groups activated and sent overseas between March 1942 and June 1944, thirty-seven were B-24 units.

British Liberators were used in various postwar roles and B-24s, C-87s and PB4Y-2s flew with the Nationalist Chinese Air Force and Privateers with the French *Aeronavale.* The Navy kept Privateers well into the '50s, some serving with the Coast Guard; VP-24, (the descendant of the wartime Buccaneers

Colonel Albert Shower lifts the restored Strawberry Bitch *from Davis Monthan's broad strip on May 12, 1959; her last flight ended* *at Wright-Patterson Air Force Base, where she stands today.*

squadron), and VW-3 were the last patrol and weather recon squadrons to operate them. A few more Privateers found their way to South American countries, and with them some of the few surviving B-24s. Most of the Australians' Liberators went into mothballs after the war and were scrapped in the early '50s after some had been used as forest-fire spotters, others as transports, and a few as fire-fighting training hulks. The Indian Air Force used bomber Liberators into the '60s, and in 1968 began giving the survivors to anyone who wanted them. Canada received one of these relics, in original condition, another called the *Pima Paisano* was flown to Tucson, and the San Diego Aero Space Museum at long last should become able to display the aircraft that was largely responsible for the growth of that city.

So it is not impossible to see a Liberator, it just requires a little effort.

Strawberry Bitch: After the Battles

The *Strawberry Bitch,* an old and now unique B-24D from the 512th Squadron of the 376th Bomb Group, holds court at the Air Force Museum at Wright-Patterson Air Force Base in Ohio. She is often painted, and each time the colors and markings seem to get a little farther from the original, but she is still real.

She's a little too pink, the grinning black skull of the 512th has gone from her nose, and the 47th Bomb Wing tail symbols have lost their style and form, and thereby their meaning. Happily the girl on the nose, one borrowed from Alberto Varga of *Esquire* fame, and one who graced a lot of Liberator noses, has not aged. She still looks properly leggy, properly out of tune with her homely background.

The Liberator might have been a heavy bomber, all nineteen tons of her, but now she is a cramped, claustrophobic airplane. Almost all the instruments are still banked across the cockpit, their faces staring blankly after years of disuse. The ball joints for the .50s down in the nose are rusting, and a few links of the ammunition belt still hang uselessly from a runner.

Her Army Air Force serial number is 42-72843, but that gives her an anonymity she does not deserve, particularly now. She was built as a B-24D-160-CO by Consolidated at San Diego, and flew fifty-nine missions between September 1943 and June 1944, hitting Wiener Neustadt in Austria, Rome in Italy, Athens in Greece, Budapest in Hungary, Bucharest in Romania, Toulon in France, Sofia in Bulgaria, and all the others. Her battles over, she spent thirteen years in Davis Monthan's Arizona boneyard before coming to the museum in 1959, a little heavy bomber from the '30s and another air war long, long ago.

III

Around the Clock

When *Suzy Q* went down a little of the Eighth Air Force died with her. The weathered green B-24D was patched from nose to tail, each mismatched piece a souvenir of any one of scores of targets from Kiel to Ploesti. She originally belonged to Captain Howard Moore of the Eight Balls' 67th Bomb Squadron, named for his little daughter in Indiana. Bill Cameron led the group to Rome in her, Leon Johnson took them over Ploesti in her, but Pappy Moore owned her.

She probably would have been junked the time she came back with two dead engines and mangled hydraulic and oxygen systems, if it had not happened to her during the early days when any aircraft was better than none; she spent two months in Ireland, came back with four new engines, a new tail, almost a new aircraft. Pappy Moore took her to Africa with the group in June, and on the pilot's twenty-fifth mission *Suzy* seemed almost ready to give up. Coming home from Naples on three engines, Moore lost the other three as he neared the desert airstrip at Benina and dropped the powerless B-24 in from fifteen hundred feet, landing a quarter of a mile short. But old *Suzy Q* bounced along, vaulting over rocks and brush and ditches until she gained the smooth strip and rolled to a stop.

It was the next morning that Captain William Cameron flew her to Rome at the head of the Eight Balls, and on August 1 Leon Johnson brought her back from Ploesti with her tail and right wing a little chewed by the boiling Romanian skies, but otherwise still old *Suzy Q*.

Before coming back to England *Suzy Q* was sent out to lead a mission to Foggia on August 16; it should have been a milk run, but the new crew in *Suzy Q* died in her broken wreckage on an Italian beach. She was the last of the original aircraft of the 67th Bombardment Squadron, a squadron which in some ways seemed to be a little short of luck. *Suzy Q* never flew one hundred missions, but she lived longer than most, and with her her crews.

October 1942: Ted Timberlake's Traveling Circus

When twelve B-17s raided Rouen on August 17, 1942, the Eighth Air Force had flown its first daylight heavy bomber mission; the event is memorable for little else. Necessarily pinprick missions followed, and it was October 9 before the new air force could put up one hundred four-engined bombers. It was on that day that Liberators filled out the formations for the first time; B-24Ds from the 93rd Bomb Group flew to Lille, fourteen aborting along the way, and the ten that made it not contributing a great deal. But again it was a beginning, and one of the aircraft out that day was to gain an enviable reputation, although the circumstances then were hardly promising. The most shot-up Liberator to come back from Lille was called *Bomerang,* and she was peppered with holes, a couple of hundred of them, big and small. They wanted to scrap her, but her pilot and crew chief fought for her and she went on to become the first Liberator in the Eighth to fly fifty missions.

General Ira C. Eaker, commanding VIII Bomber Command, was beset by problems. In November he lost his two most experienced Fortress groups to the new Twelfth Air Force, and he could see no point in having his inexperienced crews chopped down by enemy defenses and weather conditions which their training had hardly prepared them for. So they flew the so-called "milk runs" into France and the Low Countries, a sort of on-the-job training program. There were other operational problems—equipment would freeze and become useless at high altitude, and crewmen suffered from frostbite to an alarming degree. And there were accidents and mistakes . . . as late as June 1943 one bomber group could report that twenty-five aircraft had been damaged by enemy action, and twenty-four by friendly action!

The 93rd Group flew eight more missions before the end of 1942, without suffering another loss, and in November the 330th Squadron had been detached to fly antisubmarine missions under Royal Air Force Coastal Command. Another squadron followed them to help search for a plane lost carrying Brigadier General Asa N. Duncan, returning soon after, but obviously the Liberator forces flying with the other Eighth bombers were small. The most memorable event of these months was when a 330th Squadron Liberator flown by Major Ramsey Potts shot down two of five Ju-88s over the Bay of Biscay, on November 21. Two days after this squadron returned to the 93rd at Alconbury another, the 329th, was sent to Hardwick to have their aircraft equipped with Gee, a navigational aid which permitted accurate bombing through overcast. The squadron was to fly individual intruder missions, which would alert the enemy and thereby disrupt his activities. Foul weather was the best weather for these missions, and only middling bad weather forced them to turn back on several occasions. It was somewhat ironic, and the squadron returned to normal operations late in March, flying with the 44th Bomb Group while the rest of the 93rd was in North Africa earning the name "Ted Timberlake's Traveling Circus."

November 1942: The Eight Balls

The Eight Balls, the 44th Bomb Group, were the first Liberator unit in the Army Air Forces; however, before the fully trained group was sent overseas it was to form and train more Liberator units. The first was the 98th, the Ninth Air Force's Pyramiders, the second was the 93rd, and the third was the first Pacific B-24 group, the 90th Jolly Rogers. The Eight Balls flew their first mission on November 7, and traveled with the Fortresses. One of their

Lieutenant John Long had demolished a B-24D called the Texan *in Wales, after the Saint-Nazaire mission on January 3, 1943, but the crew survived. Flying this aircraft, #818, he went to Saint-Nazaire again on February 16; shortly after leaving the English coast, the aircraft in front of him slowed down and fell off to the left. Long found himself beneath the falling aircraft, and before he could move out of the way his left wing tip hit the belly of the other aircraft and locked there. A flame blossomed at the point of impact, and seconds later both aircraft exploded into flaming wreckage.*

three early squadrons was the 67th, and their story is, in essence, the Eight Balls' story and the Liberator's story . . .

Before the 67th's aircraft had settled amongst the pastures and wheatfields of Norfolk the rest of the group had flown their first mission. The newer squadron made it to Abbeville on December 6, then Romilly-sur-Seine on December 20, but after that the weather ganged up on them and missions were scrubbed day after day. Time after time the crews were awakened in the middle of the night, then told they weren't going. Two weeks passed before the Eight Balls again took to the air and headed for Saint-Nazaire.

Bristling with flak guns, Saint-Nazaire on the west coast of France was Germany's principal submarine base in Europe. The Eight Balls were carrying a lighter gas load than usual and they ran into trouble. Lieutenant John Long set the *Texan* down in Wales as his last engine quit, demolishing the aircraft. Eight Balls Liberators were scattered all over bases along their homeward route.

The 67th Squadron was commanded by Major Donald MacDonald, a quiet, soft-spoken man highly regarded by his crews. He had held his people together during the first months, a time which had been as tough for the ground crews as the airmen in some ways. The flight line at Shipdham was located around two miles from the living quarters, linked with them by muddy, slippery roads which had to be walked. The men, having squelched their way home, had to wash off the mud with helmets of water heated over barracks fires, each waiting his turn. The unlucky last was often holding his helmet into the late hours of the night. The food was lousy, particularly for people who did not like mutton, and the garbage cans were overflowing with it as the men chose to go hungry.

Yet there were lighter moments: a couple of 66th Squadron sergeants made their way to quaint Norwich on their first night of freedom and rented a car. They drove around, stopping at several friendly pubs along the way, and they were glowing as night fell, and with it the blackout. Navigating by pinpoints of light from their shielded headlamps, they noticed in the dimness ahead that people kept appearing and disappearing. This they found fascinating, and on investigation ascertained that they were no longer driving on the street, but on the sidewalk. Two days later VIII Bomber Command issued an order: "Due to complaints by Norwich Citizens of American Personnel ignoring driving regulations there will be no more renting of civilian automobiles," or words to that effect.

So Sergeants Bill Robertie and Anthony Stempkowski were stranded for a while; at least until they found a nearby farmer who was willing to rent his horse and cart.

*   *   *   *

The 44th Bomb Group, the Eight Balls, flew many bloody missions, but the run to Dunkirk on February 15, 1943, was one of the first. Major Donald MacDonald, leading his 67th Squadron, took a flak hit over the target which blew the nose completely away, and a second Liberator was hit by the same flak pattern, crippled, and shot down by fighters.

Major MacDonald led the 67th to Dunkirk on February 15, part of the Eight Balls' force briefed to strike the German raider *Tojo.* The Squadron commander, flying in aircraft 783, dropped his bombs at 3:40 in the afternoon after a bomb run that was unusually long and accurate, lasting several minutes through heavy flak. As her bombs fell away 783 took a hit. The left inboard engine streamed flames, and the right inboard was completely torn from the wing. The plane fell in a steep dive and the right wing separated from the fuselage seconds before the whole aircraft was blown apart by a tremendous explosion. Three chutes were seen. Lieutenant Rufus Oliphant's 794 took hits from the same pattern and did not break off when the rest of the formation turned away after the target. A few minutes later the sinking aircraft, under vicious attack by fighters, exploded. Inside Major MacDonald's aircraft the pilots had watched the bomb release light go, then everything flew to pieces. They knew it must have been a direct hit by an eighty-eight under the flight deck around the nose wheel section. Pilot Arthur Cullen was stunned for a few moments, then as his head cleared he looked around. They were in a dive, the sky was empty, there was nothing above their thick windshield—no cabin roof at all. Both inboard engines were burning and mangled, there was almost no control left in the wheel, and Cullen couldn't use the rudder because his leg was broken. He looked over to MacDonald in the co-pilot's seat and the Major motioned him to get out—Cullen saw blood running from a deep wound in the other's stomach. The airplane was on its right side and the pilot knew there was no chance to save it. MacDonald unstrapped himself and painfully extracted himself from the seat, clutching his stomach. With Cullen's help he went out where the roof had been, and made it to the ground to die on a Luftwaffe operating table. Cullen tumbled out and hit the mangled plane's tail, breaking his leg in a second place, and his right arm.

Lieutenant Bill Cameron was left as number three aircraft in the formation in the *Little Beaver*. He was shaken by the sight of MacDonald's Liberator flying alongside them with nothing left forward of the cockpit. He was sure it was the first flak shell which had done it . . . it was a weird and grim sight.

Suzy Q's pilot, Captain Howard Moore, took command of the 67th Squadron and led them to Saint-Nazaire the following day. Shortly after leaving the English coast Lieutenant Fred Billings in 354 was having difficulty in keeping formation, slowing down and falling off to the left. The Liberator began to go down rapidly and the following aircraft, John Long's 818, passed under Billings's ailing aircraft. Long saw the danger, tried to move away, but his left wingtip collided with the belly of 354 and locked there. A flame blossomed from the point of impact, and seconds later there was an explosion which blew both aircraft into flaming wreckage. Four men were blown clear and seen parachuting down, but British air-sea rescue searched for them without success. Leon Johnson led the group on to Saint-Nazaire.

At the target they found heavy flak, and the Germans were laying a smoke screen to the northwest. The drifting smoke was too late, and the Eight Balls bombed well. The fighters had been working over the Fortresses, but after the bomb run they latched onto the 44th. Focke-Wulfs drew up out of range of the gunners and lobbed 20-mm explosive shells at them, but most burst way ahead of the B-24s. Captain Clyde Price's 784 was heavily attacked on the way out, but the Eight Balls came out virtually unharmed.

Wilhelmshaven was hit on February 26, with Brest the next day. The 67th was now composed of five weathered aircraft and five incomplete crews. The missions went on, and no relief was in sight. Captain Price and Lieutenant Blaine and their crews went down over Rouen on March 8, and again Cameron's *Little Beaver* was in the number-three spot as the two aircraft with him went down . . . the prospects of survival became dim.

On March 18 *Suzy Q* led the Eight Balls to Vegesack, with the 67th and its other two aircraft surviving the fierce battle. Up to that time the squadron had flown seventeen missions including a few diversion flights, at the cost of five crews and six aircraft. With the arrival of the group's fourth squadron, the 506th, the prospect of replacements loomed. Four days after Vegesack the sixth original 67th crew went down over Wilhelmshaven—Captain Bucky Warne in 832 was shot up by flak and although all ten men got out only two were ever heard from again.

April was devoted to breaking in the 506th squadron, and the pressure eased. Bill Cameron's *Little Beaver* and *Suzy Q* were now the sole surviving 67th originals, and when *Suzy*'s nose wheel gave up on landing after a mission to Paris she was sent away to be restored. The original crews of the squadron were scarred too; they formed the "200 Club" in their barracks and as the missions went on Bill Cameron recalls the silence at night getting pretty deafening. Their main goal was raising hell, and a favorite party trick was dropping a few rounds of .45-caliber ammunition into the flat pot-bellied stove . . . very surreptitiously of course. Cameron remembers himself as being the quietest of the group, and he seemed to be the one who got into trouble . . . if he thought it was the right thing to do, he would organize transportation for the girls at 4 A.M. after the rest had gone to bed . . . and he would be caught and reprimanded. Another good turn he did was awakening two others for a practice mission at 5 A.M. . . . not realizing they had guests in their beds. A barrage of pistol shots zipped over his head in the dark and he retreated down the hallway on his knees. But he recalls that after they were gone no one ever quite took their places.

At the end of April the 93rd Bomb Group was selected to switch over to night operations, to be followed in due course by the 44th. In the meanwhile the Eight Balls were left as the sole Liberator group in the Eighth Air Force's daylight formations, and this was an uncomfortable place to be.

The Eight Balls were already at a low ebb, because when Colonel Ted Timberlake had brought three squadrons of the 93rd back from an eighty-day sojourn in Africa they had flown a mission to Vegesack on March 18, 1943, and both *Yank* and *Stars and Stripes* had hailed them with feature articles on the famous "Traveling Circus." This was a little aggravating to the long-suffering Eight Balls, who had been fighting what they thought was a slightly

Captain Bill Cameron, one of the last survivors of the original 67th Bomb Squadron, seemed to have more than his share of luck.

First Liberator group in the Eighth Air Force, the 93rd became known as Ted's Traveling Circus after detachments were sent to North Africa in December 1942, the Middle East in June 1943 to support the invasion of Sicily and attack Ploesti, then back again to support the operations at Salerno in September. This ship, Hellsadroppin' II, *became the black and yellow checkered lead ship of the 448th Bomb Group.*

more dangerous war. When one of the articles was illustrated with combat photos of Eight Ball aircraft there was no love at all lost between the two B-24 groups. Ever since the Circus had left in December 1942 the Eight Balls had been stuck with the missions like Dunkirk and Saint-Nazaire, and they had even been saddled with the 93rd's fourth squadron, the 329th, after that squadron's foray into bombing through overcast was completed. By Eight Ball standards the 329th Squadron was a raggle-taggle outfit, and while the rest of the Traveling Circus was still in Africa the leftover squadron's erratic activities in combat formations was causing the 44th some concern. Hardly rivalry, the aggravation prompted the gunners on *Little Beaver* to beg for permission to fire a few well-aimed rounds into the next 329th Squadron ship which drifted between their guns and German fighters.

In the end Major General James P. Hodges of 2nd Bomb Wing organized a Wing Smoker to bring the two groups' officers together in a friendly environment.

* * * *

As the sole daylight B-24 group, the Eight Balls were to be restricted to diversion missions prior to training for night operations. Instead they drew Kiel on May 14, 1943.

At four o'clock that cold black morning a small group of men from the 67th Squadron were stepping it out through the deserted streets of Norwich, just back from London and still seventeen miles from their base. A few weeks before, Bill Cameron, co-pilot on the *Little Beaver,* and Lieutenant Bob Brown, Moore's co-pilot on *Suzy Q,* had been checked out as pilots and given crews made up 'of ground personnel and RAF transferees. Brown got *Suzy Q*'s old crew, as Moore was now squadron commander, and Cameron's crew included a Royal Air Force co-pilot and navigator, a bombardier from another crew and five others who had been on *Little Beaver*'s ground crew. Cameron had got a pass so they could all go off to London, taking Howard Moore with them.

The little band back to Shipdham in time to sit in on the Kiel briefing, but too late to go. Nineteen Eight Balls made the mission, and only thirteen returned. The flak was murderous and the fighters clung to the Liberators as they dropped their incendiaries after Fortresses had bombed from above. The three 67th Squadron aircraft were at the rear: the squadron's first replacement crew, with Lieutenant Roach as pilot, went down first, one man surviving. Lieutenant Bob Brown, with *Suzy Q*'s old crew in another airplane, bailed out over a fjord with his men and was picked up by a boatload of Germans. *Little Beaver* was hit after the target, two bursts knocking out the

Six Eight Ball Liberators unload incendiaries over Kiel from beneath a Flying Fortress of the 306th Bomb Group. This mission, on May 14, all but wiped out the 67th.

oxygen system and a third bursting behind the navigator. The flight deck became a mass of flames and the Liberator went into a flat spin. The engineer, Mike Denny, could hardly keep on his feet as he put on his parachute, and could not get out of the aircraft through the hatch. He walked back and squeezed through a waist window, his chute opening around five hundred feet from the ground. He was the last man out, and Captain "George" Phillips's crew had been the last of the 67th. Now the battered *Suzy Q,* still under repair, Bill Cameron, Howard Moore, and Cameron's makeshift crew was all the 67th had left. The 67th was one squadron, in one group of the Eighth Air Force. Perhaps they suffered more than most, but the grim reaper was always ready to claim the unwary. If you could survive long enough, you learned . . . the rest paid the price. The 67th was part of that price.

*   *   *   *

Three days later the Eight Balls got a much-needed shot in the arm and morale soared as the result of a mission of Bordeaux became known. Every available Liberator from the two groups had been flown to Davidstowe Moor in Cornwall, and after refueling they left for Bordeaux on the morning of May 17. Colonel Johnson was flying as Moore's co-pilot in the rejuvenated *Suzy Q,* and the thirty-nine B-24s set out on a seven-hundred mile curved course which would keep the low-flying Liberators undetected until it was too late. In the nose of *Suzy Q* was bombardier Lieutenant "Gentleman Jim" DeVinney and navigator Lieutenant "Mike" Mikolowski, and he was the man who brought the Liberators in at the precise moment. Coming over the target at 22,000 feet the thirty-five Liberators that completed the flight hit the target heavily, shattering the lock gates and releasing the controlled water-level into the Garonne. There was minimal flak, and one German fighter was encountered. The cost was one Liberator which force-landed in Spain with mechanical problems.

Twelve days later the Eight Balls and the Circus continued the war against the submarines with an attack on La Pallice, but cloud cover sent them to secondary targets. Both May missions had been flown without loss, and the Eight Balls talked about a change of luck. Good weather held through June and the group was up to strength again, yet no missions were scheduled. All the while the two groups flew continuous training missions, tearing along a couple of hundred feet from the ground. Rumor ran wild, and when the famous Norden bombsights were removed from the B-24s and replaced with a modified gunsight, the barracks experts really went to work.

In the second week of June a new group, the 389th, arrived and moved in at Hethel in Norfolk; they soon joined the others in the mysterious practice missions. Finally, toward the end of the month, all three groups headed for Africa. Arriving in Libya they came under the operational command of the Ninth Air Force, and the Eight Balls moved in with the Pyramiders at Benina Main while the others went to other airfields in the Bengasi area. Their first job was to add their weight to the Sicilian campaign, and for two weeks they flew side-by-side with the Liberandos and Pyramiders. They hit Naples, and Rome, and finally on August 1 they went out to the target that was the real reason for their long journey . . . Ploesti, the oilfield complex in Romania.

*   *   *   *

After Ploesti the Eight Balls hit Wiener Neustadt on August 13, inflicting heavy damage, then they were again called upon for support in Sicily. One

Christened over Ploesti, the 389th Bomb Group   after the tail letter indicates the aircraft is
went to Tunisia a few weeks later to support   from the 566th Squadron.
Allied operations at Salerno. The plus sign

of the three missions cost the 44th Bomb Group the *Buzzin' Bear* and the immortal *Suzy Q;* Bill Cameron had taken over the 67th Bomb Squadron when Moore left, and had sent the *Bear* along with a new pilot and co-pilot, because his co-pilot Bill Dabney was down with asthma. All told the three missions cost the Eight Balls eight aircraft, the Circus one, and the 389th none. The jinx was still there.

Late in August the Eighth's groups shook the sand from their boots and headed for England. Refurbished, they flew the old route to Europe twice before they were told one day that they were going back to North Africa. At 10 P.M. on September 16 the still-dazed Eight Balls were airborne and headed for the desert. By the time they got there the crisis at Salerno had passed, but the Liberators were sent along to bomb the Leghorn marshaling yards and a bridge at Pisa, while the 389th bombed Bastia on Corsica. Bad weather intervened, and no missions were carried out until October 1, against Wiener Neustadt. Of fourteen Liberators lost the Eight Balls contributed eight, with another eight crashing on return and necessitating their being left behind when the group returned to England a couple of days later. Air Transport Command had to be called in to transport the remnants of the group back to England.

A fourth Liberator group had arrived in England during August, equipped with nose-turreted B-24Hs, and they had flown their first mission on September 6 with the other three B-24 groups; this was the 392nd, another unit whose luck would seem a little harder than some others'. Their lack of experience had kept them "home" during the desert sojourn, but as operations stepped up they played an even larger part.

Striped in white, black, and yellow, old Ball of Fire *became the formation assembly ship for the 93rd Bomb Group at Hardwick.*

The fourth Liberator group in the Eighth Air Force was the 392nd, which went into com- *bat in September 1943. They brought the first B-24Hs with their nose turrets to England.*

December 1943: New Blood

As the year ended, more new groups were arriving for the Eighth; aircraft of the 445th, 446th and 448th, their eighty-inch white tail circles gleaming, trundled into the hardstands for the first time.

The 446th was at Bungay, part of the 20th Combat Wing with the old Traveling Circus and the equally new 448th. Like all who had come before and all that came after, the crews were impressed by the neat, compact green countryside below them . . . there was every shade of green you could imagine, and there was a serenity which belied the days ahead. Based on a portion of a manor about five miles from Bungay and seventeen miles south of Norwich, the center of the Eighth's Liberator bases, they were also impressed by being able to look around and see airfields about five miles apart in all directions.

Henry's Pride was the brand-new Ford B-24H belonging to the 446th's Lieutenant Floyd Griesinger and his crew, and naturally decorated with a painting of a Model T. When their first mission was scheduled as Bremen on December 16, the fresh 446th crews took off in aircraft carrying enough fuel to give them about an hour's leeway over the calculated time for the mission. *Henry's Pride* blew a supercharger on takeoff, but the pilot could just keep up with the rest and decided to be in at the beginning. As he watched his power the crew was being astounded by the discovery that only four of their ten guns would operate, vital parts having rusted during a two months stay in the armament shop. Undaunted, Griesinger pressed on.

Fifty miles from Bremen *Henry's Pride* lost a second supercharger and the navigator calculated they had insufficient fuel to complete the mission even if they straggled behind the rest, so they salvoed their bombs and dropped out of formation. They could see the flak in the distance over the target and the enemy and escort fighters meeting; this grandstanding was interrupted when three black-crossed fighters headed toward them. *Henry's Pride* powered toward a protective cloud deck and escaped.

Griesinger broke through the base of the clouds fifty feet above the water and made landfall in England with a lot less fuel than was comfortable. With their radio equipment out, the Liberator was challenged by fighters as soon as she cleared the coast, and the co-pilot promptly dropped the landing gear to signal their good intentions. The fighters broke off when they saw the arming wires trailing out of the bomb bay, indicating that there was no lethal load in the aircraft.

The crew of *Henry's Pride* still had problems; visibility was bad and they were straining their eyes looking for somewhere to land before their last gallons of fuel were consumed. Suddenly bombardier Ben Kislin shouted an alarm to the pilot and they found themselves in the barrage balloon field around Norwich; Griesinger slalomed the big Liberator around the cables. The nervous crew spotted an airbase, but it was obvious for a reason—it was a dummy, rigged with wrecking devices for the German invasion force which never came. Then they spotted a green light from a camouflaged fighter field, but by the time they recognized the grassy area as a safe landing place and made an approach they'd lost sight of the field again.

Circling the area they again got the green light, Griesinger made a short approach and stopped rolling feet from the end of the strip. To his amazement he found he had enough fuel to taxi off the strip and the fledgling 446th crew then had time to watch a B-17 bail its crew out over the field, another brakeless Fortress bounce in twice and pile into the woods off the strip, and a Thunderbolt run out of gas fifty feet from the ground and deadstick in. The British at Coltishall seemed to take it all in good humor.

Another brand-new member of the 446th Group was Lieutenant Bernard Hutain, pilot of *Werewolf*, who quickly came to some conclusions about his job: "A mission could be physically tiring, but the emotional strain would be greater still. The quicker we left the enemy coastline the better we felt. We didn't think too much about the B-24's or B-17's relative ability to absorb punishment . . . it was a more personal fear of a bullet or piece of flak tearing into your body that made you apprehensive. Also, getting shot down didn't concern us as much as surviving the situation. Always the watch for *how many* parachutes. Politically I didn't hate the Germans as perhaps the English or French did; I was twenty and in B-24s because I'd always wanted to fly and I didn't want to end up an instructor in the States. Since we were sure to win the war, getting shot down in itself wasn't the big thing—it was getting out. Then a year, maybe two, in a prison camp and back home *alive*. We wouldn't quit, or land and surrender, but living through a shoot-down was almost as good a way of finishing up, if you lived, as flying your twenty-five or thirty-five missions and then home. Of course we preferred not to be shot down, but it was being killed that really got to us. There wasn't any of this feeling of wanting to get back and drop more bombs on them, because except to do the job we personally did not care that much.

"The worst part of a mission for me was before you got to the briefing. In the evening prior to a mission you'd be in your normal barracks routine—reading, writing, playing poker. Then someone would come in and announce the flight and tell you which crews were going to go. Things would go silent in a hurry. A few lame jokes and the 'lucky' ones would go to bed, ostensibly to catch a little sleep before 3 or 4 A.M. call. Getting to sleep would be difficult, and the sleep itself would be fitful and restless at best, for this might be your

Lieutenant Barney Hutain's Werewolf *in formation with the 446th during a mission early in 1944. Beneath the high right aircraft is a Pathfinder from the 482nd Bomb Group, but still carrying her original Eight Ball markings. In front is* Kill-Joy.

last night alive. Finally you were awakened before you'd hardly had any sleep, then you'd get undressed in the bitter cold, practically unheated barracks, walk to chow and then take what was to me that horrible truck ride to the briefing room. Horrible to me because as a farm boy I had seen father load cattle or pigs on a truck to take them to the slaughterhouse. Every time I got in that truck I felt just like I was one of those animals being taken out to be killed; I know it seems ridiculous, but at times I would walk rather than ride just because of this feeling."

Every man who went over Germany faced death or imprisonment, and over the several hours of a combat mission any failure of the psychological safety mechanism which shut out these thoughts could tie an airman in knots. The true horror of the Eighth's air war is sometimes forgotten, but within the stories of the various groups lie stories which have perhaps passed from many memories over the healing years. The grim reaper rode up front in many B-24s; one 467th Group crewman in a crippled aircraft was called upon to throw the dead body of a friend overboard because every expendable object had to go out if the aircraft was to make it home. There were the grim crashes, the propeller accidents, the collisions . . . there was the grinning radio opera- tor killed by a chunk of flak on his birthday, or the crew of the 491st's *Wham Bam,* which crash-landed successfully after losing an engine over Hanover . . . the pilot and five others were beaten to death by a civilian mob.

January 1944: A Pretty Good Landing

In December 1943 the Eighth had begun flying against the mysterious sites which were springing up in the Pas-de-Calais area; known as "Noball" missions, these flights soon had the crews' imaginations working, and the target area became known as the "rocket coast." The missions themselves were relatively easy, and short, with flak or fighters sometimes picking off one or two bombers. Naturally perhaps, it was the Eight Balls who suffered worst, losing five B-24s on January 21 as they searched for their target. A sixth Liberator crashed on reaching the English coast, and the story of that one airplane illustrates just how much punishment a B-24 could take and bring her crew home.

The group's target was Escalles-sur-Suchy, and Captain Keith Cookus was leading his section and carrying the command pilot, as well as the group bombardier and gunnery officer, who had come along for the ride to see how they worked.

The 44th met little opposition, the cloud cover shielding them but necessi- tating five runs over the target before they were forced to turn back, still carrying their bombs.

Crossing the coast on the way out they were tracked by mobile flak and the first feeling burst was so close Cookus could hear it. He began evasive action but thirty seconds later his plane was hit and thrown out of control. As the Liberator tumbled around the sky seven shells found her. Cookus wrestled with the controls and dropped the bomber down to eight thousand feet to get away as quickly as he could. He knew there wasn't much of his aircraft left: one of the shells had burst inside the bomb bay, ripping out the catwalk which also held the bottom of the fuselage together. It had killed the command pilot, who had been standing between the pilot and co-pilot, and blown the radio operator from the aircraft. The navigator was wounded and the top turret gunner was bleeding. There was a hole in the middle of the plane just as if a shark had taken a bite out of a fish.

Cookus and his co-pilot, Tiny Holladay, were untouched. The intercom was out, and the second direct hit had shot the number 1 engine to pieces, leaving it hanging by shreds. Cookus managed to get the prop feathered before he lost all of the oil pressure. The third hit had blown out half of the number 2 engine, leaving him nothing to feather. Number 3 was burning, set afire by the flash of a near miss, and it trailed a long streamer of black smoke, streaked with red. Cookus had to leave it burning because he would have no chance of getting back to the English Coast without it. So he looked the other way, but he couldn't forget it because the fire began filling the aircraft with gas and oil smoke.

There had been a direct hit in the base of the nose turret, splinters sailing up all around the gunner, but although it blew the top right off his turret he was not hurt. He managed to extricate himself from the mess and crawled back to the cockpit to tell Cookus about another shell which had gone clean through the right wing. That shell, the seventh, had taken the right main landing gear with it. Holladay leaned across and shouted "No use trying to get it down, Buck, we ain't got it with us now"; Cookus grunted, because all the hydraulics were out anyway.

He could not ditch with his wounded, he was relying on a blazing engine, and he was not sure the command pilot was dead. So he nursed the wrecked aircraft along. They weren't under attack, so he could devote all his energies to the aircraft. The group bombardier and gunnery officer had bailed out when they saw the middle of the ship erupt, but with no intercom Cookus could not give any orders to the others.

As the pilot settled down, his bombardier crawled up to the flight deck. They called him Junior, and he was covered in blood. Cookus could not help thinking that it didn't look like Junior at all . . . The blast had thrown him around like a leaf, but he had crawled into the bomb bay, holding onto the twisted metal and wires with his hands and toes, anything he could find that was still attached to the rest of the plane. He had been tossing out what he could of the mess of shattered bombs they still carried. The emergency release mechanism was gone, and the bombardier had cut his hands to ribbons before coming up to report that there were still some he could not shift. Unable to see, unable to talk, he collapsed on the flight deck and just hunched there, staring. He would die of suffocation in the twisted wreck of the bomber.

The ball turret gunner had somehow managed to get himself out of his mangled turret as it filled with blazing oil from the shattered hydraulic system. His clothing was afire when he got out, and as he crawled back toward the tail flames and burning oil were blowing around him. He made it back to where the tail gunner and a waist gunner were cowering, covering their faces against the blazing oil, which lashed at them like molten sleet. They began beating out the flames on each other and finally the hydraulic fluid burned out. With terrible burns on the exposed parts of their bodies they held a quick conference and decided to stay with the aircraft, although it looked like breaking in two at any time.

Up front, Cookus was getting along as best he could. The co-pilot shouted "Coast!" and at that moment there was a whoosh and a smack that shook the plane like jelly. Cookus saw he had no power at all from his number 3 engine. White hot, it had blown up. A fuel pipe had exploded and the fire was looking bad, licking furiously around the remains of the engine.

The two wounded men were up on the flight deck, losing a lot of blood. The co-pilot and nose gunner were taking care of them as best they could. Cookus could not look at his bombardier, to him it just wasn't Junior those last twenty minutes, staring at him through the smeared blood.

The Liberator was practically a sieve and nothing was working as it too quickly lost altitude. Cookus had to pick a landing place and hope for the best; he saw what looked like a fairly level piece of country and headed for it.

He cut his number 1 engine at fifty feet and switched off everything in sight. Then under the brow of a rise he saw they were going to hit the roof of a farmhouse. Headed for a rough landing anyway, the pilot swung the Liberator around and slammed it back, narrowly missing the building. The plane touched the ground, coming down fairly evenly and well, but the field undulated. Stalling speed was one hundred and forty miles an hour with all the damage the B-24 had taken, and the big wreck shot across the field like a piece of soap on a bathroom floor. Cookus knew they were all right and slowing down well when he saw a wire fence coming toward them. They took it and it shook them up. Cookus and Holladay looked up from where they had ducked their heads and saw a ditch and a hedge ahead. They finished up in the ditch.

When the Liberator stopped the silence was complete, and Cookus won-

The 453rd Bomb Group leaves the target on February 21, 1944, the second day of Big Week.

dered if even he was still alive. The front of the Liberator's nose section was twisted 45 degrees off center—a cable from the fence had started the twist as the plane went through. Cookus looked through his side window at the sky, and three feet away from him Holladay was looking out his window at the ground. But behind them the wings were level and it had been a pretty good landing.

Smoke was pouring from the remains of number 3 engine, and Cookus wanted to get out fast before it spread to the wing tanks. From the nose the navigator shouted, "I'm stuck." Cookus got caught trying to squeeze through his window, and dived into the mud. Clambering to his feet and wiping his hands across his muddy flight suit he saw that the three burned men from

The 446th flies through flak in February 1944;
their target is Frankfurt and the center air-
craft is Desperate Desmond.

the back of the aircraft were out. Terrified the plane might go up at any minute, Cookus handed them a fire extinguisher, then tore a hole in the engine paneling and shoved clumps of sodden earth into it to smother the fire.

The earth had piled up under the plane, crushing the floor of the flight deck, and the top hatch was crushed; the navigator and top turret gunner shared their cramped trap with the dead command pilot and bombardier. The navigator's legs were held in a vice formed by the roof and floor, and he was bent double with his head forced between his knees. Holladay was inside the cabin tearing away things to reach them. With the help of British crane trucks they were released after nearly three hours. Their Liberator had got them home.

February 1944: The Big Week

The possibility of good weather in central Germany in February meant that the long-awaited plan called Argument could become reality. On February 19 the meteorologists were watching a high-pressure area move to the southeast across Germany, and the aircraft factories which had been priority targets for so long seemed about to be laid bare.

The weather was not perfect, but it was good enough to permit the sustained attacks which caused the period after February 20 to be called Big Week. During the morning of that cold Sunday, England was blanketed by cloud, with snowflakes drifting down onto the broad shoulders of the Fortresses and Liberators in the hardstands, but soon a thousand heavies were airborne, bound for a dozen targets deep in Germany. The major force, Second Air Division Liberators following the First Division B-17s, headed for central Germany, accompanied by all the available long-range fighter escort. To facilitate fighter cover the bombers would stay together until west of Brunswick, then divide to attack their targets, and link up again for the flight back. Hindered at some targets by cloud, the operation was still a success, and the next day a similar force was dispatched to repeat the dose. The main targets were at Brunswick, but weather intervened and the bombing had to be blind. Only Diepholz air depot was hit as planned, and some of the bombers were forced to resort to targets of opportunity.

The Eighth flew its third mission in as many days on February 22, breaching very bad weather to get to the targets. Assembly was so hazardous and so ragged that the Second Air Division's Liberators were recalled; some B-24s, already over the Low Countries, sought targets of opportunity, and one group mistook Njimegen for a German town and killed two hundred Dutch civilians.

On February 23 less than ideal conditions over the targets and the need for maintenance and repairs to the bombers caused the Eighth Air Force to stand down, but on February 24 the Liberators made amends for their previous mission. They waded through the most savage Luftwaffe interception to that date to bomb their snow-covered targets at Gotha. While a brand-new group, the 458th, flew a diversion over the North Sea, the eight B-24 groups set out to destroy the Messerschmitt 110 factories in three unwieldy wing formations. The 2nd Wing went in first, and met the enemy fighters over an hour before the target. At the Initial Point the leading 389th Bomb Group aircraft slid off course and released her bombs when an oxygen failure caused the bombardier to fall over his sight and trip the bomb release. The other Sky Scorpions naturally also dropped, but the 445th behind them realized it was a mistake and carried on. After they had bombed they received special

A new number 4 engine for Dead End Kids *of the 448th. This group departed from tradition with their squadron identification, which consisted of a geometric symbol centered in the black stripe on their yellow tails. A triangle was used by the 712th Squadron, a circle by the 713th, a square by the 714th, and a diamond by the 715th.*

The first crew to complete twenty-five missions with the 445th Bomb Group at Tibenham was led by Lieutenant Sam Miller. The event was always notable.

attention from the German fighters and in sixty minutes of turmoil thirteen of their twenty-five aircraft were blasted away. The leading Sky Scorpions lost six.

Behind them, the 14th Combat Wing had been battling with fighters since the Dutch coast. Up front the 392nd Group planted 98 percent of their bombs within two thousand feet of the aiming point, and the Eight Balls added to the good bombing. The mission cost the 392nd seven B-24s.

The final day of Big Week sent the Liberators to Fürth, and fine weather gave good results before the clouds came back to western Europe.

The Liberators met less opposition than the Fortresses during the March 6 attack on Berlin, the most costly Eighth Air Force mission of the war. Less than two days later the bombers were being readied to go back to the German capital again, but the city was covered by cloud and the enemy fighters stayed on the ground. In the middle of March the Eighth was able to make its first visual attacks since Big Week, but the smoke screen at Friedrichshafen on March 18 was so effective that radar bombing was still necessary. Smoke floats on Lake Constance contributed to a screen which completely blanketed the city, and the fighters knocked out most of the forty-three bombers which went down. A dozen Liberators landed in Switzerland, a neutral haven for crippled aircraft which received around eighty Eighth and Fifteenth Air Force Liberators before the air war ended.

Another new group, the 466th, flew its first mission in March, joining the Eighth attack on Berlin on March 22. This group was suffering casualties which could not be afforded—on the first mission two of its B-24s collided on the way in, and the following day two more slammed into one another near Osternburg. On March 27 still two more collided in cloud while assembling, bringing the group's losses to six Liberators in five days; perhaps the pilots had let their attention to the job of directing the lumbering bombers ebb, perhaps their training had not prepared them for the conditions, but either way it could not be allowed to happen.

One answer to the assembly problem, which one 446th pilot likened to Russian roulette, was the use of gaudily painted, flare-firing assembly ships. Old war-weary Liberators, stripped of their armament and bedecked with lights, the planes in clown make-up at least partially solved a real problem. The 466th received an old and battered veteran from the Traveling Circus called *Ready and Willing,* which had survived the low-level mission to Ploesti; they scraped her bare and painted red lightning flashes all along her. But what the 466th really needed was the experience that their Judas goat had in such abundance.

April ushered in yet another new group, the 467th, and they joined in the assaults against aircraft production which took the Eighth into France, the

Low Countries and Western Germany during the first few weeks of the month.

On April 22 the 467th's mission was over, and their Liberators were coming home as darkness crowded in on them. They had been to Hamm's marshaling yards late in the day, where they dropped their bombs into the smoke and fire left by the preceding groups. As the lighted Liberators swung in over their field they were warned off, and the antiaircraft guns began firing. There were German fighters there in the darkness with them. The crews jumped to their guns and snapped off bursts at fleeting shadows. An intruder passed over the field at fifty feet, heading for a floodlit B-24 being repaired at the south end of the field. Another zoomed across the runway, chasing the tracers that streamed from its wings. Two bombs hit the lighted area, killing a soldier, wounding a ground crewman and wrecking a cottage. The antiaircraft fire shot down one of the 467th's planes and another went down northwest of the field.

It was obvious what had happened: weather had delayed the mission to the marshaling yards, meaning a return after dark. Single intruders had been used before, but this time the Luftwaffe had clearly seen a golden opportunity and about fifteen Me-410s followed the Liberators home, striking at around 9:30 that night. Confusion reigned as the crews in the Liberators, in darkness, realized that the fighters were there too. Five bases were attacked, and five Liberators lost as guns fired in every direction. The total loss was nine aircraft, and thirty-eight men dead; one Liberator had managed to shoot down an Me-410.

Overlord, the Normandy invasion, came to the fore in May, and the Eighth's initial task was to shatter the railroad systems of Belgium and France. of the heavies using them against targets which could be handled better by medium bombers, and second that the casualties to civilians could be heavy, and mar goodwill when it would be needed most.

In the end it was agreed that the heavies would continue with their battle against the Luftwaffe, but would share the load of the transportation targets. Bad weather during the first days of May kept the Eighth at the close Noball Late in April 191 Liberators had rung in the campaign, but there had been serious objections to it, both of them logical. The first was that it was a waste targets, where increasingly concentrated flak was forcing them to bomb from higher altitudes. The 486th and 487th Bomb Groups, the first two Liberator outfits to fly with the Third Air Division (until then all Flying Fortresses), flew an introductory mission to the marshaling yards at Liége on May 7, 1944. They were the focal point of another problem: for obvious reasons it was considered undesirable to have both types of bomber in one column, but because of the chopping and changing in theater distribution, the Eighth found itself with more Liberators than it could use in the Second Air Division,

Chief Wapello *carries the white square of the Third Air Division; she flew with the 487th Bomb Group, one of five which were* the result of an imbalance in bomber strength. By September 1944 these groups had all converted to the Flying Fortress.

The 486th steers around the smoke pall at Lutzkendorf in May 1944. These aircraft are from the Zodiacs, the 834th Squadron—each Liberator was decorated with an astrological symbol and named accordingly.

Lieutenant Hugh Shalvoy brought this 492nd Bomb Group Liberator in at Bury St. Edmunds in one of the most spectacular crash landings of the war.

Shalvoy waits for attention in the wreckage of his cockpit. The B-24 ran out of fuel after the 492nd's first mission on May 11, 1944.

but not enough Fortresses to make Third Air Division as large as the other two.

It was during the first week of May that the Eighth was able to dispatch a thousand bombers for the first time, sending them to Berlin and other targets. On May 11 over nine hundred ranged out to attack marshaling yards, and the ill-fated 492nd Bomb Group's silvery B-24s made their debut. On their fourth combat mission, the 487th Group wandered over a flak concentration at Châteaudun and lost their group commander, Colonel Beirne Lay, Jr., and became so shaken up that they aborted the mission.

Oil. The commanders had realized the possibilities that destruction of Germany's oil supply would mean, but their forces had not been capable of waging the necessarily sustained offensive against the far-flung targets. But with air supremacy and the Fifteenth Air Force the picture had altered. For the moment General Dwight D. Eisenhower had the full use of the strategic bombing forces, but there was a wedge that could be used. Attacks on oil would certainly bring the Luftwaffe up, and destruction of those forces by any means was the Eighth's first priority, obviously. The Eighth was more closely tied to Overlord than the Fifteenth, and General James H. Doolittle

The first Liberators in England carried no identification except their serial numbers, but early in 1943 a letter was added. In August each group was given a letter which was to be painted on the tail in an eighty-inch ball, and in March 1944 they received two-letter squadron codes. April brought a color and bar combination to more easily identify wing and group. Pathfinders in the 446th went a step futher and carried a circle in yellow and black, over their usual markings, to single themselves out.

With the invasion approaching the Eighth's target lists changed; on May 25, 1944, the Third Division's 34th Bomb Group hit the marshaling yards at Charleroi in Belgium.

wanted to send them out whenever visual bombing would be possible. It was May 12 before the conditions were right, and nearly nine hundred bombers set out for targets in the Leipzig area. Two hundred fighters met the formations and hacked at them for thirty-five minutes, scattering the B-24s of the Third Division at Zwickau. The Second Air Division had better luck at Bollen and Zeitz.

Bad weather meant canceled missions, but, on May 19, 331 Liberators went to Brunswick, and the usual reception. One force of fighters tangled with the American escort, the other went for the bombers, and the old jinx stuck with the 14th Bomb Wing. The new 492nd Bomb Group lost eight planes, a harbinger of doom that the group could not know about.

During the last week of May a little band of 389th Bomb Group Liberators, with Fortresses from the other two divisions, made a radar attack on the French coast. The mission was unusual because it was a bright, clear day, and the gunners and other uninformed participants were left to resort to rumor for the answer. Naturally the flight was a test, in case cloud covered the coast on D-Day; the results were not really good, but would improve before the crucial day.

Oil was in the offing on May 28, and just over a hundred Third Division Liberators, some of them from the organization's newest group, the 34th, trailed in a huge formation of nearly thirteen hundred bombers. More than three hundred Second Division Liberators filled out the force, which was aimed at seven separate targets. The next day 224 Liberators went to the synthetic oil plant at Politz, northeast of Berlin.

The early June days were completely filled by tactical missions against France, and two more Liberator groups, the Third Division's 490th and the Second's 489th, added their weight. The last Second Air Division group, the 491st, made its debut with the 489th on June 2, and by flying a direct route instead of the undulating briefed route, they found themselves in a flak

Colonel Frank Bostrom's 490th Bomb Group was the fourth of five B-24 groups in the Third Air Division's 92nd and 93rd Wings.

concentration. One 491st aircraft went down, the 489th lost four, and fifty-eight more from both groups were damaged.

June 1944: Spearhead of Overlord

There were three phases to the aerial participation in Overlord: first was the period from D-Day minus 50 to D-Day minus 30, and this involved the decimation of the Luftwaffe. The second ran from then until D-Day minus 1, and targets were to be the Luftwaffe, railroad centers, coastal batteries and airfields within a 130-mile radius of Caen, in that order. Third was the assault phase, which would begin the night before D-Day. At the end of the second phase half of the Eighth's bombers were to be kept in reserve to support the landing, while the rest would strike selected targets in Normandy and the Pas-de-Calais. On June 4 the second phase ended on a good note . . . then D-Day was postponed for twenty-four hours.

So on June 5 the dose had to be repeated. Twenty-nine-year-old Colonel Leon Vance was chosen to lead the B-24s which would hit Wimereux, one of the selected targets in the Pas-de-Calais, in an effort to keep the enemy guessing about where the troops would land.

His group, the 489th, was in the air on schedule and headed for the target. Approaching Wimereux, Vance's ship was hit again and again by flak which mangled the aircraft, killed the pilot, and wounded Vance and other crewmen. Vance's right foot was practically severed, but he led the formation over the target. Holding the aircraft on her one good engine, Vance applied a tourniquet to his leg with the help of the radio operator. Obviously the aircraft was doomed, and at the edge of stalling as the remaining engine faltered. Vance squirmed to a semi-upright position beside the co-pilot and took over the aircraft. He cut the power and feathered their last engine and set the aircraft in a glide that was steep enough to give him some airspeed. As the aircraft sank she neared the English coast, and Vance ordered the crew to jump. He heard an interphone message that led him to believe one of his crew could not get out, so he decided to ditch in the Channel.

In the bomb bay there was a 500-pound bomb that had hung up, adding to the risk. Vance's foot was lodged behind the co-pilot's seat and he could not move into the vacant seat. Lying on the floor and using only aileron and elevators for control, he watched out the side window of the cockpit and somehow ditched the wreck successfully.

The plane began sinking quickly, with Vance pinned in by the upper turret, which had torn loose when the ship hit the water. As the aircraft settled there was an explosion which threw Vance clear, and he clung to a piece of wreck-

The 448th Bomb Group was commanded by Colonel Gerry L. Mason, whose briefings always ended with a little talk, perhaps "Do me a good job today, boys, this is my birthday." Most crews in the group remember him having several birthdays between April and November 1944.

age until he could inflate his Mae West. He began searching for the crewman he thought had been in the ship, but found nothing. He started swimming and was picked up by Air Sea Rescue about fifty minutes later. He was awarded the Medal of Honor.

The last Eighth Air Force Liberator group, the Third Air Division's 493rd, would fly its first mission on Tuesday, June 6, 1944. The crews had been flying practice missions every day and had watched the ships and barges in the Channel and wondered what was happening, or perhaps only when it would happen. At their briefing they were told what it all meant.

Colonel Gerry L. Mason's 448th Bomb Group was given a little talk by their colorful commander: "Do me a good job today, boys, it's my birthday." The seasoned crews in the audience had been present on several of Mason's birthdays since he had assumed command in April. The group had already begun a strenuous series of invasion missions, and one pilot would fly six in seven days. Two or three days after the landing, he wearily brought his crew down and noticed Liberators with vertical black bars on their yellow tails zipping past. This was strange, as the 448th's marking was a diagonal bar on their yellow fins. With some embarrassment he realized that he had landed by mistake at Hardwick, home of the 93rd.

The honor of leading the big show went to the 446th at Bungay, and the machines were taxied out onto the runways and lined up to avoid anyone leaving a revetment going off the runway and fouling up the timetable. The Field Order to the Liberators had clattered endlessly from the teletype, telling the groups of their part. Four wings were to put up 450 aircraft—the new 95th was not in the initial attack. There could be no short bombing, as the troops would be just four hundred yards from the shore as the bombers unloaded. The Liberators would go over in waves of three six-plane flights in line abreast, with a radar-equipped ship in every third flight; everything had to be perfect. There could be no errors. There was bright moonlight, but the 446th's ships had every available light on as they waited. The group's yellowy orange assembly ship, an old B-24D called *Fearless Freddie,* took off

June 6, 1944, and at Bungay in Suffolk every aircraft had been lined up on the runways with every light on. Fearless Freddie, the bold yellow 446th lead ship, was first into the air a little before 2 A.M., and the 704th Squad- *ron's Red Ass, flown by the group commander Colonel Jacob Brogger with Lieutenant Charlie Ryan, prepared to lead the Second Air Division to Normandy.*

first to form the group shortly before two o'clock in the morning. Close by a 389th Group radar ship, Colonel Jacob Brogger and Charlie Ryan of the 704th Squadron droned along in *Red Ass,* leading the entire D-Day force.

Five minutes before 6 A.M. clouds moved in and necessitated radar bombing for the trailing Second Division Liberators, and the overcast worsened during the day. The crews were disappointed that they could not see their contribution, but it hardly dampened the exhilaration of the momentous events. Four missions were flown that day, and the only loss to enemy fire was one B-24 from the 487th; two 493rd aircraft veered toward each other and collided in cloud, bringing the total losses to three airplanes. The Luftwaffe was never sighted, as Eisenhower had promised.

The next day the 487th again suffered the only loss over enemy territory, but the 34th Bomb Group, returning from the second of two five hundred bomber tactical missions, was hit harder. Reaching home in twilight, they were attacked over their field by intruders, and as aircraft scrambled around the sky four Liberators were shot down, and two 490th Bomb Group aircraft were written off when one landed almost on top of another as they scurried for shelter at a convenient Royal Air Force base.

Out of the Night

As in all other air forces, the Eighth's Liberators were involved in special duties and the D-Day operation meant much to do; in November 1943 a couple of squadrons of the disbanded 479th Antisubmarine Group had joined

Toll on the high road: Lieutenant Hansen's Little Warrior, *from the 493rd Bomb Group at Debach, took a direct flak hit over Quakenbruk on June 28. Staff Sergeant Cliff Stocking, a waist gunner on* The Green Hornet, *happened to have an aerial camera in his hands as the wing tanks exploded. The burning B-24 veered in toward him sharply and he quickly forgot his photography and snapped on a chest pack chute, but Hansen somehow maneuvered the torching B-24 away from them. Sudden, terrifying, this chance picture paints a grim portrait of the Eighth's war.*

the 801st Bomb Group to fly "Carpetbagger" operations, the supply of equipment and agents to underground organizations in western Europe. They began early in the New Year, flying glossy black B-24s which had been stripped of nose, waist, and ball turret armament, the space where the latter had been providing a convenient exit for parachutists. With the increase in the demand for their kind of work two more squadrons were added late in May, one from the 467th Bomb Group and one from the 490th. After the invasion workload was over they were returned to their previous owners.

On June 19 a squadron of the 492nd Group was ordered to Cheddington to become a night leaflet squadron, but it was actually mainly a paper changeover because the planes and crews of the squadron were left to be dealt out among the remainder of the 492nd. Removed from daylight operations in August, this group took over the Carpetbagger duties.

July 1944: Business As Usual

The Eighth flew on twenty-seven days in July, occupied with tactical targets and oil. On July 27 twenty-three of 373 Liberators were shot down, and for the third time the greatest loss was suffered by the 492nd Bomb Group, operational for just two months. The group had the highest loss rate of any, and had been mauled by fighters when the rest of the bombers had been unscathed. The Eight Balls had been jinxed, the 392nd was not the luckiest group in the ETO, and the bad luck seemed firmly imbedded in the 492nd. The 14th Combat Wing was regarded with a macabre awe.

Bad luck was not restricted to any one group: on July 24, supporting American troops near Saint-Lô, a bombardier in a Liberator accidentally hit his release switch, and the bombs fell on a landing strip, killing four men and destroying two Thunderbolts. A day later a lead bombardier made a mistake on a visual run and twelve Liberators dropped 47,000 pounds of bombs into American positions. Minutes later another bombardier mistook gun flashes for smoke markers and eleven more Liberators added their bombs to the previous error.

By August the 486th and 487th Groups had converted to Fortresses, and the other three Third Air Division Liberator groups would follow suit before the end of September. On August 7 the unfortunate 492nd Bomb Group ceased operations, the 491st moving to North Pickenham to take their place in the 14th Wing. The grim reputation of the group, which was obviously "marked by the Luftwaffe," caused the incoming unit to insist on retaining its green tail markings; there was no way they would change over to the

East side, west side . . . a photographer on a 492nd Bomb Group Liberator over Saarbrucken on July 16 took these pictures of That's All Brother *and* Umbriago *from the waist windows. Both aircraft are from the 859th Squadron, and* Umbriago *wears a dual fin marking—both the black-circle and the later black diagonal.*

492nd's bare black diagonal. The 489th was then made the fourth group in the 20th Wing, and the 95th Wing ceased to exist.

As the Allies bolted across France, the heavies backed them up. Bridges, transportation, and communications were often the targets, to cut off retreating troops and reinforcements. Supplying the rapidly moving Allies became a problem, and the transport groups could not meet the demands. Impromptu duty for the B-24s began when the "new" 492nd Bomb Group at Harrington, a special operations group bearing little resemblance to the original, and a couple of hundred Second Air Division Liberators were diverted to flying transport missions. The four 20th Wing groups were stood down from bombing operations on August 28, and next day they began delivering food and other supplies to France. On September 12 the 96th Wing took over from them, and five days later the 2nd Wing lent a hand. The situation eased, but Patton's armor was hindered by a lack of fuel, and beginning on September 20 the 96th Wing spent eleven days "trucking" over two million gallons of eighty octane fuel between England and France.

Initially this was loaded onto the bombers in five-gallon cans, passed through the waist windows, but as pumping equipment became available at the French bases the load was carried in the Liberators' own bomb bay tanks and P-47 drop tanks in the waist. The Liberators were manned by the two pilots and a crew of three, and competition amongst "passengers" was keen, with a limit of two tourists per plane. The 467th Group at Rackheath went off operations on September 11 and the multicolored fins and rudders of other groups contributing war wearies for the job dotted the field. Before the operation was over, Rackheath's Officers' Club was well adorned with swastikas clipped from wrecked Luftwaffe planes, and other mementos of overnight stops in France abounded. Lieutenant Ben Marshall of the 458th Bomb Group got more excitement than he had bargained for on September 26. Arriving at Lille around 7 P.M. he found a nightclub and settled down to absorb some cognac and champagne. An overzealous American flyer was showing his Colt automatic to a young French girl and shot himself in the foot; the Germans had only left the premises a day or two before and Marshall was pretty sure they'd come back. He reached for his .45 and thought, "what a hell of a place to die fighting a war." The Liberators flew 2,248 trucking trips in all, and delivered nearly ten thousand tons of supplies ranging from liquid coffee to jeep tires.

While the various groups had been flying transport missions the rest of the Liberators had carried on in their usual role, and it was generally considered that trucking was a rest. Hovever, one supply mission in mid-September proved exactly the opposite, when Allied paratroops were dropped at Arnhem, Eindhoven, and Njimegen to secure a foothold over the Rhine.

A Liberator from the 489th Bomb Group over the Schulau oil refinery near Hamburg in August.

Supplies were dropped the day after the landings and the 14th and 20th Wings were selected to add their Liberators to the transport force. After some practice low-level missions the B-24s were loaded with containers during the night of September 17. A dropmaster from Ninth Troop Carrier Command was put in each plane to direct the emission of the containers through the now empty ball turret openings and the rear hatch. The plan called for an altitude of fifteen hundred feet to the Initial Point, three hundred feet for the actual drop, then a climbing turn to fifteen hundred feet or more on the way out. Twenty-eight squadrons of nine aircraft would fly over at thirty-second intervals at 150 miles per hour.

Early in the afternoon 252 B-24s formed up, after great consternation caused by the fact that the crews' briefing documents and maps for the 14th Wing had gone to the 20th, and vice versa, which meant pilots and navigators had to catch up on the details on the way to the target. After an unscheduled turn by the leading 20th Wing Liberators the 448th Bomb Group lost sight of the rest and proceeded alone, and five lost 93rd Liberators aborted. At the Initial Point there was more confusion when the radio location beacon in the 20th Wing's drop zone was inoperative, and visual markers were hard to spot. The 448th dropped five miles short, some 489th aircraft had to make three runs. The 14th Wing was a shambles when it reached the area, with their spacing shot to pieces, but almost every one of their aircraft dropped in their correct zones, although the containers were scattered and 80 percent were lost. The German groundfire was savage, and seven B-24s were shot down; the Liberator gunners were hard pressed to respond because the enemy used little tracer ammunition.

Although the Luftwaffe was seemingly beaten, flak was taking an ever larger toll. In August 131 aircraft were lost to antiaircraft fire, compared with thirty-nine shot down by fighters. In June, the Eighth had ordered the removal of the ball turrets from all the Liberators to improve stability and permit higher altitude flight; by that time the Liberators were all B-24H or later models, lumbering beasts with jutting power turrets which could not answer the flak gunners. The fighters were still a problem, and more vicious than ever, almost always singling out one particular formation for a mass assault. The success of the *Sturmgruppe* tactics, which had decimated the 492nd, caused Adolf Galland, Hitler's fighter commander, to advocate similar units in all his *Jagdeschwaders*. By August *Jagdeschwader* 4 had its *Gruppe* II specially equipped with the Focke-Wulf 190A-8, a heavily armored fighter with the sole design of shooting down four-engined bombers. Their cannon armament was formidable: two 13-mm and two 20-mm guns complemented by wing mounted 30-mm cannon. The tactic was a simple line abreast attack from the rear, to swamp the bombers.

The green-tailed Firebird, *another exception to the rules by having her 853rd Squadron code letters, T8, painted in black on a white patch. She had been transferred from the 852nd Squadron and perhaps the 491st had more* white paint than olive drab paint that day. Over Holland on September 18, she has just dropped her load of supplies in the glider strewn drop zone.

The group that would learn about *Gruppe* II of *Jagdeschwader* 4 was the 445th, which had not been hit hard since the Gotha mission in February. The 445th was to be involved in the greatest blood bath any single Eighth Air Force group ever suffered.

On September 27 they were part of a force of more than three hundred Liberators flying over solid cloud to the Henschel works at Kassel. The 445th's thirty-seven Liberators, wearing their ominously black tail bands, were leading their Combat Wing when they took a wrong turn at the Initial Point. This led them away from the main column, and it was all that was needed. The Liberators dropped through the murk on what they thought was Kassel and moved on, unaware of their mistake of almost twenty miles. Following the plan, they placed themselves behind the rest of the Liberators and ten minutes after bombs away the first fighters came in. The Focke-Wulf's, almost impervious to fifty-caliber hits as they closed, charged the Liberators, and behind them came Messerschmitt 109s to finish off the stragglers. The German fighters hit them like a rock in a still pond, and the Liberators scattered like ripples. The crews estimated there were ninety fighters, and they took three minutes working over the 445th. Twenty-five B-24s went down in the sky full of smoking wreckage and dying aircraft before Mustangs could lend a hand, and the survivors formed a sorry, loose parade. Two crash-landed in France, another two made it to Manston's crash strip, and another gave up just before her base. Two hundred and thirty-six men were missing, and the returning aircraft carried one dead and thirteen wounded. It was a black day.

The Liberators had flown most of their oil missions in northwestern Germany, to targets like Hamburg and Misburg, while the Fortresses took care of the rest, and it was at Misburg that the Luftwaffe again made its presence felt. The 491st Group had just turned at the Initial Point on November 26 when FW190s dropped on them from the clouds above. The low squadron

A 564th Squadron Liberator streams blazing pieces over the target as the fuselage screws itself from the wings. December 12, 1944.

had bombed early after an accidental release and left the other squadrons to begin their flak evasion. It was the opportune moment that the fighters sought. Twenty Liberators fell to the onslaught, fifteen from the 491st and the rest from the unfortunate 445th. Oil was costing more airplanes than any other target system, but by November it was having an irreversible effect. Oil and transportation were the targets throughout the closing weeks of 1944.

The Battle of the Bulge began on December 18 and the Germans had been helped by gloom which prevented aerial intervention . . . until Christmas Eve. The Field Order called for a total effort, a mission in which every machine that could lift itself off the ground was to participate. The Eighth was to destroy every airfield that could possibly provide German support for Field Marshal Karl von Rundstedt's troops, and the largest force ever to fly from England was airborne on the clear, cold morning. More than two thousand bombers cluttered the skies; the 467th even sent up their assembly ship, the gaudy black, red and yellow *Pete the POM Inspector,* flown by a pilot who had completed his tour, and defended by two men in the waist with carbines. The other groups added their war wearies and assembly ships and the Liberators set out for fourteen communications centers to the west of the Rhine. As the last of the Liberators droned from the English shores the

Gas House Mouse *from the 458th was lucky. She made it back to Manston, one of three special "crash strips" built near the English coast. Manston had a 9,000 foot runway, 750 feet wide, with heavily grassed over and undershoot areas. This red-tailed ship came in in good order on three engines, using* one of the two "white" runways for aircraft under partial control. The "green" strip was for straight-in emergencies, and sometimes Manston handled up to six planes in thirty minutes. Sharing the haven are a British Lancaster and a B-17.

When the Third Air Division Liberator groups converted to the Fortress their aircraft went to the Second Air Division as replacements. The Shack from the 487th ended up with the 458th at Horsham St. Faith. The 458th was the group chosen to try out the Azon bomb from England, with ten specially equipped B-24s. The rigid requirements of the technique could not be met, and after mid-June, less than three weeks after the first mission, the attacks were abandoned.

spearhead of B-17s was already penetrating Germany, and the mammoth mission had the desired results.

For eleven straight days the 467th and the other groups flew these missions against small, hard to find targets. On Christmas Day they returned to Rackheath less three of their number, but a report that one of them was lying complete and abandoned in a marsh in Wales raised some eyebrows. The plane had been returning from Germany when fighters struck and set an engine on fire . . . the pilot ordered the crew to get out and everybody in the waist and flight deck areas jumped over Germany and were taken prisoner. The navigator and bombardier, up front, had not heard the bailout order and found themselves alone in the pilotless aircraft. The engine fire had blown itself out, and although neither man could fly a B-24 the navigator knew the direction she was supposed to be going and the bombardier could work the autopilot. So they set her for France, and as soon as they were sure they were across the Allied lines they bailed out. Meanwhile the plane carried on, settling gently into the Welsh bog when the fuel was exhausted.

The New Year meant more attacks on tactical targets, and infrequent attacks on oil and other strategic targets. February and March offered some fair weather, and the incessant hammering of German communications went

The 458th forms up on the white-fronted, red, black and yellow polka-dotted assembly ship. This was the group's second lead Liberator, and in March 1945 she came in for a one- *wheel landing, spun around and demolished a small construction shack belonging to some British workmen. Next day the workmen were at 458th headquarters with their bill.*

on. During the first week of March the weather got worse, and Liberators seeking targets of opportunity mistakenly bombed Basil and Zurich in Switzerland, haven for hundreds of their fellow crewmen.

Fighter interceptions during March were almost all carried out by jet Me-262s, and the attacks grew in strength. On March 18 Berlin suffered its heaviest attack, but the jets took advantage of the heavy contrails following the bombers, and slipped in unseen on the trailing groups; so although air supremacy belonged to the Allies, the use of successful tactics and new airplanes could still harm them badly. What the Germans lacked in quantity they were compensating for in quality to an alarming degree.

A campaign against airfields which would deny the enemy all bases from which they could interfere with the Allied offensive across the Rhine was initiated on March 21. During four days of fine weather thirty-four fields were hit and the airborne assault across the Rhine three days later saw Liberators delivering supplies to the troops on the east side of the river. The news that this was their assignment met a tepid welcome from crews who could recall the Holland job in September, and the 240 Liberators again met savage small arms fire. Fourteen did not return, but almost all the force successfully dropped their supplies.

April 1945: The Fortunes of War

Colonel Troy Crawford, commander of the 446th Bomb Group, was riding in a Mosquito on April 4, 1945, shepherding his group to their target, a jet fighter base near Dortmund. The intercom crackled with talk of "bandits" and the Mosquito pilot winged over toward the bombers to see what was happening. The blue fighter, with its twin engines, was not unlike an Me-262 head on . . .

Her bomb bays loaded with supplies for the airborne troops east of the Rhine, a garishly painted 448th Bomb Group B-24 lifts off from Seething.

In Lieutenant Don Disbrow's plane the gunners saw the aircraft coming in and poured fire into it. The Mosquito corkscrewed past Disbrow's B-24 and scooted through the formation, followed by the clatter of .50-calibers as men on the other planes became caught up in the error. The Mosquito went down.

Back at Bungay the error was discovered, but by then Colonel Crawford was a prisoner in Germany. He was finally taken to an airfield near Stendahl for interrogation, and Stendahl was a target he knew his own group was going to hit hard within a week. Sweating out that upcoming mission, he was approached by some Germans who knew the Allies were moving nearer and wanted to make a deal. So Colonel Crawford talked quickly and he and nearly forty other American prisoners lit out for the woods, finally linking up with American armor. On April 25 he was back at Bungay.

*　*　*　*

The war was nearing an end, but on April 7 something new was added. Over a thousand bombers ranged out over various targets in Germany and the escort fighters tangled with a score of jets and a potent force of Me-109s and FW-190s, the first they had met for some time.

About half the interceptors managed to break through the fighter screen, and a Messerschmitt 109 screamed into the nose of the 389th Pathfinder leading the Second Air Division to Dunenberg. The decapitated Liberator lurched into the left wing of the deputy leader, and both fell in a horrifying torrent of flame and torn metal. In the wreckage was Colonel John Herboth, the 389th's commander.

There had been other collisions during the forty-five minute battle, and it was thought that these were the result of overly zealous attacks by poorly trained fighter pilots or damaged aircraft gone out of control. Intelligence reports showed it was something else, something the Americans found hard to comprehend. Volunteers had been formed into a group known as *Sonderkommando Elbe;* they had been filled full of Nazi propaganda and sent out to win the war and turn back the bombers by ramming them. The one concession to the civilized mind was that they were permitted to bail out once their planes were certain to hit their target. Of eighteen bombers lost on April 7 eight were believed to be victims of the suicide force, which was evidently never sent against the Eighth again.

A few German batteries were still holding out on the French coast near Royan, denying the use of Bordeaux to the Allies, and on three April days the Eighth was sent to knock them out. The weather was crisp and clear,

At Royan on April 14 the 458th Bomb Group was one of the units making the first napalm attack: Liberators and Fortresses dropped the jellied gasoline in fighter-type drop tanks.

Like an arrow into Germany's heart, the thick trail from a smoke marker streaks down, followed by a shower of bombs from red-tailed Liberators of the 466th Bomb Group.

As the months passed, scores of Liberators and Fortresses from the Eighth and Fifteenth air forces found a haven in neutral Switzerland.

The colored tails of nearly every group can be found somewhere in this photo of the collection. (Roger Freeman)

the targets were little islands in Allied territory, and the flak was not going to be much of a problem. It was to be a series of genuine milk runs. But on April 14 one of Third Air Division's Fortress groups made a second run over the target, and as they dropped the 389th Group's Liberators passed beneath them. Fragmentation bombs hit five Liberators, blowing two to pieces while two more crash-landed in France and a fifth dragged herself back to England.

Colonel Albert Shower's 467th Bomb Group at Rackheath had always been a good group, but at Point de Grave the next day they proved they were among the best. Twenty-four Liberators bombed a coastal battery and every one of their two thousand pounders fell within a thousand feet of the Mean Point of Impact, and half of them within five hundred feet. No other group had ever achieved this, and although conditions were ideal it was a historic occasion; the 467th had been building toward it, leading the Eighth in bombing accuracy since November 1944.

The 467th was unique in another way . . . they were the proud owners of *Witchcraft,* a B-24 which flew 131 missions, more than any other in the

When the victorious Eighth flew across Doolittle's headquarters at High Wycombe it was the 467th that was chosen to lead them. Their outstanding record possibly also led to their being chosen to put an aircraft on display under the Eiffel Tower in Paris; Witchcraft #2 acted as stand-in for the famous original. (Air Force Museum)

Eighth. Over the Hermann Goering steel works at Brunswick she had set an earlier record by being the first to fly one hundred without an abort, and she dropped half a million pounds of bombs between April 10, 1944, and April 21, 1945, four days before the final Eighth Air Force mission of the war.

The Eighth held a showoff parade on May 13, flung across High Wycombe and General Doolittle's headquarters; it was not surprising that the 467th was in the lead position.

So the Eighth had won its victory. Over the years they had fought for and achieved absolute aerial supremacy, and although post war investigations proved daylight strategic bombing had fallen somewhat short of its goal, there is no way any credit can be taken away from the men and planes, a lot of them Liberators, that did the job.

IV
War at the End of the World

Pearl Harbor was half a year into history when the Japanese launched the first planes against Dutch Harbor in the Aleutians. Having no intention of invading the United States through Alaska, their main goal was the occupation of the islands of Kiska and Attu in order to block any American invasion of Japan through the Aleutian chain and the Kuriles, a goal they quickly achieved. Accordingly, when their two-day attack of June 1942 was over, the Japanese task force withdrew. A second goal had been to bring the remnants of the American fleet north, but intelligence was aware that the main Japanese action would be against Midway Island; what was to be another victory turned into a disaster costing four Japanese carriers and turning the tide in the Pacific war.

The Eleventh Air Force, defending the vast wastes of Alaska and the Aleutians, was short of aircraft, short of men and short of bases, though they had been bolstered since Pearl Harbor. Until June 1942 they had had one heavy bomber squadron, the 36th, flying Liberators and Fortresses, two medium bomber, one transport and three fighter squadrons; the three bombing units were combined to form the 28th Composite Group, and backing them up were Navy and Canadian Air Force planes. A mixed bag and a small bag.

In the beginning all American forces in the Pacific were on the defensive, but in the bleak north they would remain that way. The Eleventh was not destined to receive the flood of men and machines which would have vaulted them to Tokyo, and it was not that the island chain was not "a dagger aimed at the heart of the Japanese Empire." It was simply that the difficulties of distance, terrain and weather made it impractical to imbed the dagger. The Eleventh was headquartered at Anchorage with their advanced base at Umnak, some 800 miles away. The Aleutian chain stretched 2,400 miles out into the gray Bering Sea—rocky volcanic upheavals, ugly, barren, and covered with a thick layer of either tundra or muskeg which was incapable of supporting a runway on the rare flat areas.

Aleutian weather is best represented by a persistent clinging overcast which is virtually perpetual, and the few clear areas are small. The weather conditions have a wanderlust which makes forecasts of limited value, and Attu sometimes records only a dozen clear days in a year. Winds from Siberia flustered navigators in their fogbound aircraft and the cruel silhouettes of the islands themselves added to the turmoil in the air. The Aleutians are also unique in the fact that they alone can produce a combination of thick fog and high winds. Though usually neutral, it was the weather which ultimately forced the Aleutians into the background. Neither combatant ever attempted a strategic offensive, although there was painful island hopping by both sides. This backseat role was bad for morale when airmen realized they could die without firing a shot at the enemy, and generals and admirals found themselves left to gather icicles.

*   *   *   *

After their initial strike the Japanese Task Force had retired east, waiting to intercept any American force coming from Midway to contest their Kiska and Attu landings. American planes did not have much success in finding the enemy fleet, but they did know where Kiska was supposed to be, and on the night of June 10 the crews of four B-24s and an LB-30 were briefed at Cold Bay in Alaska; next morning they picked up their bombs at dark, depressing Umnak and took off again to pound the shipping in Kiska Harbor.

The leading Liberator, flown by Captain Jack Todd, took a flak hit in her open bomb bay and erupted, shredded pieces slamming into her two wing ships. A wing crumbled away and the ball of wreckage smashed into a mountainside. Without planting one effective bomb the pioneer raiders headed home, two of them crippled.

Liberators on the Kiska run, 1943.

Between that attack and the end of June only six successful missions were flown, with indeterminable results. One three-plane group tried a time-elapsed run from the Kiska volcano, which somehow managed to jut through the soup, and dead reckoning runs became an accepted method. The flak over Kiska was always heavy, and bombers seeking holes in the cloud were predicting their positions for the waiting gunners. The Liberators flying these missions were equipped with bomb bay fuel tanks, which reduced their bomb load to around 3,500 pounds. Their bases at Cold Bay and Umnak were less than desirable, Umnak's strip being 150 feet wide with little revetment area, meaning the bombers had to work as if they were on an aircraft carrier, landing and taxying to the strip's edge to park before another could follow.

The bombers of the 21st and 36th Squadrons headed out on fifteen days in July, but were turned back seven times by solid overcast. On one of the other eight missions hits were claimed on shipping, but on the rest nobody saw exactly where the bombs went. Finally the commander in the area, Admiral Robert A. Theobald, suspended the bombing through overcast because the results were hardly worthy of the effort and the cost.

The Eleventh Bomber Command had been bolstered in July when the 404th Bombardment Squadron arrived; their B-24Ds had been slotted for Africa and were quite correctly painted desert pink, a splendid touch of color in the gray world of the Eleventh. Soon known as the "Pink Elephants" they took over flying the Bering Sea patrols, flying thirty-nine missions without a single mishap. This record proved so outstanding that the squadron remained in the Aleutians long after others rotated home, and in fact they were still there in 1947.

So the crews flew the long dull missions when they could, and cultivated a characteristic called the Aleutian Stare. It was a miserable life. With only a few old faces hunched around the bleak barracks even conversation became a chore. One replacement pilot found that nobody even told jokes in the Aleutians any more . . . they'd just say "twenty-one" or "thirty-nine" and there would be a chuckle, or perhaps a groan. The new man enquired why and was told that they had given each tale a number—it saved time. After thumbing through the Aleutian Joke Book he thought he would give it a try, and said, "Eighteen." Silence. He tried again with "Thirteen." Bleak stares. He took his colleague aside and asked him why he'd been so poorly received. His friend looked at him knowingly and replied, "It's not the

Aleutian night life, 1942. The Eleventh Air Force did have one entrepreneur who gathered some money and went back to Anchorage to get some whiskey to brighten life up, but he flew commercial back to the States and had a good time with the money until it was gone.

joke—it's the way you tell it." Lieutenant Lawrence Reineke found similar problems as an Intelligence Officer in the 21st Squadron. Reineke arrived with visions of crisply flicking a pointer over a highly detailed map, but found a briefing truly brief in the Aleutians: "The target for today is twenty-three." The pilots had been to twenty-three before and that was all they needed to know.

An LB-30 made the last flight from Umnak to Kiska on September 13 and battle damage forced her to make an emergency landing at the new field on Adak, where a more powerful force had already assembled to surprise the nearby Japanese. It was to be a low-level attack by a dozen Liberators from the 21st and the Pink Elephants, armed with a combination of incendiaries and 1,000-pound bombs. Escorted by twenty-eight fighters they left Adak the next morning and whirled in low over their target, setting large fires and hitting shipping. The mission was a success and although the B-24s were grounded for the next ten days it alleviated some of the Aleutian gloom.

Between June and October the Eleventh lost seventy-two planes—nine of them in combat. At one point the 36th Squadron had had no aircraft at all, and flew a second shift in the 21st Squadron's aircraft. The weather was a deadly adversary. November brought 80-knot winds and a foot of water covered Adak's strip. Nothing flew. The weather ship got off on November 7 and strafed and bombed some float-plane Zekes washed into a creek bed on Attu, but through November and December the Eleventh was all but immobilized.

Adak was only 250 miles from Kiska, but this kind of weather necessitated an American base even closer to the priority target if the air war was to be waged effectively in the few hours available each day, week, or month. Amchitka was a logical possibility and the fear that the Japanese might occupy this island, only 80 miles from Kiska, added the necessary motivation. A small survey party landed from a Catalina on December 18 and confirmed that fields could be laid for the B-24s in three or four months. The invasion of Amchitka was set for January 5, 1943, and the island was secure within twenty hours of the landing.

The New Year weather prevented all but ten tons of bombs dropping on Kiska and Attu in January, at the cost of four Liberators. Two simply disappeared, a third cracked up on Great Sitkin, and a fourth overshot the flare-lit Umnak runway and mangled a couple of fighters. February was a little better, but in April the greatest storm ever recorded hit the Aleutians.

From the beginning of May, Attu became the prime target, in preparation for the invasion in the second week of the month. It was a bloody little campaign for the men on the freezing ground, and weather prevented the air forces from playing more than a minimal part in the battle. While the

After a heavy rain Adak's airstrip sometimes seemed to revert to the bottom of the lagoon from whence it came. These 21st Bomb Squad- *ron aircraft wear the Walt Disney designed squadron insignia, "Wee Willie," a bomb-throwing bumblebee.*

fight went on the engineers were building an airstrip 25 miles away on Shemya, the only flat island in the Aleutians. At the same time they had marked out an area on the east side of Massacre Bay on Attu, and that strip was ready for use by the second week of June.

If Kiska could be invaded and won on schedule the Aleutians would be secure by late summer, and by staging through Adak and Attu the invasion of Japan from the north would be possible in the spring of 1944. For its part in the great plan the Eleventh was hitting Kiska whenever weather permitted, and sometimes when it did not.

Paramushiro: One Man's War

Hardly a part in the "great plan," Lieutenant Lawrence Reineke, the superfluous assistant Intelligence Officer in the 21st Squadron, was passing his time as best he could. Looking past Attu and Kiska on the charts he had seen

Paramushiro and Shimushu in the Kuriles and had checked with one of the navigators, Lieutenant Irwin Smith, who confirmed that it would be possible to make the round trip in a B-24. Because he did not look like ever getting to give a briefing, and because the bomber crews knew much more about Kiska and Attu than he did anyway, he had begun a project . . .

The Air Force had no maps or data on the islands, but, sometime in late May, Reineke had found out about the naval intelligence unit on Adak, and there he talked an ensign into allowing him to delve into their files. He found books dating back to the nineteenth century which gave elevations, currents, harbors and other naval details; it was enough to produce a large outline map of the two islands. Somewhere along the way the ensign had mentioned a bunch of Japanese diaries they had captured and were translating, so Reineke looked over the Navy's shoulder and found the fatalistic Japanese entered most interesting facts in their diaries. They wrote about earth moving equipment here, a gun battery there, more guns coming in, more shipping . . . Reineke began sketching detail on his outline maps.

As expected, orders came down to mount a mission against the Kuriles and Reineke went to his squadron commander. Captain Frederick Ramputi, a hulking former wrestling champion and one of the few men who could fly a Liberator with one hand, listened briefly then told Reineke to do the briefing on the mission.

After giving that briefing in a darkened Nissen hut Reineke found himself being well chewed out by his embarrassed superior and briskly assigned to Shemya, where he was put in charge of pulling muskeg and tundra to provide a firm base for forthcoming 21st Squadron housing. He was not to know that the brass would be at the briefing, nor that they had been told by Reineke's senior officers that there was no information available on Paramushiro. It was to be some time before he found out exactly what had happened after his fateful briefing . . .

Six B-24s led by Major Robert Speer of the 36th Squadron had left Attu on July 10 to make that first land-based attack on Japan, and spirits were high until a Catalina spotted four transports midway between Paramushiro and Attu. From Adak, Major General William O. Butler ordered Speer to divert and go after them.

Pappy Speer was furious, particularly when he arrived and found that Mitchells had already sunk two of the transports and the others were scooting around under an umbrella of flak. The Liberators went in on the deck but found the transports too nimble. Low on fuel, the Paramushiro force turned away for home, but as they did a parting shot from one of the ships blew up in Lieutenant Lucian Wernick's face. It injured nobody but the plane filled with smoke and the 36th Squadron pilot was left with an aircraft with a mangled nose wheel and no hydraulics. The emergency raft had been destroyed, Wernick's crew never carried life preservers and there was a life expectancy of possibly ten minutes in the freezing gray water below. There was no choice . . . Wernick had to land on two wheels, without brakes, on a slippery steel mat. He told his crew they were going to Adak . . . Adak, where the runway began at the edge of Kulak Bay and ended at the foot of a mountain.

Wernick began instructing his crew. After cranking down the main gear by hand they left the pilot alone at the controls and gathered in the fuselage aft of the wings to add their weight to keep the tail down.

Wernick dropped the Liberator to sea level to come in on the runway in a nose-up attitude. At the edge of a secondary stall he popped her up over the lip of the runway and stalled her in, with the big rudders almost skidding along the ground. The main wheels bit and the nine crewmen began slowly walking toward the tail as the bomber sped across the strip. The center of gravity kept shifting with the crew's weight and the bomber's nose stayed

On the way back from Kiska this Liberator found home too fog bound and was fortunate to find this flat space for a successful belly landing.

Kashiwabara Harbor on Paramushiro, beneath the Eleventh's Liberators on August 11, 1943. This second B-24 mission to the Kuriles cost two aircraft of the force of nine. (Lawrence Reineke)

in the air as Wernick kept balance with the elevator and rudder and let the ship have her head. The tail gunner was squeezed into his turret, the crew bunched up behind him, as the Liberator slowed down and began to tilt. Stopping within a few feet of the end of the runway the aircraft sighed and the smashed nose clunked to the ground.

Weather cleared for the Liberators again on July 18, and again Speer was slotted to lead the 1,700-mile round trip to Paramushiro. When the B-24s finally arrived over the Kamchatka peninsula of Siberia the crews rubbed their eyes to see if those really were trees down there . . . the first trees some of them had seen in a year. Arriving over the target at 18,000 feet three of the Liberators peeled off to bomb the air base. Wernick, Ramputi, and Major Richard Lavin made a straight run over the harbor, sighting a big concentration of several dozen warships, transports, and fishing vessels. A few flak positions opened up as the bombs tumbled down but the Japanese were numbed by surprise.

The three Liberators over the harbor had to make a second run after the bomb racks had frozen the first time, and Lavin was having engine trouble. Wernick and Ramputi got rid of their bombs, but Lavin's hung up and he tried to follow them with an engine feathered and a full bomb load.

The other three B-24s over the airfield were watching five Zeros dodging craters as they took off, and a couple of float-plane fighters were boating across a lake. As the bombers joined up and raced off, Lavin struggling to keep up, the Zeros seemed to be gaining on them, but they gave up the chase after a few minutes. Speer throttled back to Lavin's speed and the six aircraft reached Adak at dusk.

The aircraft had no damage of any kind, and the target photos showed that the Paramushiro raid had caused enough damage to shake the Japanese and probably make them bleed other fronts for extra defenses.

Butler asked Wernick to lead a second Paramushiro mission, but he refused to volunteer again, pointing out that they had only achieved what they did by surprise. Next time would not be so easy.

The second Paramushiro mission took off on August 11, 1943, with six B-24s from the 404th and three from the 21st, led by Major Louis Blau, Pappy Speer's co-pilot on the earlier mission. The target was overcast, so the Liberators went in at low level. The Japanese were waiting.

Flak was fierce, filling the sky with smoke. Fighters were up and forming as a shower of incendiaries and explosives struck buildings, a pier and a cargo ship . . . mushrooming fire and smoke followed the B-24s across the target. And through the flak the Zeros were waiting. One Liberator blazed into the ground and the other eight fought their way out for forty-five minutes. Every bomber was perforated by the stream of fire. Lieutenant Robert Lockwood's ship, limping on three engines, was being shot to pieces. His crew was throwing stuff overboard as the B-24 lost height. At two hundred feet fuel starvation stopped all three good engines dead. The pilot's hands flicked out, jabbing tank selectors, booster pumps, and turbos. The ball turret skipped on the water as the engines came back in and Lockwood thundered along a few feet above the waves. Lieutenant Leon Smith's Liberator had taken the brunt of the flak and the fighter attacks, flying at the rear of the formation. They

One of the survivors of the September 11 Para- *craft, a crippling blow which halted missions*
mushiro mission; this attack by seven B-24s *against the Kuriles for five months.*
and twelve Mitchells cost the Eleventh ten air-

thought they were finished when they reached some cloud cover after diving
to 1,500 feet. As he felt his way through the soup Smith kept remembering
Lieutenant Reineke's assurance that the highest elevation on Shimushu was
620 feet, so Smith tiptoed along on eight hundred. When they got back Smith
made a point of thanking Reineke for the information.

Somehow all eight Liberators survived and there would be no more Paramushiro raids without strong fighter escort. And no more until the next step
in the Aleutians, the invasion of Kiska, was complete.

Kiska was invaded on August 15, about a fortnight after the Japanese
garrison had been withdrawn, and the Aleutians were essentially ours. As
one of his last acts as Alaskan air commander General Butler ordered a
full-scale bombardment of Paramushiro on September 11, but withdrawal
of two of his Liberator squadrons had left Butler under strength and he could
only raise seven B-24s and twelve Mitchells. During the savage battle three
went down and seven force-landed near Petropavlovsk in Soviet Kamchatka
. . . the crews came home but the Russians kept the aircraft. The Eleventh
was decimated.

During the fall and winter the tiny air force trained for missions against
the Kuriles and it was February 24, 1944, before the 404th Squadron sent
six B-24s against the islands; five aborted and the sixth jettisoned its bombs
through the overcast.

While the Pink Elephants struggled along an added blaze of color came in with the Blue Geese, aquamarine F-7s from the 2nd Photo Charting Squadron, sent along to photograph the Kuriles. Unusually good weather blessed their first mission, but it was more than two months before their job was completed late in August. Their pictures revealed that the Japanese bases in the Kuriles were hardly dangerous to the allies at this stage of the war.

Time passed, and the Pink Elephants were flying the longest overwater missions of the war. On June 19, 1945, they flew their longest run, the 2,700 miles from Shemya to Kruppu, fifteen long hours.

Although the Eleventh's Liberators never amounted to a full combat group they had helped tie up several hundred planes and the forty thousand Japanese troops who were deployed against a northern invasion. On August 13, 1945, they flew their last mission, against Paramushiro, and as the official history says, they were always "at least a considerable nuisance value."

V

Cactus to Kyushu

The Japanese crew in their mottled bronze Betty bomber could relax. Their landing gear was down and locked, their airstrip on barren Nauru was straight ahead, and their mission was over.

Three or four miles behind, and rapidly closing the distance, a battered Navy Liberator bearing the legend *Whitsshits* was roaring in to spoil their day.

Lieutenant Whitney Wright had drawn Patrol Sector 11 and Nauru that day, and that was always a hot mission. Two VB-104 aircraft had just never come back from this patrol; bearing that in mind Wright had flown a long, indirect route, heading directly for Nauru from the direction of Ponape, the next major enemy base. With luck the Japanese would think he was one of theirs.

The day belonged to flyers, with a brilliant clear sky. The water, far below, was smooth and alive with the sun. Life aboard the Liberator had assumed a temporary serenity by the time Wright stuck her blunt nose right into Nauru's business. He methodically reported the merchant ship loading phosphate at the pier on the west side of the island, and the destroyer lazing a mile or so out from the beach. Pretty targets, but not for a lone Liberator.

Wright, a lean and taciturn Yankee from Hyde Park, Massachusetts, was feeling well satisfied when one of his crew called in that a twin-engine Japanese Betty was coming in to land. It was decision time, and there was little of it. Wright threw discretion to the wind at the sight of the fat, dawdling, unsuspecting target. Knowing that by now Nauru was watching him as closely as he had been watching it, he still found the temptation too great and manipulated the Liberator down and around to slightly below the Betty's

Equipped with a Consolidated tail turret in the nose, Air Force style, one of VD-1's photo *PB4Ys takes off from Carney Field, Guadalcanal, in December 1943.*

course. Closing the few miles between them he brought *Whitsshits* up, gave his sparse orders in his broad twang and felt the bow and top turrets open up with a teeth-rattling roar. Four streams of fire laced into the trapped Japanese; the left engine burst into flames as the bomber staggered about a mile or so from the haven of the airstrip. Wright couldn't figure out why the fuel tanks didn't blow, but his musing was cut short by fighters scrambled from Nauru while he was stalking his quarry. The pilot had seen a flurry of dust as they took off and by the time the seven Zeros homed in on the PB4Y Wright had her down on the water, his best chance for survival. The Liberator churned along the surface, her engines straining as the pilots poured everything on. Wright forgot to raise the ball turret and gave the gunner, cocooned a few feet above the waves, a ride he would long remember. This slight oversight also cost him about five knots he could have used.

The Zeros formed lines on each side of the fleeing Liberator, three on one side and four on the other, staying just out of range as they paralleled Wright's course. Turning in they made head-on runs at a 30-degree angle, one from each side and coming down as Wright sat sweating in the cockpit, watching twin lines of water spouts from their hits coming toward him, and flinching as the turret behind his head punctuated the rhythmic roaring of the engines.

Each time it looked as if the Liberator was going to fly right into the lines of enemy shells the fighters would break off, discouraged by the heavy return fire. For more than fifteen minutes the duel continued, with Wright straining as he manhandled the big plane at the perilously low altitude.

Back in the waist the one gunner, Tony Conti, was bounding from side to side and gun to gun to ward off the periodic beam attacks. Luckily for Wright, the Japanese never co-ordinated their beam attacks and Conti was always there waiting for them. Finally the Zeros went home, and Wright came to the conclusion that he had not come out too well at all . . . they could not claim any of the fighters, and that damned Betty never did catch alight properly . . .

July 1942: The Navy's Lake

The Pacific Ocean area encompasses nearly 64,000,000 square miles; an area larger than that covered by all the lands of the earth. Contemplating the vastness of the Pacific, the Navy had recognized the need for a truly long-range patrol aircraft, and the Liberator was their answer. Capable of carrying the necessary fuel, capable of defending herself, capable too of inflicting damage, the Liberator, called PB4Y by the Navy and Marines, was without doubt the best Patrol Bomber of World War II.

In July 1942 the Army had agreed to the Navy receiving a quantity of B-24 Liberators, and the first aircraft went to the Transitional Training Squadron, Pacific, a couple of months later. The first Navy squadron to receive one (repeat, one) aircraft was Bombing Squadron 101, and after training and fuller equipping they left for the South Pacific in January 1943, led by Commander Bill Moffett, Jr. On February 13 they went looking for their first targets, and in those bleak days that part was easy—they didn't have to range far to find Japanese. The PB4Ys sighted two destroyers and a transport between Bougainville and New Guinea, dropped a few bombs, skidded around some flak, and all came home. The following day nine Liberators, with fighter escort, attacked Kahili. They thundered in on a transport and it was carpet-bombing in miniature as the ship was lost from sight in a huge, undulating cloud of spray. When the water settled the transport was gone, leaving behind, Moffett recalls, "a magnificent belch" of smoke. By then the anti-aircraft fire was picking them up, a swarm of fighters was heading their way, and two of the Liberators were shot down before they could get clear, one of them Lieutenant J. D. Bacon's ship. Bacon had a case of whiskey back in his tent, so that night 101 toasted him and a bitter victory; then and there they decided that until their fighter escort could be stronger they would fight only at night, and it was July 1943 before VB-101 flew another daylight mission.

VB-102 was next "down," in April 1943. Their skipper was Commander Bruce Van Voorhis, who would win the Medal of Honor in July. His squadron had Liberators fitted with nose turrets, in part the result of sadder 101 experiences. This squadron moved to enchanting Guadalcanal, a Pacific paradise code-named Cactus, where the hours could be whiled away filling 2,700-gallon Liberator tanks from seven-gallon cans . . . 360 of them.

Commander Van Voorhis was lost trying to sink a seaplane tender off Kapingamarangi, a tiny atoll northwest of the Solomons, and Lieutenant Commander Gordon Fowler assumed command. One VB-102 pilot, boyish, uncommunicative Burton Albrecht, established quite a reputation for himself when he singlehandedly took on a convoy of nine armed cargo ships and sank three, then beat off fourteen enemy fighters, his gunners claiming three of those too. Albrecht decided to see what he could do at Kapingamarangi, which had taken other crews since Van Voorhis's. One evening, right at dusk, his lumbering aircraft left Henderson Field and headed out to follow his theory that the Zero float-planes, 102's Kapingamarangi nemesis, would be impotent on the beach when he arrived.

He was right. As his Liberator closed in he could see ten or twelve of the fighters and his gunners opened up with everything they had. The Liberator made haste back to the Canal, leaving the beach littered with six fiercely burning Zeros and a few more that were adequately sieved.

*   *   *   *

The first Navy photo squadron with Liberators was, appropriately, VD-1, sent to the South Pacific in April 1943. Commander Robert J. Stroh, who had been Executive Officer during the formation and organization phase in San Diego, was held back when the squadron moved out. His new job was to organize a second photo squadron, VD-3, on the same self-sustaining basis as VD-1—and while the latter went to the South Pacific and Guadalcanal, VD-3 and its six aircraft would go island-hopping in the Central Pacific. Setting up at Canton and staging through Baker Island, they covered Wotje, Jaluit, and everything else in Japanese support range of Tarawa. When the Marines captured the airstrip on Tarawa's bloody Betio, it was Bob Stroh who landed the first heavy bomber there. He had been asked to get a coxswain's-eye view of Roi Namur; pictures of what the landing craft commanders would see as they approached the beach. This was obviously an extremely low-level mission, so Stroh and his wingman planned to arrive late in the afternoon, with the sun low in the west to shield them. Everything went fine, but as the two Liberators passed their target at wavetop height they saw twelve Japanese fighters taxiing out for what must have been a routine patrol. The enemy spotted the two intruders and buzzed out angrily, making pass after pass as the PB4Ys lit out for their lives. Stroh watched his wingman lurch and hit the water, spinning and breaking apart in a way that told him there could be no survivors.

As time passed ever so slowly in the remaining Liberator the Japanese pursuits were finally forced to break off and go home, leaving Stroh with the pictures the Navy needed. Even so, scant time was available for counting their blessings, because the aircraft, although undamaged, had guzzled much too much fuel during the fire-walling run across the ocean. With darkness encroaching on the final glow of day, Stroh decided he would make an emergency landing on Tarawa.

The Seabees were still working on the runway as the Liberator neared the naked island and was cleared to come in. The second the wheels touched Stroh knew they were going to make it, but by the time they stopped rolling there was no landing strip left beneath them. That was the tropical evening of December 10, 1943, and two days later yet another stricken Liberator would frustrate any chances at all of an official heavy bomber christening of Betio strip, when an Air Force pilot would bring the beat-up *Belle of Texas* in.

From Apemama VD-3 supported the Kwajalein campaign, then moved to Eniwetok in the Marshalls to cover the Marianas, and finally Guam, where VD-5 relieved them as the allies prepared for the final assault on the home islands of the Japanese Empire.

August 1943: Corned Beef, Spam, and a Place Called Guadalcanal

When VB-101 went home in August 1943 they were replaced by Commander Harry E. Sears's VB-104, the "Buccaneers." Before they finished their two tours, the Buccaneers racked up an enviable record, including two Presidential Unit Citations. They began their war at fabled Guadalcanal, where during the rainy season their clothes mildewed overnight, and while they staggered through the mud they could gaze upward and watch the palm trees creak as the gentle tradewinds all but tore their roots from the sodden earth. There was the nauseating stench of rotting breadfruit, and as the ground around the foxholes and slit trenches dried, the odor of decomposing bodies would rise up and embrace them. The jungle itself was a rusting junkyard of remnants of the battle for the island, and at night there was the dissonant whine of Washing Machine Charlie, early Japanese version of psychological

Harry Sears, commander of VB-104, the Buccaneers.

Shot up by enemy fighters, Lieutenant Gordon Gray took this VMD-154 Liberator into Henderson Field for emergency repairs. Then they sent her back to Espiritu Santo for major work and #31940 returned fitted out with a formidable 37-mm cannon, (from a less fortunate P-39 Airacobra), fired by the pilot. (Al Bibee)

warfare, to keep them awake and nervy with the sound of his unsynchronized engines and occasional bombs.

Harry Sears had his share of problems right from the start. Bombing 104 had been formed from a Catalina squadron, but instead of the entire squadron transitioning to the Liberator, one half was taken as the nucleus of VB-104, while the other half was left to rebuild with Catalinas again. So there was transition training for the old crews, plus full operational training for the new people. Volunteers made up the nucleus of 104, the crews having been given the choice of staying with Catalinas in their relatively safe operations, or going out with the Buccaneers; Harry Sears attributes much of the squadron's success to this.

When Guadalcanal wasn't muddy it was dusty, and Sears found "a sick bay full of malaria cases, one shower head for a camp of a thousand men, little screening in the camp, and lousy food." To make matters worse, the Japanese usually bombed twice nightly and there were not enough trenches or shelters. Sears says that "the answer was simple. This was an All Hands job with top priority. I had already put everybody on atabrine and vitamin pills, and long sleeves and pants were the order of the day after sunset. We screened our camps, felled trees, made gravel walks to get out of the mud, and dug slit trenches. A few bottles of whiskey in the right places with our local Seabee unit got us a beautiful shower room with several stations, an adjoining washroom with a couple of washing machines, improved messing, men's club and other facilities. We started to live."

Sears's plan worked. The Buccaneers' first tour ended without a single case of malaria or serious illness, the squadron produced its own tomatoes, roasting corn, lettuce, and an officers' club which was so desirable that it was promptly turned into a chapel when 104 left; a chapel without a bar, or the beckoning red light (which was purely and simply the port running light as any sailor knows).

Spare parts were a problem, but Sears took that in hand too. He remembers the answer first came to light when he was dining with the local Air Force group commander, who apologized profusely for the dinner of Australian corned beef. Sears ate it with obvious enjoyment, prompting his shocked host to enquire, "Do you like that stuff?" "I sure do," Sears replied. Naturally he returned the favor soon after, and found himself apologizing for the Spam platter he offered. To his amazement he saw his Air Force guest relishing it and, ascertaining that he did indeed like the stuff, initiated a case-for-case trade of Spam for bully beef. This led inexorably to trading in other items— particularly B-24 spare parts. The Buccaneers ended up with the best airplane availability record in the South Pacific.

While all this was happening, Buccaneer crews were flying nine to fifteen

Commander Harry Sears, skipper of VB-104, in his second aircraft, Mark's Farts.

hour missions every second or third day. Lieutenant John Alley and his crew in *Open Bottom* scored first for the squadron on their first patrol, shooting down a giant four-engined Mavis seaplane. This led to a wave of shoot-downs, mainly hapless Betty bombers unfortunate enough to be patrolling the area. Lieutenant John Humphrey got two in one day, Andy Anderson, Bob Van Benschoten, John Burton, Whit Wright, and Harry Sears all made their presence felt.

Another Betty killer was Lieutenant W. D. Searls, who washed out the commander's aircraft, *Sears Steers,* on an aborted takeoff with full gas and bomb load. After that Sears took over Lieutenant Mark Montgomery's air-craft, # 61. The plane was renowned for having the most luscious girl in the squadron painted on her nose, but was rather indelicately christened *Mark's Farts,* one reason press reporters always refer to her as *Sally* or the *Buccaneer.* The name of *Open Bottom* had to be tactfully obliterated when VB-104 flew Eleanor Roosevelt from the New Hebrides to Guadalcanal . . . Harry Sears was the pilot, and surprisingly the naked young lady touching her toes was allowed to remain. In their area 104 was quite an attraction, with nearly all its aircraft decorated by nude women. Sears well remembers New Zealander P-40 pilots nearly putting their wingtips through the PB4Y cockpit windows as they drooled over the Buccaneers' painted ladies.

It was in #61 that Harry Sears caught six Japanese ships running supplies from Truk to their besieged garrisons. Roaring in at masthead level, he sank four and probably five, and badly damaged the sixth, getting an engine shot out along the way. The message promptly came through from Halsey: FOR THIS ONE PLANE BLITZ, WELL DONE!

*   *   *   *

Gordon Fowler's VB-102 and Sears' Buccaneers formed the Navy Long Range Search Group, Solomons, and as Senior Squadron Commander Sears co-ordinated their operations. That co-ordination was at its best on November 4, 1943, beginning when Sears sighted two 10,500-ton oilers and two *Shigure* class destroyers. It was shortly after daybreak and he went in over their masts, leaving one oiler dead in the water on his first run, and the other ablaze on his second. At 8 A.M. Lieutenant Andy Anderson came upon the scene and set up a low-level run on the burning oiler, scoring several hits and wrapping a length of the ship's antenna around his rudders as he passed by.

Fowler, meanwhile, was hunting a supposedly damaged steamer when he picked up a radio message from Sears, indicating that he had four ships cornered. Fowler immediately headed for the fray.

Arriving at noon, he came across one tanker dead in the water, and a destroyer. He decided to go in low, with the sun at his back, and catch them off guard. The destroyer was not to be caught that simply, and zipped into position between the PB4Y and the tanker, twinkling of life with a barrage of flak. Two miles away Fowler set up his run and stuck to it, watching flak blossom dangerously a couple of hundred yards in front of his aircraft. For ten or fifteen minutes the destroyer and the aircraft jockeyed for position, but always the nimble Japanese ship managed to keep between the Liberator and her prey. Frustrated, Fowler decided to look for another target. The Japanese destroyer, flushed with victory, actually chased him for a mile or so, lobbing shells after him. So Fowler gleefully doubled back, got the tanker between himself and the destroyer, went in low, dropped six bombs, and left the destroyer to escort a rather large oil slick. Fowler's aircraft didn't even have a hole in it.

*   *   *   *

Commander John Hayward of VB-106, which moved into the South Pacific in November 1943. In their first tour Hayward's Hellions lost eight men, less than one full crew, and managed to destroy twenty Japanese planes and sink or damage ninety-seven craft, including a rather incautious trio of submarines. Chick's Chick won her decoration when a Seabee offered to paint the likeness of his girl friend on the PB4Y; she turned out to be stripper Beryl Wallace, and Hayward and his crew were most impressed by the artist's memory. Hayward was a man who left no stone unturned in his search for targets . . . proudly emblazoned on Chick's Chick was the tiny silhouette of a rowboat sunk with its contents, four enemy soldiers.

Rest and relaxation, South Pacific style — cigar stub firmly clamped between his teeth, Whit Wright gives his full attention to a soft ball game on Guadalcanal.

Rangy, shaven-headed Whit Wright, Executive Officer of the Buccaneers, found plenty of trouble in the Nauru sector, and these actions, like the incident with the Betty in the traffic circle, won him the Navy Cross.

On one remarkable day, November 3, 1943, Wright found a ship steaming toward Nauru from Ocean Island, attacked low, and saw and felt the ship explode in a huge burst of fire and smoke. He had hit a munitions ship, obviously. The tremendous blast tossed the Liberator like a leaf, peppered her with 154 holes, caved in the bow window breaking bombardier Tom Dempster's jaw, and blew the bomb-bay doors askew. One pair of shutters just hung down, flapping in the slipstream.

Up front Wright thought they had taken a direct hit in the bomb bay and was pouring on the power as the air, ramming back into the aft section of the aircraft, tried to pull her back from her straining engines. They were 750 miles from home with a wounded man on board, and Wright knew without calculating that their fuel would not get them back in their condition. The crew knew too, and behind him his plane captain, Tony Conti, was manhandling the doors more-or-less closed. The one flapping in the aircraft's slipstream was the main drawback so Conti, with another crewman holding him firmly by the ankles, hung out from the narrow bomb-bay catwalk and coolly pulled the errant door in and tied it down. Several hours later Wright landed back at Gaudalcanal with no flaps or brakes and rolled gently to a stop against a grassy gun bunker. Surprised mechanics and crew found the bomb bay coated with a sticky, powdery substance and scraped out about a pound of it. Lieutenant Jock Sutherland, co-pilot on *Pistol Packin' Mama,* took some to analyze it, and within twenty-four hours announced that it was a type of nitrate used in munitions . . . the Navy confirmed some months later that it was indeed a tiny part of the unfortunate victim's cargo.

The Lonely Sea and the Sky

In any evaluation of the Navy's Liberator operations it is important to understand that their primary mission was long-range patrol. It was not their job to attack enemy task forces—in fact during many operations they were strictly forbidden to do so because their possible loss in action would result in the loss of vital intelligence gained by their patrol activities. So in a lot of cases any enemy shipping sunk or planes and installations destroyed were gravy.

Thumbing through the action reports of these squadrons it is possible to gain the impression that they fought a hell-for-leather war, "slapping down Japs" without a moment's respite. That is simply because these are *action*

Shadow of death. A Navy Liberator sets up on a Tess transport.

Commander Eddie Renfro's Sugar. *She was the flagship of VB-108, which was the first of the Central Pacific Liberator squadrons. Starting out less than a week before the Marines went ashore on Tarawa, VB-108 adapted the method of attack used with such success against shipping and employed it against fortified islands. In January of 1944 Renfro led a formation of ten Liberators over Kwajalen, clipping the palm tops. Only one Japanese gunner responded to them and fire from Renfro's aircraft killed him before he could do any damage; Tokyo Rose gave the Liberators credit for more destruction than they had noticed themselves, and their real mission was magnificently camouflaged. The attack was simply a diversion so the two VD-3 camera planes with them could get low oblique shots of the shore for the upcoming invasion.*

Japanese shipping at Kwajalein gets the treatment from Central Pacific PB4Ys from VB-108 and VB-109.

reports and they do not convey the weariness, the numbness, the discomfort of a twelve- to sixteen-hour flight over thousands of miles of water where virtually nothing breaks the monotony. A smooth shave turns to stubble, the mouth gets sticky, eyes seem determined to close, clothing is clinging and clammy. Every muscle aches and a pilot feels that if he moved beyond an uncomfortable squirm his bones would creak. The sight of an enemy ship on that great expanse of nothingness eradicates every one of these symptoms, and the elation of success could carry a crew all the way back to base, but on many patrols no bombs were dropped, no guns were fired . . . there was only monotony, hours upon hours of monotony.

1944: Stepping Over the Stones

When the Marianas were captured in mid-1944 the Japanese Empire came within range of the Navy's bombers, and once these islands were secured Liberators moved to Tinian and covered northwest, north and northeast sectors to a distance of a thousand miles. Two VPB-116 Liberators took the initiative in the Bonins, shooting down six of eight Japanese fighters scrambled from Iwo Jima to get them. After that, patrol planes were virtually unmolested in the area.

Prior to the initial landings in the Philippines, at Leyte in October 1944, long-range patrols had been flown from each succeeding base in the Southwest Pacific campaign, beginning from Guadalcanal. Pre-invasion patrols were flown from Biak and Morotai to cover the approaches to Leyte, then when Tacloban airstrip was secured the "Blue Raiders," VPB-117, moved up from Tinian and flew the long patrols to the west and north. From there they and the Buccaneers covered not only the coast of French Indochina but also sometimes ranged north beyond Okinawa, flying patrols as long as 1,200 miles.

By early in 1945 five Liberator and Privateer squadrons were covering the enemy coastline every day, from Singapore north almost as far as Shanghai. Two squadrons at Puerto Princessa on Palawan covered the west coast of Celebes, both the east and west coasts of Borneo, and from Singapore to the tip of French Indochina. A squadron based on Mindoro took the French Indochina sectors as far north as Hainan, and two more squadrons from Clark Field in the Philippines covered the China coast from Hainan almost to Shanghai.

*   *   *   *

Justin Miller took VPB-101 down for their second tour and in midafternoon on October 19, 1944, his Liberator was returning from its sweep of the South China Sea when the pilot decided to take a crack at a seaplane base in the Philippines. Going in at around one hundred feet he put ten bombs around two small ships moored at a pier and strafed forty planes on an airfield, then came back around to photograph his work. "We found ourselves heading for half a dozen seaplanes south of the wharf," Miller dryly recalls.

A flak position on top of a large mission house got their number, its fire severing a rudder cable and setting the Liberator's right wing on fire. The starboard aileron was burning away and the plane smacked into the sea and broke up three or four minutes later, about ten miles northeast of the target. One wounded crewman died a couple of minutes after the crash, two more

The finishing touches are put to Lieutenant Oliver Glenn's Urge Me, *from VB-109. During a pre-invasion patrol of the Marianas an escorting carrier pilot noticed the painting and liked it so much that he called his squadron by radio and they filed past to check it out, departing with happily leering faces pressed to their cockpit windows.*

Commander "Bus" Miller of VB-109 became a legend in the Central Pacific. He and his airplane, the Thunder Mug, *took a tremendous individual toll. Among other things, Miller is credited with being the first man to really lift the lid of Truk, Japan's fabled fortress. The story began on April 4, 1944, when Miller was out looking for a carrier in the Hall Islands. It wasn't there, and the next thing his crew knew was when they heard Miller call to his bow gunner: "Keep an eye open for reefs. We're going into Truk." Entering the lagoon at sea level they bombed an enemy destroyer at anchor in the first attack on Truk by a lone aircraft.*

Flying Lieutenant Hal Belew's aircraft while Thunder Mug *was resting, Miller attacked Puluwat, an atoll 120 miles west of Truk. Puluwat was singlehandedly devastated by Miller, who always argued that it "wasn't supposed to be there". For six weeks he waged his war, and by the middle of May a battered lighthouse was all that was left. On this mission he got involved with a flak gun mounted in the light-house, and after that he was preparing to knock out a radio station when a three-inch shell exploded above the cockpit. Miller, bleeding from dozens of small wounds, lands safely at Eniwetok.*

Back at Eniwetok, VB-109 found out exactly what had happened over Puluwat. The blast from the exploding shell kicked the blocks from under the top turret and depressed the barrels. The dazed gunner kept firing, and the fifty caliber bullets streamed through the cockpit ceiling, wounding Miller and co-pilot Bill Bridgeman as their instrument panel disintegrated and muzzle blast singed their hair. The VB-109 commander flew painfully home to the Marshalls—eight hundred and fifty miles and seven hours.

Last flight for the Thunder Mug. *Hit by flak over Ponape, she landed on Eniwetok without brakes. Commander Miller tried to ground-loop her to avoid ploughing through a stack of aircraft, missed them and slewed off the field, crossed a road barely missing a jeep, and rolled down a fifteen foot embankment into three feet of water, mangling the bow turret. The whole crew heard her sigh.*

were last seen floating in life jackets, and Miller and seven others, all hurt, clung to a bobbing bomb-bay tank. Paddling and drifting for three hours, they struggled to reach a tiny island about seven miles off the main island, covered with dense foliage and about a mile and a half in circumference. Coconuts were the only food to be had and the four crewmen who could walk could hardly manage to climb the trees.

At 3 P.M. the next day another PB4Y, piloted by Lieutenant Hamilton Dawes, shot down a twin-engined enemy bomber over their little island as the four men waved frantically to the rescuer they had waited for. The Japanese aircraft hit the water a hundred feet offshore and skipped into the little group of Americans before they could scatter. The wrecked enemy plane killed one of them and injured two others, and its whirling right engine tore loose and seemed to chase the fourth, Lieutenant William Read, gashing his ankle as he leaped for cover.

In the burning wreckage Miller's crew counted fourteen dead Japanese, but a fifteenth had been tossed clear and crawled ashore brandishing two long knives. Read grabbed a couple of coconuts and hobbled toward him, shouting and gesticulating that there were many Americans on the island. He was convincing, and the Japanese headed out to sea on the Liberator's bomb-bay tank.

Miller's crew managed to salvage a pistol, swords, two parachutes, a map, tools, four cans of fish and ten packages of candy mints, and that night two of them tried to swim to the bigger island, only to be forced back. They then settled down for a week, seven Robinson Crusoes, until, on October 27, Miller and the co-pilot got away on a raft they had built. After a week of island-hopping and all-night paddling the pair reached the larger island on November 2, where fishermen took them to the local Filipino guerilla officer. He arranged the rescue of the other five, and then they were taken to guerrilla headquarters. The submarine USS *Gunnell* picked them up on December 2, with four carrier airmen they had collected along the way, and left them on Saipan on December 15; they bummed rides on various aircraft and reached their squadron again on December 19, exactly two months after they had taken off on their doomed patrol.

November 1944: The Buccaneers Revisited

Redesignated VPB-104 in accordance with new Navy practice, the Buc-caneers began their second tour of duty in November 1944. Commanded by Whit Wright, with Lieutenant Paul Stevens as his Exec, they got right back to work and, on December 26, Paul Stevens was assigned the patrol sector from Leyte westward across Cebu, Panay, Mindoro and over the South China Sea to Cam Ranh Bay in French Indochina.

Operating from Tacloban on Leyte, the Buccaneers were flying their PB4Ys at 68,000 pounds gross weight, three thousand pounds more than the emer-gency war overload. Tacloban field, with loosely lashed Marston matting, undulated to such an extent that every takeoff became an uphill run. So that night Stevens lined the airplane up between the flare pots along the runway edges and applied full power. As she rolled down the strip the Liberator gathered speed—Stevens as always trusted that it was enough speed to fly. When they ran out of runway there was a two-foot drop to the water and upon reaching the end of the strip it was a case of pulling the aircraft up and hoping.

Carefully retracting the gear as the aircraft bounded across the water, Stevens gradually gained altitude to begin the climb across the mountains of the central Philippines.

When they reached cruising altitude at 8,000 feet the waist guns were swung out and the radome extended from its belly position, their added drag now permissible.

Dawn was just breaking as the Liberator reached Mindoro, invaded by American troops a few days before. Stevens expected a warm welcome, knowing from bitter experience that the ship and shore-based flak batteries would fire at anything with wings on, and a lone Navy Liberator could expect mistakes to be made. Stevens warned his crew on interphone to fire at *any* aircraft approaching in a menacing manner. Then he moved the radio control to the frequency of the area's fighter controllers to advise them of his presence, but could not raise any response. An enemy air raid was in progress and American fighters were just being launched as Stevens monitored the fighter channel and followed the action, surmising that he might encounter Japanese aircraft returning from their strikes as his Liberator passed over the northern portion of Mindoro. He hoped for a straggler or two, but none came their way.

To ensure complete coverage of this search sector during the critical time of the landings on Mindoro, Stevens was flying without bombs and under strict orders to make no attacks. He had already been mildly chided due to his destruction of several craft on a previous "no attack" mission, but it somehow went against his grain to ignore any opportunity to do the enemy harm.

Passing out of the Mindoro area the Liberator ran into heavy weather and violent turbulence and sporadic heavy rain blanked out their radar, partially negating their coverage of the area.

As they neared the French Indochina coast Stevens let down as a caution against fighter attack, confident his gunners could handle any number of attacking fighters at low altitude. The weather had improved to heavy overcast and occasional showers so Stevens decided to proceed far enough into Cam Ranh Bay to give it a thorough inspection, remembering that a large portion of the Japanese fleet had sortied from Cam Ranh for the Second Battle of the Philippine Sea.

Approaching the anchorage he advanced the throttles to maximum power and started a low-level run. Passing through the harbor entrance the Liberator met a small anti-sub vessel going out, but Stevens ignored it and pressed on. Nine twin-float Jakes sat on the water and the PB4Y pilot was delighted to find this "easy meat," telling his crew to fire at will. One Jake was slowly taxiing and as the PB4Y opened up its three man crew abandoned ship and were left treading water behind their chugging airplane. The Liberator's top and bow turrets laced the other Jakes while the right waist gunner poured fire into the buildings lining the beach.

*Paul Stevens shooting up Jake float-planes in
Cam Ranh Bay, December 26, 1944.*

Stevens's usual rule was "make one pass and keep right on going," but there had been no ground fire and he decided on a second run. One Jake was sinking and another was listing, but none were burning, frustrating for the Liberator crew. Considering a third run Stevens saw Japanese scrambling to their gun positions on a ridge and decided to go. Looking back he saw one float-plane sinking, two listing, and the pilotless plane still taxiing along its merry way.

Heading north, Stevens sighted four tankers at anchor and kept going. At Na Trang airstrip a group of Japanese were apparently undergoing an inspection, lined up in their whites in front of the hangars, but Stevens had to pass that one up too.

A little farther north he turned back toward Leyte and began his return flight. About 170 miles west of Mindoro, at 4:10 in the afternoon, the PB4Y broke out into clear weather and Stevens could not believe his eyes. Beneath them was the heavy cruiser *Ashigara*, with two light cruisers and five destroyers, headed for Mindoro. Sending a flash message, Stevens began worrying about being caught up high by the Japanese fighters based close by at Manila.

A minute after first sighting, the heavy cruiser opened up with its main batteries, also discouraging to any bomber.

At Mindoro the landing support forces had been withdrawn for replenishment and the amphibious forces were still on the beaches in large numbers, along with their usual mountain of supplies. Turning toward Mindoro, Stevens repeated his message several times to ensure that it was received and understood. As he drew nearer he made voice contact with the ground forces and agreed to land and confirm his report. The airstrip was simply bulldozed dirt, and short as well, but as the PB4Y rolled along it she sank so deep Stevens found himself increasing power to keep her moving. Shutting down, he ordered the crew to fuel her and loped over to the strip's operations tent. The Army commander wanted Stevens to attack the force, but he replied that he was under orders not to engage the enemy. The colonel thought Stevens might not mind slipping out to "pick off a destroyer," a suggestion which brought a wry smile to the Navy pilot's face.

The Army considered it a life-and-death matter and finally Stevens bent and requested four 500-pound bombs, in a hurry. The field was under intermittent Japanese attack and he was beginning to wonder if he would get off at all.

When he returned the PB4Y had been refueled but no bombs had arrived, so Stevens and the aching crew adjourned for some cold beans and lukewarm coffee with the Army. They got back to their aircraft just as the bomb truck arrived, and were in time to watch a P-38 crash-land and come slithering to a crumpled stop just in front of their Liberator . . . reducing the usable runway by around a thousand feet.

There was no bomb hoist, so three of the crew began rolling the bombs under the bomb bay. With the forward bays full of fuel tanks, only three men, Lieutenant Garner Culpepper, Lee Little, and bombardier Lee Weber, could fit into the cramped area aft to load the bombs. They achieved this by Weber and Little getting on each end of a 500-pounder and lifting it about two feet. Then Culpepper would slide under it on his hands and knees and hold the bomb across his back while the other two got a new grip on it. Then all three would heave and latch the bomb onto the shackles. By the time they had all four bombs hung it was completely dark.

Stevens was worried again as he set his plane up on the unknown, unlit runway. The takeoff would be hard, but the mission looked impossible. At full power the straining Liberator started to roll . . . the left wheel stuck in the loose dirt and the ship groaned and lurched around toward it. Stevens hit the right brake and the right wheel sank, pulling the plane around in the opposite direction. They pivoted along for a while, their ungraceful gargantuan slowly accelerating until Stevens saw trees ahead and knew the time had come. He pulled hard on the controls and the ship staggered upward.

Fifty miles north he was at 8,000 feet and in the moonlight he could see Air Force Mitchells beginning their attack on the Japanese ships. They were taking a terrible beating from the gunners, and Stevens swung around to the west to better his chances of getting in undetected. He told Weber to pick out the largest ship as his target and make sure of a hit, even if it meant another bomb run.

At the words "Bombs Away" Stevens made a hard right turn, heavy flak feeling out for him, its random flashes eerily etching deeper lines into his boyish face. Rolling out of the turn he looked back and saw one bomb burst in the wake of the heavy cruiser, and at least two on the big ship itself. Weber was overjoyed at the sight of the big ship streaming oil, repeating over and over "Let's go get more bombs, let's go get more bombs!"

The Japanese reached the beachhead about midnight and found only a blazing Liberty ship, a victim of an earlier air strike. Not sighting the other ships, which had slipped to sanctuary a few miles away, and seeing little to shoot at, they retired at high speed, shadowed by Stevens until dawn, when he left them minus one destroyer and with their pride still streaming her black blood.

Bound for home after twenty-two out of twenty-four hours spent in the air, Stevens and his crew were completely drained of energy. At Tacloban the pilot was sent to Admiral Frank D. Wagner, Commander Air Forces Seventh Fleet, who seemed well pleased with the results but a little puzzled as to why the Liberator had not picked up the Japanese force on the outbound leg of their patrol. Stevens didn't find out until later that these enquiries were made to ascertain whether he deserved a court-martial or the Navy Cross. He got the Navy Cross.

* * * *

In January 1945 the PB4Y-2 Privateer came into the forward areas, slowly replacing the older Liberators. With elaborate radar equipment and commanding fire power, Privateers could go places where the Liberators feared to tread. Enemy aircraft and shipping were in short supply and after February virtually the only shipping targets left were small wooden vessels which hugged the Malay, China, and Indochina coasts. Many of these were built in the rivers of Borneo, moving only at night and tying up under camouflage during the day. They were excellent targets, the hunting was sometimes very good, and once VPB-109 Privateers destroyed more than sixty in three successive patrols.

The invasion of Iwo Jima in February brought the Japanese homeland within range and two weeks after the invasion the Liberators and Privateers commenced daily searches of the Japanese coastal waters. It was not until over a month later that aircraft could be based on Iwo, for obvious reasons. One VPB-116 pilot flying a patrol from Tinian to the mainland in March needed a fuel stop at Iwo on the way home . . . he found the landing "especially hazardous due to a soft mat and uncleared mines." The sniper fire directed at the aircraft on takeoff was equally unnerving.

The waters between Iwo and Japan were extensively patrolled by picket boats, an early warning system against American bombing raids. Well defended and heavily armed, these mean and maneuverable little vessels were a tough quarry for the search planes. With Iwo available a PB4Y on Empire Patrol could call in rocket-firing Venturas and follow them in for a low-level strafing and bombing run. Thirteen of these attacks resulted in nine sinkings.

As the Japanese were forced back and resistance over the Empire proved less potent than anticipated the search planes began attacks on the homeland itself. VPB-108, with fixed 20-mm cannon jutting from the noses of their Privateers, went after ground installations with devastating results. One day VPB-116 found a prize opportune target on a low level run to Honshu—rolling over a small hill they saw several hundred Japanese troops lined up for

A couple of VD-5 Liberators go to work near Iwo Jima, February 1945.

Hyuga, *a 30,000-ton battleship modernized by the Japanese in 1937, tempted Commander Whit Wright on February 16, 1945. The VPB-104 commander recalls it as his "best day." Intelligence had alerted 104 that two battleships,* Ise *and* Hyuga, *had left Singapore and were heading through the China Seas for home. The weather was foul, and neither surface ships nor other aircraft had seen the elusive quarry anywhere, except on radar. In his regular search sector, Wright thought he might have a last chance of seeing them before they got right through, and toward the outer limit of his flight he found clear weather, with a little cloud around two or three thousand feet. Wright pressed on another hundred miles, and there they were, with a lonely Jake flying antisub patrol in front of them. A PB4Y did not attack two battleships and their escort in daylight, so Wright closed in on the Jake and drilled it, plus a little ship ten miles ahead of the main force, spotting another convoy in the distance to the north. Controlling his natural urge Wright turned back, shivering in his tropical clothing as the Liberator left snow-covered shores behind her. Wright's "loss" was the carrier planes' gain—this is how they left the* Hyuga *at Kure naval base.*

Looking just as pretty as the Varga girl on her nose, one of VD-5's photo-recon aircraft poses for a sister ship in March 1945. She survived the war and turned up at Alameda in 1946 as the Rovin' *Redhead.*

a dress inspection. The Privateer came in strafing and bombing right along the line, by the numbers.

March 1945: Get the Admiral

On March 17, 1945, Paul Stevens of the Buccaneers was briefed for a specific mission: intelligence had information that a high-ranking Japanese officer was moving from Batavia on Java to Shanghai.

Stevens was more nervous than usual as they took off from Clark Field at noon, because he didn't like the fact that they would be working after dark. His patrol area was up the eastern side of Formosa, through the straits, then south down the China Coast.

After passing Formosa he let down through some clouds and was surprised to see a Pacific rarity, ice forming on the Liberator's wings. He headed for China right on the water, but there was a fog bank along the coastline and he could only get so close, so he proceeded cautiously, searching about three to five miles offshore.

As the miles passed the Liberator was zipping along, aided by strong tail winds. About 150 to 200 miles along the coast Stevens spotted a Japanese freighter leaving a harbor, and farther out to sea a destroyer. Like all Navy pilots he had a lot of respect for Japanese destroyers, but this one looked to be just far enough away to be out of effective gun range so he decided to try it. The destroyer opened up as the Liberator hurtled toward the freighter at 200 knots. Above him Stevens's top turret was roaring, deafening the men in the cockpit. The bow turret was shooting too, and Stevens could see the streams of tracer converging on the freighter, chipping away at her. There was no return fire as the PB4Y lobbed its 100-pound bombs. As they zoomed over at masthead height Stevens looked back, pressing his face into the bubble of the cockpit window like a kid at a store window on Christmas Eve. He knew he had his freighter as he went around for another pass. The furiously blazing ship turned a half-circle, her crew going over the side as the PB4Y hared past.

Two or three minutes away from the sinking ship Stevens's crew spotted

Second prize to Admiral Yamagata's Emily was this ship, the Koshu, *caught by Paul Stevens on March 17, 1945.*

two Jake float-planes going in the opposite direction. Stevens stayed low on the water and joined their formation, holding his crew's fire until they were right on them. Flying along as number three in the formation, the Liberator drew close enough for Stevens to see the Japanese gunner, facing him, look in his direction, look away, then look back again, pure, classic disbelief on his face. It was like a silent movie until the PB4Y turrets cut loose. The first Jake went down hard and Stevens prepared to take out the second. The Japanese pilot, using his best weapon, dashed to the destroyer and circled his protector until the Liberator went away.

Twenty or thirty minutes passed and the coast whipped past the Liberator. Stevens's eyes were following their normal scanning pattern when they clicked onto something about five miles ahead, and three or four thousand feet above them. It was a big four-engined Emily seaplane and Stevens noted it was a fat cat, slicked up and with all the guns removed. He knew this was the target they had been told to watch for.

He yelled to his crew to stand by, and put on full power. He wondered whether he should close headon with the aircraft or come around on her beam to stay with her and make sure. He made his choice.

Making a zoom climb he turned into the other aircraft with his gunners firing into it at point-blank range and saw the flashes of light along the big plane as tracers chewed into it. He realized that he should have told his crew to get an engine to slow her down, because at the end of the zoom climb the PB4Y stalled out and Stevens lost height and distance recovering. The Emily was heading north, descending slowly, and Stevens raced after her; but even with full power he was gaining too slowly. The co-pilot asked him how far they were going to chase her. "To Tokyo if necessary," Stevens snapped excitedly, but the question stuck in his mind. He had used up a lot of fuel on the freighter and the Jakes and now he had to decide whether to get the Emily and risk an almost certain night ditching after their fuel ran out. He was heartsick as he reluctantly turned homeward and let the big Japanese flying boat draw away. The sight of that plane slipping farther away nullified the exultation over the freighter and the Jake . . . Stevens felt like any gambler who wins then loses his gains. The Liberator arrived back at Clark Field after more than thirteen hours in the air, and a dejected Stevens went to make his report.

It was at lunch two days later that he noticed Whit Wright and Captain "Doc" Jones, Commander of Fleet Air Wing Seventeen, chortling and furtively glancing in his direction. Finally they called him over to their table and Wright said, "You got him, Steve, you got him! The admiral went down!" Stevens just looked at them and mumbled, "No shit!"

When he finally coaxed the Intelligence Officer into giving him the details he found that his firing pass had killed the Japanese pilots and the navigator had tried to land on a river near the Chinese coast. The Emily crashed, but Admiral Seigo Yamagata and some of his staff survived. Realizing that capture was close at hand he took the honorable way out and fell on his sword. It was a hell of a way to shoot down a Japanese admiral, but Stevens and his crew had done it.

One of Bunker Hill's *Hellcats wheels past*   *April 1, 1945.*
a VD-5 Liberator over Okinawa on L-Day,

April 1945: The Missile That Wouldn't Be Guided

The "Bat" was basically a plywood glider shell encasing a 1,000-pound bomb, and one was supposed to be suspended under each wing of a Privateer, controlled from the aircraft until its inbuilt radar was locked on the target for directional homing. VPB-109 was selected as the first Bat unit, specialists were attached to the squadron, and in April 1945 they joined Fleet Air Wing 10 and were based at Palawan. Operations began immediately, but the Bats seemed worthless, traveling erratically and falling short. Still, on April 28, two aircraft surprised themselves during a shipping strike against Balikpapan harbor; their intended target was a large transport, and three Bats were released. One traveled true but struck a small freighter tied up at a dock, falling somewhat short of the transport but destroying the freighter and part of the dock. The second missile struck another freighter in line with the transport and destroyed it, and the third turned 45 degrees to the right a quarter of a mile from its target and zipped ashore, blowing up a large oil storage tank at the Pandansari refinery. The first truly successful Bat attack was on May 27, when Lieutenant Leo Kennedy sank a destroyer on the high seas, the missile blowing the entire bow off. The Bats had flown through typhoons, been pulled apart and put together again, stacked in the sun and dust of Palawan, then the mud and mould of Okinawa . . . unprotected. It was not really surprising that negative Bat attacks went on.

Although there were many hiding places in the myriad islands off the coast of Korea, the attacking search planes kept pounding until this last line was cut. On May 30 four VPB-109 Privateers sank a tanker and a picket boat and damaged a freighter, two cargo ships, a tug, nine picket boats, two lightships, a tanker, and two transports. But antiaircraft fire from the ships was accurate, and Lieutenant Clifton Davis's plane, strafing at low level while another aircraft lined up for a Bat attack, was hit and severely damaged. His co-pilot was wounded and his Plane Captain badly hurt. With his radio equipment shot out he could not warn the following planes and Lieutenant Joe Jobe was hit as he came in at low-level, then Leo Kennedy, following him, was killed instantly when a 20-mm shell exploded in the cockpit.

On May 31 the squadron was relieved by VPB-123 and moved back to Tinian for rest and repairs.

Patrol Bombing 123 encountered similar problems with the Bats, and pilots carrying them were chagrined because aircraft using the good old ways were scoring, while their missiles floundered. Arriving at Okinawa in June, VPB-124 was reluctant to use Bats at all except under ideal conditions, and soon the project was dropped. The subsequent investigation cleared the

Fleet Air Wing 17 aircraft ranged all over Formosa, pecking away at targets of opportunity.   *This Nate and its companions were caught flat-footed at Koshun airstrip.*

missiles and each day two planes were loaded up with the remaining Bats and stood alert waiting for suitable targets.

The first Privateer squadron was VPB-118, mainly moulded around a core of experienced crews from seasoned squadrons like the Buccaneers. On May 3 six crews were briefed for a special strike on the heavily defended Kanoya Airfield on southern Kyushu, where a concentration of Baka suicide bombs and their Betty delivery aircraft were based. Lieutenant Commander Art Farwell led the first section and Lieutenant Mark Montgomery led the second, but Farwell's flight was forced to turn back. One hundred miles from the target Montgomery dropped down so low that the Privateer left a trail on the water beneath her; his two wingmen were stepped up slightly as he pulled up to two hundred feet about ten miles from the target. The field's lights

Captain C. B. Jones, commander of Fleet Air Wing 17, had become aware of the schedule of an airline the Japanese were running from Japan to Kiirun on Formosa. Takeoffs and landings were at sunrise and sunset, so he put one Liberator over Kiirun at 10,000 feet at those times . . . seven planes were shot down and the airline ceased to exist. Lieutenant

George Waldeck from VPB-104 got this Sally on April 22, 1945. Seeing her from fifteen miles away, Waldeck crept up to within five hundred feet unobserved. His bow and top turrets poured four hundred rounds into her, setting fire to both engines. The entire tail section broke off as she fell away.

A wart-nosed Privateer from VPB-106 on Palawan in the Philippines, July 1945.

were on, the Privateers found themselves in the landing circle, and down went sixty 100-pound bombs on the revetments and aircraft. The PB4Y-2s strafed hangars and buildings in the glow of the fires and as the flak chased them from the target they peppered a railroad locomotive. Rounding the southern tip of Kyushu they spotted a small freighter. The Privateers turned on their formation lights, formed a traffic pattern around the ship and poured the rest of their ammunition into it, leaving it burning furiously.

One of the VPB-117 Blue Raiders' pilots at Tacloban, Lieutenant Arthur Elder, established one of the outstanding individual records of the war. In seven weeks beginning in February 1945 he reportedly destroyed 26,000 tons of enemy shipping and damaged another 30,000 tons, shot down two aircraft, destroyed twelve more on the ground and raided shore installations from Sarawak to Borneo to Tourane on the Indochina coast. One of his most spectacular flights was when he penetrated the Mekong Delta, bound for Saigon. Following the deep channel he found ten large merchant ships with escorts at anchor. In three bombing and strafing runs he sank eight large ships and ten smaller ones. Heading south again Elder saw a Japanese seaplane bound for Saigon at 300 feet and shot him to flaming wreckage as an afterthought.

One of VC-5's Liberators causes a traffic jam somewhere in the Philippines.

As a one hundred pounder demolishes a dock, the tail gunner on this Liberator gets in a few shots at junks in Hoi How Bay on Hainan Island. (C. B. Jones)

The first reconnaissance of Singapore by the Navy was by two VPB-106 Privateers from Palawan, who looked it over in May 1945. After that they and VPB-111 repeatedly checked the progress on repairs to four Japanese cruisers which had retired there after the Battle of Leyte Gulf. There were still fighters defending Singapore, and patrol planes were always sent there in pairs for mutual protection. Finally the PB4Y2s gave the green light and two of the cruisers were sunk by British submarines shortly after they left the haven of the harbor.

An End in Sight

With so few aerial and shipping targets, the patrol planes began to go inland. The Blue Raiders (VPB-117) became an anti-railroad squadron, their daily patrols including attacks on the Saigon-Tourane Railroad; shortly afterward the railroad shut down.

The Japanese had problems, the answer: highway transportation. So sorry . . . the Navy knocked out so many trucks that one crew proudly reported the destruction of one 1937 Ford V-8 Tudor Sedan. Not to be outdone, Intelligence pored over the photo and came up with a correction . . . it was, in fact, a Fordor! In the meantime the patrol bombers were hitting blockhouses on Hainan and strafing the numerous troops evacuating the coastal areas . . . on foot.

* * * *

Privateers moved up to Okinawa in April and the crews lived, ate and slept in mud. Yontan Field was miserable, but by May there were usually two full squadrons there, rotating every few weeks between Tinian and Okinawa. These aircraft harassed Japanese shipping crossing the China Sea to Tsushima Straits, the Inland Sea and the home ports and this was the last opportunity for the crews to get more shipping. Flown in two-plane sectors, Privateers by day and Martin Mariners by night, these patrols were so effective that the bedraggled convoys were forced to follow the coast of China north to the Shantung Peninsula then across the Yellow Sea to Korea, and down the west coast to Tsushima Straits, crossing to the home islands in darkness.

The July 1945 carrier plane strikes against Japan put the patrol planes into the role of flying as a barrier between the fleet and any outgoing Japanese force and covering fleet refueling operations. They also flew special weather flights, air-sea rescue missions, anti-submarine patrols and "super-Dumbo" flights covering Superfortress and P-51 strikes. The four Iwo-based squadrons were flying some crews two days out of three, which was asking much of them.

Strikes were flown against industrial and railroad targets in Korea as the shipping disappeared, and by war's end the Liberators and Privateers had accomplished an incredible record. Twelve fifteen-plane, eight-crew squadrons, each flying six routine patrols a day—a total of seventy-two daily flights—had provided complete daylight search coverage from Singapore and Borneo to Korea, Kyushu, and Honshu . . . these were the anonymous, almost forgotten "Navy land-based bombers."

Flying Tail?, *Lieutenant Commander Art Farwell's aircraft. Farwell, skipper of VPB-118, twice ditched a Privateer, the second time under less-than-ideal conditions . . . having sunk one tanker he was attacking another when twenty millimeter flak set fire to the number 3 engine and number 4 died completely. The* *hydraulics were gone and the emergency flap system was out. The lop-sided PB4Y-2 hit the water at 105 knots without flaps and with the bomb bays wide open. All thirteen crewmen got out and within thirty minutes were aboard a Martin Mariner which had raced and beaten a Japanese vessel to pick them up.*

VI

Over the Hump

The flight across the Hump began at a field called Chabua, in the Indian province of Assam. When the Japanese cut the Burma Road China's forces were isolated from the Allied supply line which meandered to them through the Middle East, and the prospects were grim unless an airlift could be organized, over the Himalayas from India to Kunming, China.

The terrain was the most malevolent of any that ever passed beneath an airplane; the deadly peaks of the tallest mountains in the world lay to the north, and the winds which lashed down from Tibet spent themselves on the rocky heights between Chabua and Kunming. These mountains, while not four-mile-high monsters like Everest, were high enough to make it necessary to fly at 20,000 feet to ensure clearing them. The route through the passes was deadly in anything but perfect weather, and perfect weather on the Hump route was a rarity.

During the monsoon the thunderheads built up in thick, smoky pillars to 20,000 feet and more, and within the dense, clammy masses lurked every kind of circumstance conceived by Thor to strike an aircraft from the skies. The mountainous jungles were littered with the gleaming wreckage of Hump flyers who had faltered.

The path to Chabua is traced by the Brahmaputra River, soon known to the regulars as the "Brahmaputrid." There is beauty and tranquillity in the soft mirrors of the rice paddies, the lush gentility of the tea plantations—even beauty in the heavy layers of cloud and the bluish mountains, dimly visible. But to the Hump flyers those clouds were full of rocks.

* * * *

One of the most tenacious B-24Ds of them all was the 308th's Chug-a-Lug, *back at Kunming from a mission in 1943.*

Led initially by Brigadier General Caleb V. Haynes, some of the best pilots of Air Corps Ferrying Command were given the job of setting up the India-China route, and Haynes was in Assam by April 1942, just two months after the Japanese boasted of their successful closing of the Burma Road.

Of the sixty-four aircraft used during the first eight months seventeen were wrecked, shot down, lost or otherwise written off. The fields were inadequate, parts were scarce, and the route was from a narrow strip rising out of a tea plantation. Any deviation to the west brought an aircraft into contact with the area housing the highest mountains in the world, and any to the east meant two hours over Japanese occupied territory.

The India-China Wing, one of nine under Air Transport Command, was organized in December 1942, and eventually took greater tonnage over the Hump route than had been carried over the Burma Road. That cost a lot of men . . . the India-China Wing was the first "non-combat" outfit to receive a Presidential Unit Citation, which speaks for itself.

The 450-mile flight could vary in time, depending on the winds; it was standard operational procedure to make no concrete appointments. The temperature at takeoff could be around 120 degrees, with the cockpit like a Turkish bath, but after the four-mile climb to clear the peaks the crew would be sucking oxygen in their heaviest flight gear, and watching the undulating Davis wings for the first signs of ice.

The Japanese fighters could be a problem if they could find the transports, but generally the Hump flyers were too busy reading instruments to look for them; later some C-87s were equipped with two fixed .50-caliber guns, fired by the pilot, just in case a Japanese fighter happened to pass directly in front of the aircraft.

* * * *

The 7th Bomb Group

On the Indian side of the Hump, General Brereton's Tenth Air Force had one Liberator group, the 7th. The Tenth had traveled around with LB-30s and B-17s during the blacker, earlier days of the war, and ended up in India in March 1942, with their motley collection of Liberators and Fortresses. Later in the year they converted to B-24s, and were allotted thirty-five aircraft in four squadrons. Accordingly, the Tenth Air Force had thirty-two B-24s by the end of 1942. In October a small flight from the 436th Squadron, led by Major Max R. Fennell, had carried out the first offensive strike north of the Yellow River. Fennell had been borrowed from the Ninth Air Force because of his familiarity with the target region and the mission left Chengtu on the afternoon of October 21 to loose their bombs over the Lin-hsi mines, hoping to destroy power plants and pumping stations. Had this mission been successful these mines, which produced 14,000 tons of coal per day, would have been flooded and immobilized for several months, but though the bombs fell around the target they failed to destroy the crucial parts.

Of that early 7th Bomb Group, 75 percent was paper. Their 9th Squadron was still in the Middle East, and the 492nd and 493rd were cadres waiting for airplanes, so in essence the 7th Bomb Group in India was the 436th Bomb Squadron. In November they reinstituted a regular run to the Rangoon area, and on three days dropped their loads into the midst of six or seven hundred railroad cars in the Mandalay marshaling yards. Two days later six aircraft attacked again, and on November 28 nine aircraft led by the 7th's commander, Lieutenant Colonel Conrad F. Necrason, made a 2760-mile round trip to Bangkok to seriously damage an oil refinery. On the last day of the month the Liberators extended their attempted interdiction of the water approaches to Burma by initiating a series of strikes on Port Blair in the Andaman Islands.

By January 1943 the 7th was up to strength, with two squadrons at Gaya and two more at Pandaveswar. The protection of the Hump route would be shared by the air forces at either end, but at that time Arnold was against

General Claire L. Chennault's China Air Task Force ever becoming the Fourteenth Air Force, believing that it should continue as an arm of the Tenth. Arnold's main concern was the problem of supplying fuel, and while he acknowledged the craggy Chennault as a brilliant commander, he made his reservations clear. He did offer substantial help, including promising the 308th Bomb Group and their Liberators, originally destined for the Eighth Air Force. In March 1943 they were in China and took off on their first mission in May; the 308th was probably the unluckiest bomb group in all the Army Air Forces . . . it had been "anticipated" that their operations would impose no additional strain on the air transport line, because they would double as transports, carrying their own supplies.

1943: The 308th Bomb Group and "Supply to China"

General Arnold called supply to China the "greatest single challenge to the efficiency of the Air Forces . . . a C-87 Liberator transport must consume three and one-half tons of 100-octane gasoline flying the Hump over the Himalaya mountains between Assam and Kunming, getting four tons through to the Fourteenth Air Force. Before a bombardment group in China can go on a single mission in its B-24 Liberators, it must fly the Hump four times to build up its supplies." That "bombardment group" was the 308th, and all their bombs, ammunition, gasoline, oil, and whatever else they might need had to be flown to them across the Hump, and because they had B-24s which were akin to C-87s somebody decided they would supply themselves.

So the 308th's crews flew over the Hump between missions and picked up enough gas and bombs for the next mission. General Arnold's figures seem a little erratic, at least for one 308th Liberator, the *Doodlebug*. This old B-24D carried eleven stenciled bomb symbols, ten little Japanese flags below those, and *one hundred and twenty* tiny snowcapped mountain peaks. *The Pelican*, another B-24D, flew the Hump thirty-six times in five months, in addition to her bombing missions. Her pilot, Lieutenant Jack Keene, recalled one trip from China to Chabua: "We went to 28,000 feet and right into solid, overcast weather. The ship started icing and soon our radio compass went out. We knew we were some place over the field, and we fooled around for a half hour trying to find a hole in the clouds. Then we gradually descended, thinking we were in a valley. At 13,000 feet a peak appeared directly in front of us. We missed that one by a few feet."

They were sure they were hopelessly lost and kept flying for an hour and a half until their radioman finally picked up the bearing signal flashed from the field.

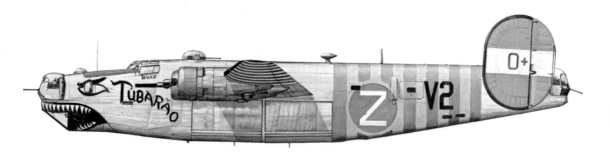

Tubarao *was an original 491st Bomb Group aircraft, serving her time with the 854th Squadron before "retiring" to become the group's assembly ship. She was a B-24J-145-CO, serial number 44-40101.*

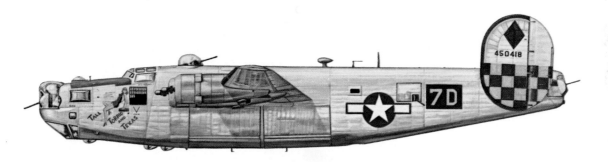

Lieutenant Carl McKinnon's home was Iowa Park, Texas, but his B-24M-1-FO, 44-50418 was actually named for a long-forgotten starlet who was said to possess these three qualities in abundance.

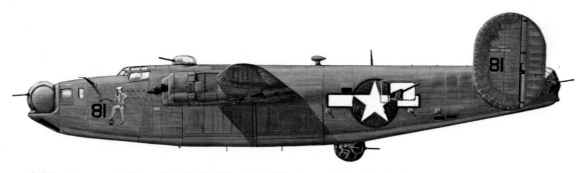

Whitsshits *was built as B-24D-90-CO 42-40726, but with the Navy's Buccaneers squadron she wore the Bureau of Aeronautics Number 32081, and the Erco bow turret.*

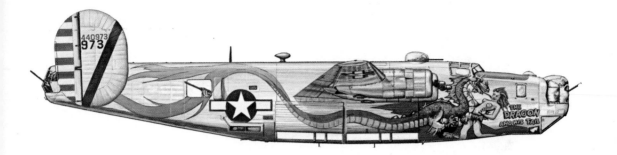

Probably the most lavishly decorated B-24 of them all, The Dragon and His Tail *flew with the 64th Squadron of the 43rd Bomb Group. Beneath it all she was a B-24J-190-CO, serial 44-40973.*

The Mitsubishi A6M3 Model 22 "Zero-Sen" Reisen, known to the Allies as Hamp. This plane flew with the 251st Kokutai in the Solomons in 1943.

A heavily armed and armored Focke-Wulf 190A-8 from Gruppe II of Jagdeschwader 4. This aircraft had engine trouble on New Year's Day, 1945, and was forced to land at the 404th Fighter Group's forward base in France.

The Flying Fortress got most of the glory, but in this case it was deservedly so. Nine-O-Nine *flew one hundred and forty missions with the Eighth Air Force's 91st Bomb Group.*

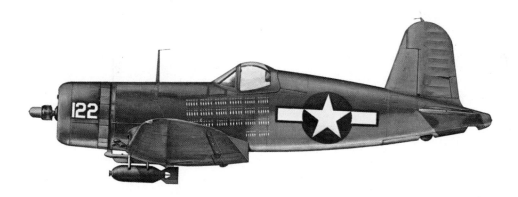

"Ole 122" flew more than one hundred dive-bombing missions with the Marines' VMF-111, the Devil Dogs, and had an official citation varnished into her cockpit. The Corsair was one of the finest fighters of the war, and many Liberator crews were glad to see them.

Little friend to the Eighth and Fifteenth's bombers, the P-51 Mustang changed the face of the air war over Europe. This P-51B, The Iowa Beaut, *flew with the 355th Fighter Group.*

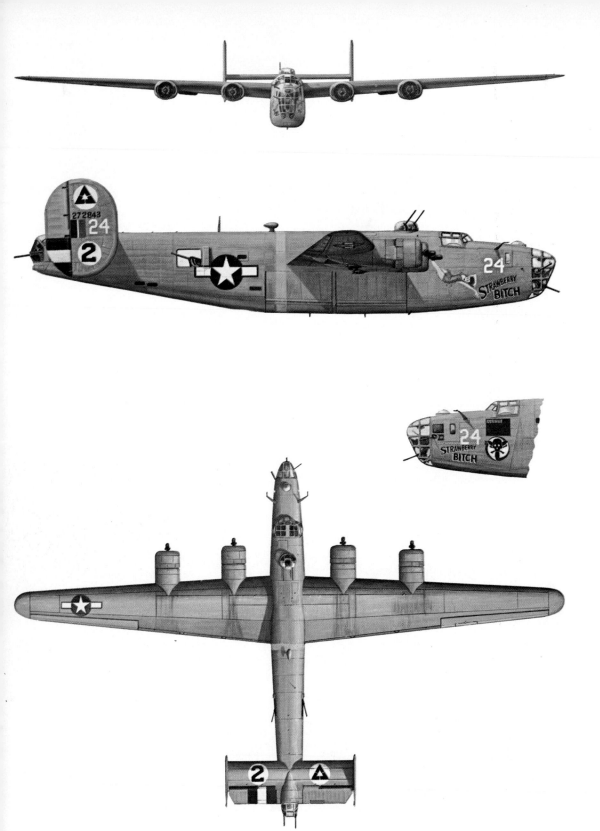

The last surviving B-24D, 42-72843, the Strawberry Bitch, *in her full Liberandos regalia. The skull and crossbones is the 512th Squadron insignia. Now on display at the Air Force Museum, she flew fifty-five missions.*

Lieutenant Jack Keene's Pelican *was a Hump veteran. About mid-October of 1943 fighters began to attack cargo planes, so 308th Liberators flew the Hump in loose formation, hoping to be mistaken for C-87s. They continued using the southernmost route while the regular transport ships flew farther north. It was a great success, with the B-24s getting eight fighters in two days.*

Doodlebug, *with the Chinese equivalent beneath (if there is one), displays the 120 Hump symbols which made her something special in the 308th Group.*

"By that time," Keene went on, "we had just ten minutes gas supply left and we were ready to hit the silk. However, we swung around at about 600 feet and tried coming in on the final approach, but we lost the field and had to climb back again to 2000. The next time, and how I still don't know, we landed safely."

And there was *The Mighty Eight Ball* and the *Snowball from Hell*, whose crew had brought her from the States. The latter made more than thirty-five trips over the Hump before the end of 1943, and on one of these she hit a downdraft so vicious that she plummeted a thousand feet in three seconds. Everything in the aircraft flew up and hit the ceiling, including her nervous crew. Another time, ten inches of ice crusted onto the top of the wings, the ailerons constantly froze and had to be wrenched free, and icicles dangled from the radio antenna; once they landed in China with two engines out on one wing, a nerve-wracking way to complete any flight, but moreso a Hump flight.

Having flown no missions except supply runs since July 29 of 1943, the 308th went back into action on August 21. The plan called for fourteen B-24s from Chungking to be joined at Hengyang by Mitchell medium bombers and P-40s for an attack on Hankow, but it was one of those days when nearly everything went wrong. Shortly before the Liberators were due over Hengyang, Colonel Bruce Holloway, commander of the 23rd Fighter Group, had to send his shark-mouthed P-40s up to meet an incoming flight of Japanese planes. After the enemy was driven off Holloway called his fighters in for servicing, but time was short and only six of the promised twelve could be made ready for the scheduled rendezvous. The Liberators missed Hengyang altogether anyway and flew on to their target, where they were immediately jumped by a swarm of fighters, estimated at somewhere between sixty and one hundred. The Japanese were unusually daring and determined and on their first pass shot down the plane carrying squadron leader Major Bruce Beat, and wounded the pilots in each of the lead planes. For twenty-seven minutes the battle raged. A second Liberator crash-landed with three dead and two wounded, while a third was so badly damaged it force-landed at Ling Ling. The others reached Kweilin, all but two were badly shot up. In the battered airplanes a gunner was dead and three pilots and a co-pilot wounded.

Three days later fourteen more Liberators took off from Kunming for a similar Hankow attack and again the mission was doomed. Seven planes ran into bad weather and returned home, leaving the other seven, from the 425th Squadron, to go in alone. The fighters and Mitchells joined in on schedule this time, and all looked fine until the bombs were away . . . heavy, accurate flak was followed by forty enemy fighters, singling out the lumbering B-24s. In forty-five fierce minutes the Liberators went down one by one. When the Japanese finally broke off only three remained in the air. All crippled, they got home to Kweilin, with one pilot and a crewman dead, and six more wounded. One of the three surviving aircraft one crashed on returning to Kunming the next day, killing ten and injuring two, and the 425 Squadron had ceased to exist.

* * * *

A Grand Plan

From the beginning of 1943 until the monsoon, Rangoon had been regularly attacked by the Liberators; oilfields, airstrips, port facilities, rail centers and shipping were the priority targets. Aside from shipping, all strategic targets worthy of attack by B-24s and within their range lay in the vicinity of Rangoon, and the greatest effort of the 7th Bomb Group was aimed in that direction. The Japanese had built up their defenses until Rangoon became one of the most heavily defended targets in Southeast Asia, with heavy flak and searchlight installations; the greater part of enemy fighter strength

The 7th Bomb Group adopted a checkered rudder marking to identify their aircraft, with the placement of the patterned area indicating the squadron.

in Burma was based at Mingaladon and other nearby airfields, adding to the hazards.

Rain and fog had cut down the number of Rangoon missions in the summer, but in July, weather permitted the bombing of the Syrian refineries. In September both the refineries and the Sule Pagoda docks were bombed and better weather in October brought regular missions.

South East Asia Command, uniting the British and American forces, had become a reality in November 1943, with Admiral the Lord Louis Mountbatten, the youngest supreme commander since Napoleon, as leader. Major General George E. Stratemeyer became chief of Eastern Air Command, headquartered in Calcutta, and he had always been eager to use the American and British air forces closely together. In November he had planned the most significant CBI missions of all when he proposed that the combined strength be used to completely destroy the vital installations around Rangoon; with the danger of enemy attacks on Assam and Calcutta growing with enemy strength in southern Burma, everyone was enthusiastic. The 308th would need to be moved to India, but as they were hamstrung by lack of fuel and would return fully loaded by the Hump route, Chennault had no objections.

Specific targets were given priority based on the results of earlier bombings. The locomotive works at Insein and the Mahlwagon marshaling yards were selected as good night targets because of their easily seen position between two bends in a river, with the lucrative docks at Rangoon as the third major objective. The night attacks would be flown by Royal Air Force Liberators and Wellingtons, and the rest by day by the Americans.

When the 308th came over the Hump it was divided into halves, with a pair of squadrons going to each of the two 7th Bomb Group bases. The plan was for the maximum strength of Mitchells and Liberators, escorted by Lightnings and Mustangs, to attack in two waves on November 25. The 7th's Liberators would hit the Insein locomotive shops in the first wave, with the 308th Group and the Mitchells bombing fighter airfields in the hope of catching aircraft on the ground, particularly fighters still being refueled and armed after intercepting the first force. Then that night the British would mount a maximum effort against the Mahlwagon yards, followed up by an American attack the next day. After that, day and night attacks would concentrate on wharves, until the entire port was destroyed. As planned the missions would last for six days and five nights, then the Americans would mine the shipping lanes at Rangoon and Moulmein.

On November 25 the weather was worse than usual, but the die was cast. From the very takeoff, when two B-24s crashed, the mission looked grim. As the Liberators passed their rendezvous point with the fighters overcast prevented a contact and forced the heavies to proceed alone. The Insein shops

were totally socked in and the first wave was unable to attack; the second
wave met similar weather at their target and also abandoned the mission,
losing one B-24 as they dawdled around in the flak, looking for a break in
the soup.

The results were disappointing. The initial surprise element was gone, three
B-24s were destroyed, the major target was untouched, and the whole schedule
upset.

On November 26 weather grounded the missions, and with two days fouled
up, the timetable was thrown to the wind. The Liberators hit Insein the
following day, and despite spirited resistance by the enemy fighters the results
were excellent. Brigadier General Howard C. Davidson, commander of the
Strategic Air Force, estimated that 75 percent of the target was destroyed.

Next day the heavy bombers attacked Botataung docks, encountering far less resistance and returning without loss after inflicting heavy damage. The next two days were set aside for maintenance, but on December 1 the B-24s were back over Insein, with all "available" fighter escort. The Japanese had brought in heavy reinforcements and the bombers, coming in from the north to avoid thick flak, came under concentrated attack by sixty enemy fighters. Coming out of the sun, they were firing before they were even sighted. The 7th Group took the weight of the first attack—on the first pass their leader, his left wingman and a squadron leader were knocked out of formation. Three planes pulled up to close the gaps, one of them going down soon after. Three more tried to cover the crippled group leader as he slowed down and lost altitude.

When the 308th arrived the fighters were waiting for them too; sometimes three came in abreast on one plane, sometimes they came in a loose string, and the leading Liberator went down after the first pass. Bombing results were hard to gauge because of the fierce interception, though the pattern was believed to have been good. Yet the losses were unbearably high for this theater: six Liberators lost and five more heavily damaged.

The British missions, flown at night, cost three Wellington medium bombers, and seemed better value. The 7th and 308th's part of the campaign came to a close on the afternoon of December 4, after a successful mining mission, and the total cost had been twelve B-24s. The objectives were not fully accomplished but there had been some success, particularly at Insein, and the two B-24 groups had operated together without a hitch.

Rangoon was left alone for a few weeks, and in the meanwhile the potential of another target had increased. Information had leaked through about the expansion of the dock facilities at Bangkok and the building of a railway to connect the port with the Ye-Moulmein Railway and accordingly, to the railway system of all Burma. Liberators had attacked the port a year before and on the night of December 19 twenty-one B-24Js from the 7th headed for the new docks. One failed to reach the target, but shortly after midnight the rest rained their bombs down. Some were caught by searchlights but the flak was ineffective and no fighters were seen as the B-24s droned over for more than an hour, dropping 50,000 pounds of bombs. Two nights later a second attack was made, with the railway terminal as the aiming point; nineteen Liberators scattered 55,000 pounds of explosives and incendiaries, huge fires illuminating the accuracy of their bombing. The 7th Bomb Group's morale improved after these two fourteen hour night missions without loss . . . particularly, they helped erase the memory of that bloody day at Rangoon.

In January 1944, one month after the creation of General Davidson's Strategic Air Force, there were within the command forty-eight American

Mergui Harbor, a few hundred miles up the Malay Peninsula from Rangoon, became a haven for enemy shipping. These six 7th Bomb Group Liberators hosed it down on January 23, 1944.

Daedalus, a Liberator VIII of 356 Squadron, Royal Air Force, hovers over her target, a Japanese headquarters. This squadron and 159 Squadron shared the greatest shipping prize in South East Asia, a 10,000 ton tanker, destroyed in June 1945.

One of the best examples of improvising equipment came at the end of the Burma war, when 7th and 308th Bomb Groups were placed under the operational control of Air Transport Command to haul gasoline into China. To convert B-24s into gas carrying aircraft, kits to install droppable bomb bay tanks were made up under the supervision of the Southern India Air Depot. A standard piping manifold was designed to allow withdrawal of gasoline from the tanks through two outlets at the same time, and to facilitate emergency use of bomb bay gasoline during flight through a connection with the engines. By means of a manifold, gasoline could also be drained from the auxiliary wing tanks into the bomb bay, achieving maximum safety in flight and rapid unloading of the maximum amount of gas in China. This 7th Bomb Group C-109 (a converted B-24J) is being unloaded at Kunming in September 1944.

Liberators of the 7th Group and thirty-one British Liberators in three squadrons. Their main strategic goal was the disruption of the Japanese transportation system, on which the enemy in Burma was entirely dependent; they went to work.

Priorities ran in an accepted order: first came shipping, followed by communications leading into Burma or within Burma, third were enemy air bases, fourth ports and dock facilities, and finally military installations such as supply dumps and depots. The reasons were obvious . . . partially severing overwater communications to Japan would blockade the enemy in Burma and destroy his power to resist.

The attacks on the priority target were not particularly fruitful, because enemy shipping was not concentrated within the radius of the bombers. So actual tonnage sunk in the Andaman Sea and the Gulf of Siam was negligible, but the payoff came after mid-1944, when Allied air superiority was so complete that Japanese shipping was not prepared to face the risk of sailing in these waters.

Burmese railways were especially vulnerable to bridge-busting aircraft, and in the country there were over three hundred bridges that were more than forty feet long. Cutting two in succession isolated the intervening track and anything unlucky enough to be using it. This was tactical work, and the Liberators backed it up by hitting the larger rail centers with their marshaling yards, turntables and repair depots, at Bangkok, Rangoon and Mandalay.

May 1944: Give and Take in the CBI

In May of 1944 General Joseph W. Stilwell's forces appeared to have Myitkyina, main enemy base in northern Burma, well within their reach. However, although the troops captured the airstrip, they failed to take the town. And so began a long siege until August, during which the 308th Group was called in to hit crucial targets on shuttle trips between China and India.

After Myitkyina fell to the Allies nearly two months passed before they were ready to get their offensive rolling again, with Rangoon as the final objective. Strategic Air Force's Liberators were given targets ranging into Malaya, Indochina, and all of Thailand.

During October the mining of Japanese ports and the crippling of their land and sea communications took priority, and the Liberators were more effective than ever. Whereas early in the year the 1000-mile flight to Bangkok had restricted the Liberators to a bomb load of about three thousand pounds, by late 1944 a variety of ways and means of conserving fuel allowed them to carry up to eight thousand pounds.

The Azon bomb received its first combat test by the Tenth Air Force on the mission of December 27, 1944. The weapon proved especially successful in the interdiction of rail lines, and the radio-controlled bomb reduced the number of aircraft needed for this work. The 493rd Bomb Squadron was selected as the Azon unit, and best results were obtained by dropping the bombs singly from eight to ten thousand feet. The meandering required over the target with the Azon technique was possible because of the weakness of Japanese ground defenses, and by April 1945 Stratemeyer would be able to report that "the 7th Bomb Group's Azon bombing continues to be highly successful, with one mission getting four bridges with four bombs, and another getting six direct hits on two bridges with six bombs."

The liberation of Burma had begun in October 1944, with an outstanding mission to mine the inner approaches to Penang in Malaya. The Liberators of the Tenth were fully occupied with their all-out program to strangle communications and supply movements. During December special attention was given to railway communications with Thailand, and bridges, roads, railways, and canals were broken more rapidly than the enemy could repair them through January, February, and March 1945. The climax was reached on April 24, when the 7th Bomb Group sent forty aircraft against the Bangkok-Rangoon Railway line, claiming thirty bridges destroyed and eighteen damaged in that one day.

China in the Balance

Chennault had convinced Chiang Kai-shek that air power alone could save China, but the Japanese offensives in the summer of 1944 proved General

A shark-mouthed B-24J races away from smoking Hengyang on September 16, 1944.   *Her rudder markings identify her as an aircraft of the 308th's 375th Bomb Squadron.*

A flying autograph book, this Azon B-24 served with the 7th Group's 493rd Squadron.

Bridge-busting 7th Bomb Group Liberator pauses to reflect on her job on the Bilin railroad in Burma. November 1944.

A Zero soars angrily up from the smoking inferno of the Kowloon docks, hit by the 308th on October 16, 1944.

Stilwell had been right in believing that without effective ground forces the Chinese airfields would be overrun by the enemy. Chennault and Stilwell had already fallen out over the distribution of supplies coming over the Hump, but the former had gained President Roosevelt's support and the lion's share of Hump tonnage. As he had predicted, Chennault quickly and expertly gained air superiority over central China, but in May 1944 a quarter of a million Japanese troops attacked south from Hankow, and then west from Canton.

In June they captured Changsha and Chinese opposition was crumbling; the Fourteenth Air Force could not hold them alone. The enemy advanced steadily as far as Hengyang, which held out until the second week of August, then moved on again, snapping up Chennault's airfields as the Fourteenth used up most of its precious stores of fuel and ammunition. The Liberators of the 308th, which Chennault had hoped to use against enemy communications along the China coast, were on the defensive, supporting the hard-pressed Chinese armies.

In November the Japanese captured Kweilin, Liuchow, and Nanning, driving the Fourteenth from eastern China, and virtually completing a corridor between Manchuria and Indochina. While the enemy had overrun many key airfields, they had also besieged others. A ragged Chinese army was still fighting in the area, and that month Chennault organized the East China Air Task Force, a fighter outfit supported by a detachment of 308th Group Liberators. Again the 308th suffered an indignity—these planes were denied the "luxury" of ground crews to ease the ever-present supply problem. Only a counterattack in December finally stopped the Japanese advance and saved China.

One Man's War

On the night of October 26, 1944, Major Horace Carswell, a twenty-eight-year-old Texan, had volunteered to make a one-plane strike against shipping in the South China Sea. The enemy force of twelve ships, escorted by a couple of destroyers, was taken by surprise as the lone B-24 made a bombing run from six hundred feet, near-missing one ship and escaping into the darkness without drawing fire. Carswell circled, fully realizing that the convoy was now fully alerted and would meet his next attack with a barrage of flak, and began a second low-level run which paid off with two direct hits on a large tanker. A hail of steel from the ships riddled the bomber, knocking out two engines and damaging a third, crippling the hydraulic system, puncturing one gas tank and wounding the co-pilot. Carswell managed to control the plane's plunge toward the sea and carefully forced her into a halting climb in the direction of the China shore. On reaching land one of the crew discovered his parachute had been ripped by flak and was useless; so Carswell, hoping to cross mountainous terrain and reach a base, continued on until a third engine failed. He ordered the crew to bail out while he struggled to maintain altitude, and rather than save himself, he chose to remain with the stranded crewman and attempt a crash landing. They died when the aircraft struck a mountainside. Carswell, from the 308th Bomb Group, had earned the Medal of Honor.

1945: China, India—a Bang and a Whimper

The Fourteenth was kept supporting the struggle on the ground in China as new Japanese offensives in the first three months of 1945 moved westward on a broad front between the Yellow and Yangtze rivers, but by

February they had been able to begin an interdiction program to cut off supplies to the enemy. Three squadrons of Liberators were taken off coastal sweeps and added to a fighter wing for missions against repair centers in northern China handling battered locomotives and rolling stock, but because of no great superiority in the job over the fighters the heavies were taken back in April and transferred to India for ferrying work over the Hump, setting up at Rupsi in June. A month later the black-painted Snoopers of the 373rd Squadron had been sent off to Okinawa to join Kelly's Cobras, a Seventh Air Force Liberator group.

It had been planned to move the Tenth Air Force across to China after the conclusion of the Burma campaign, so both the Tenth and Fourteenth could co-ordinate with the Far East Air Forces in the Philippines; but Hump tonnage was still a problem and the move was not easily brought about. In July 1945 Tenth Air Force Headquarters was in Kunming, but the war ended before the 7th Bomb Group and the other units had completed the crossing.

With their two Liberator groups the tiny air forces had done a remarkable job as their war dragged by in the vast China-Burma-India Theater, against more than the usual odds. And while the 308th flew their appointed missions during the final days of the war, the 7th was fully occupied with another major movement . . . over the Hump.

VII

Down Under

A bitter, grudging retreat by a handful of weary bombers from the Philippines through Java to Australia . . . the Fifth Air Force was born into bad times.

From Australia the new force played a small part in the Battle of the Coral Sea, the first turning point in the Pacific war, but there was really no Fifth Air Force until later in 1942, when General George C. Kenney took command.

Australia had to be saved, and that meant moving air bases forward, into

General George C. Kenney, commander of the Fifth Air Force, inspects a repair job on Con- nell's Special, an old B-24D which was scraped back to the bare metal and flown by Colonel Arthur Rogers. The old stager survived the battles of the Southwest Pacific and went back to the States to be fitted with a multitude of remote-controlled turrets for the training of Superfortress gunners.

Colonel Arthur Rogers's 90th Bomb Group was the first Fifth Air Force Liberator outfit, and flew its first mission against Buin-Faisi at Bougainville on November 16, 1942.

Virgin II, *taxying out at Jackson Strip near Port Moresby in December, flew more than fifty missions and shot down four fighters.*

enemy territory. Port Moresby had to be made secure, and this was accomplished by the Papuan offensive through Buna and Gona, a bloody struggle against terrain and a confident, well-equipped enemy. Just five hundred miles northeast of Port Moresby was Rabaul, the huge supply base for all the enemy forces in the Bismarcks, New Guinea, and the Solomons; Rabaul had to be blockaded.

The air war in the South and Southwest Pacific was complex: two theaters of war, side by side, divided by an imaginary line, the 159th Meridian East. Eventually Kenney's Southwest Pacific air force would gain four Liberator groups—the first being Colonel Arthur Rogers's 90th, the Jolly Rogers. They would be followed by the 43rd, an old ex-B-17 group known as Ken's Men. In May 1943 the 380th Flying Circus would set up in Australia and finally the 22nd Bomb Group, the Red Raiders, would become a B-24 group early in 1944.

The Long Rangers and the Bomber Barons were the 307th and 5th Bomb Groups, forming the heavy bomber arm of the tiny Thirteenth Air Force, which was created in December 1942 to ease the complexity of the situation of a two-theater air war without a unified command. This South Pacific air force fought the long and bitter air war which led them, with the Fifth, from the shores of Australia to the shores of the Empire; always complementing one another, often supplementing each other, these two air forces played their parts in every important campaign against Japan.

The battle for Guadalcanal had reached and passed the critical stage by October 1942, when eight Liberators of the new 90th Bomb Group made their way from Hawaii as a replacement for the war-weary Fortresses which had fought nearly all the way from Pearl Harbor. By January 1943 the new group had taken over the major share of the Fifth's heavy operations, although of the sixty B-24s then on hand only fifteen could be counted on at any one time. There were severe maintenance problems, and the aircraft needed modification.

As Colonel Rogers and his crews learned to live with the Liberator, the tide began to turn in the Pacific. Papua was secured with the occupation of Sanananda in mid-January of 1943, and while the last Japanese resistance was beaten down the Fifth ranged out to attack the New Guinea coast around the Huon Gulf, battering Lae. In March the Liberators found and shadowed the convoy bound for Lae, which culminated in the Battle of the Bismarck Sea, an outstanding aerial victory which all but isolated the enemy forces in the Lae and Salamaua areas.

The Snoopers Show the Way

The Long Rangers joined the Thirteenth on Guadalcanal in February, and flew their first mission in the second week of the month. This and another the following day cost them five of the fifteen aircraft involved and put a stop to daylight missions in the area. At the end of the month the Bomber Barons began receiving their first B-24s as replacement aircraft, and the group flew a mixed bag of bombers into the latter half of the year. Most successful were the specially equipped Liberators they called "Snoopers," which were the direct result of a low-level radar bombing project begun in 1942 by Colonel Stuart Wright and the Radiation Laboratory of the National Defense Research Council. These Liberators carried special radar sighting equipment and Arnold assigned ten of them to the South Pacific, where they arrived late in August with their guardian, Colonel Wright. At Carney Field on Guadalcanal it was decided to make them the 394th Squadron of the Bomber Barons, and within a week pilots and radar men were ready to try out their planes against the enemy ships forming the "Tokyo Express." From August 27, 1943, they flew almost nightly missions averaging eleven hours of cruising up the Slot at around twelve to fifteen hundred feet, covering the shipping lanes leading to the Buin-Faisi area and hitting convoys or barges moving down the east and west coasts of Bougainville.

A veteran Bomber Baron in for repair at the   the background is Munda Belle, *a black-*
Thirteenth Air Depot on New Caledonia. In   bellied Snooper.

Each mission seemed better than the last and the highly secret "Colonel
Wright's Project" gained quite a reputation. Their best night was probably
September 28, when five of the eight Snoopers in the air hit an eleven-ship
convoy north of Cape Alexander, sinking a destroyer and pummeling the rest
enough to force them to reverse course and run. Brigadier General William
A. Matheny, who led a daring B-24 strike against Wake Island on December
22, 1942, and had since become chief of Thirteenth Bomber Command, was
delighted with the squadron, but some problems had cropped up. Top secret
and weakly defended, the radar aircraft could not be flown with the other
Liberators in daylight, in effect sapping the Bomber Barons' strength. There
were maintenance and supply troubles too, and eventually the solution came
in the formation of a new squadron, the 868th, activated in January 1944
and operating independently in the Thirteenth.

The Snoopers' successes continued, forcing the Japanese to give their shipping air cover, and plane-for-plane the SB-24s were sinking and damaging more shipping by night than the rest of the heavies were by day. Admiral William F. Halsey naturally put it more colorfully, dispatching this message after an October sinking: MY HAT IS OFF TO THE BAKER TWENTY-FOUR SNOOPERS ON SUCCESSFULLY BOMBING ANOTHER JAP SHIP FROM A LIGHT RED GLOW TO A SIZZLING WHITE SMOKE.

* * * *

July 1943: The Flying Circus

Late in the summer of 1943 the Fifth was busily attacking targets in northeast New Guinea, and in July the Flying Circus flew its first missions. They took over from a squadron of the Jolly Rogers which had been covering the Netherlands East Indies by hitting targets such as Amboina, Koepang, and even distant Makassar on Celebes. As the Circus took over they made even deeper penetrations, the most sensational being the August 13 attack on Balikpapan, the rich oil center of the Netherlands East Indies. Twelve Liberators left Darwin in the evening and crossed the Timor Sea in heavy

Lieutenant Dave Brennan's Deliverer, *from the 531st Squadron of the Flying Circus.*

weather, and between midnight and 1.45 A.M. eight aircraft bombed, claiming forty-eight hits. Colonel William Miller, Circus commander, arrived late in the attack to see burning oil rolling down the hillsides and spreading into the harbor, causing heat so intense that he chose to bomb from seven thousand feet. After a 2,600-mile flight completed in just under seventeen hours seven of the eight aircraft returned to their base. The eighth, Lieutenant Doug Craig's *Shady Lady,* tangled with fighters and force-landed on the first smooth-looking stretch of sand at the Australian coast. The nose wheel managed to find a hole and the front became a little caved in, but a two man crew managed to fly the aircraft off again before high tide would have swamped her.

The Circus sent two aircraft back to Balikpapan on August 16, then two days later eleven more made the journey. When it was over General Douglas MacArthur radioed that it had been a "magnificent performance" and the Flying Circus had earned its first Presidential Unit Citation.

During August, the Fifth struck heavily at the Wewak airfields in support of the Huon Gulf campaign, and, by September, Salamaua and Lae were surrounded by the Allies and taken, and Nadzab was captured by paratroops before the first week of the month was over. Finschafen fell on October 2, and the Huon Gulf was Allied territory.

*   *   *   *

Fred Hinze loved to fly the Liberator, and called his own the *Golden Gator.* Whenever there was a B-24 to be slow-timed and checked out it was he who took it up . . . he had a regular rendezvous for dogfights with an Australian Spitfire pilot. Originally wanting to fly fighters, he was happy enough in the leaden Liberator . . . once getting himself grounded for two months by buzzing a Dutch trawler and capsizing it when his wing tipped the mast.

Hinze had come to Australia with the 380th Bomb Group, the Flying Circus, and on October 26, 1943, he and *Golden Gator* were part of a mission against the open-cut nickel mines at Pomelaa in the south-east Celebes. The mission had begun badly when a Liberator lost an engine and crashed on takeoff, and of eleven bombers which got into the air only four reached the target.

The Japanese bounced the Flying Circus flight as they came off Pomelaa, and promptly shot down *Fyrtle Myrtle,* carrying the 531st Squadron's Operations Officer, Captain John Farrington. *Golden Gator* became separated from the others, and all the group heard from Hinze's aircraft were brief messages: CAN'T MAKE BASE. WILL EMERGENCY LAND MOA ISLAND. Then finally: HAVE PASSED MOA ISLAND. UNDER ATTACK.

The next day the Flying Circus combed the area around Moa, but found nothing. Then on the second day they spotted rafts, and an Australian Catalina landed and picked up four survivors—bombardier Bob Jones, navigator Ed Green, radio operator Bob Statland, and Bill Fansler, the engineer. All were wounded but alive, and they told this story:

Jones had spotted a large merchant vessel and chose it as a target of opportunity, scoring a direct hit, before all four Liberators left the target area in loose formation. A flock of fighters caught up with them near the southern tip of Celebes, getting *Fyrtle Myrtle* on the second pass. Hinze followed the burning plane down to give some cover, but as they lost altitude they received a message from the stricken B-24: "Go on home boys, you can't do us any good."

The *Golden Gator* was under determined attack as she started to regain altitude, and a hit in one engine set the wings ablaze. Hinze searched for cloud cover, found some, and while they were cloaked the crew got an extinguisher onto the seeping fire and put it out. Breaking out of the cloud again they were jumped by ten fighters, and for forty minutes the Liberator was fighting for life. The *Gator's* gunners claimed eight of them and the others were trailing smoke when they gave up and headed for home.

The *Gator* had lost another engine, and a third was rough. She was going down, so Hinze put her into a dive to try to windmill an engine back in. The aircraft broke through clouds over a small island, right on the deck, and as Hinze frantically pulled her out he clipped off the top of a tree, wedging it into the stabilizer where it stayed for the rest of the flight.

The young pilot tried to skirt Timor on the way home to keep out of trouble, and ordered his crew to throw out all the guns and ammunition except 25 rounds for the top turret. For three hundred miles *Golden Gator* managed to stay up there, but Hinze knew they could not make Darwin and decided to go in to Moa, taking the chance that there were no Japanese there.

Over Moa two Nicks appeared. Sergeant John Wine in the top turret blasted his 25 rounds through in one burst and the *Gator* was unarmed. The Nicks came in again and again, raking the Liberator. She was holed all over, pounded and mangled. Wine was still in the top turret, tracking with cold guns, when it exploded around him. The bullet which shattered his turret went into his head, killing him instantly.

The waist area was in bad shape. The photographer riding with the crew went back to get his chute and was cut in two by machine gun bullets. Nose gunner Mark Mitchell came back to help out and was working over the generator when a hit exploded it—he died in the arms of gunner Howard Collet. Collet sat down and pulled a Bible from his pocket and was reading it over the intercom when a bullet hit him in the stomach, choking him into silence. In the tail turret a cannon shell blasted the gunner as he hunched behind his useless guns.

Bombardier Bob Jones was crouched between Hinze and the co-pilot on the flight deck. A cannon shell exploded, blasting away the left side of Hinze's boyish face, and another took away his left foot above the ankle. The co-pilot, Francis Herres, on his first mission, was hit in both legs and his set of controls was shot away. Hinze had to fly the aircraft, so Jones applied a tourniquet while the pilot used his one foot on the rudder pedals.

Jones was still working on the smashed ankle when shrapnel tore up Hinze's hands; a fighter came zipping by without firing and Hinze tried to grin through his blood as he croaked "Dry run." He told the survivors of his crew he was going to ditch, so Jones moved back to get the escape hatch off. Another bullet hit Hinze in the chest, but he still managed to get the *Gator* down onto the water. The aircraft floated a couple of minutes, water spurting in from everywhere through the hundreds of holes. Bob Jones reached for his pilot but he was dead. The life rafts did not release as they should have, but the five survivors were grateful for that when a fighter swooped over them, saw nothing and moved on. Herres, not realizing everybody else was already dead, swam back to the waist section of the aircraft and squirmed in. The others never saw him again.

*   *   *   *

General Kenney had been pressing for blind-bombing equipment for his Liberators, and in October thirteen specially fitted aircraft arrived and were assigned to the 43rd Group's 63rd Bomb Squadron, the Fifth's pioneer anti-shipping unit. These Liberators were just part of the payoff for Kenney, whose early fears about the B-24 were dissolved—in fact the impending conversion of the old medium 22nd Bomb Group delighted him.

Rabaul had been consistently bombed since 1942, but in October 1943 the pressure was applied. The immediate airfields such as Vunakanau and Lakunai and other installations on New Britain and New Ireland were bombed and strafed into paralysis. Initially bad weather hampered the Liberators' part in the reduction of Rabaul, but over Christmas 1943 both air forces were able to join in the offensive. Cape Gloucester was invaded in December and as the battle against Rabaul went on the Thirteenth's Liberators were hitting the whole range of targets in the Bougainville, New Ireland, and New Britain areas. The Jolly Rogers and Ken's Men also played their part, beginning with the pre-invasion bombardment of Arawe and Cape Gloucester through December, then the assault on Kavieng, New Ireland until February of 1944.

In February 1944 the Bomber Barons moved to Munda, with the Navy's Buccaneers squadron. The rain on Munda sneered at the men's tents, and it was reliably reported that it really leaked on the outside and rained in the tents.

Betsy carries a Consolidated tail turret in her nose as she heads for Wewak early in 1944. The Jolly Rogers tail insignia, the most distinctive marking of the war, was designed by Sergeant Leonard Baer, and it saved the crew of Mission Belle after they bailed out on the way back from a Rabaul mission in October 1943. All the crew landed safely and three of them got through the jungle to a mission at Kerau. To attract the attention of rescue planes from Moresby they formed their parachutes into the skull and bombs symbol. For the gaping eyes and mouth they convinced two natives to squat where the eyes should be, and another to lie across the lower part of the skull. They were immediately recognized. Flushed with success, they began appending messages like "Coffee" and "Cigarettes."

The Japanese had occupied the Admiralties since early 1942, with airfields on Manus and Los Negros, the two major islands, which were separated by a tiny, narrow strait. Seeadler Harbor, enclosed from the eastern end of Manus by curving Los Negros, was a fine anchorage. The Jolly Rogers and Ken's Men began hitting the airfields in January, and recon revealed that the enemy made no attempt to repair them as the attacks continued through February, without opposition. It was not until later that the Allies learned it had been the plan of the Japanese commander to give the impression that the islands had been abandoned.

American troops landed in the Admiralties on February 29, and after D-Day on Manus the Fifth Air Force's part in the campaign was essentially over. With these airfields in Allied hands Kavieng, Rabaul, and the northeast coast of New Guinea were blockaded.

By April plans had been completed for moving the two Thirteenth Air Force Liberator Groups up to the Admiralties, from where they could be employed in the crushing of the Carolines. They were to be in their new bases as soon as possible, because it was hoped to get at least "one good strike out of them" at Hollandia as well. Construction of suitable bomber fields was underway at Momote and Mokerang on Los Negros, and on April 11 Kenney established the Thirteenth Air Task Force under the command of Major General St. Clair Streett. Movement of the Liberators to the Admiralties came too late to bring their weight in at Hollandia, but they were not needed there anyway.

Beginning on March 26 it had been their task to neutralize Truk and Satawan, which meant unescorted missions of 1,700 miles to attack heavily defended airfields. The first two strikes had been abortive, but the Long Rangers got through on March 29; two dozen Liberators had left Munda the day before, staged through Piva on Bougainville, and twenty of them arrived 19,000 feet above Truk's Eten Island shortly after midday.

Led by the Long Rangers' Operations Officer, Major Lucky Lundy, they were met by around twenty-five fighters ten minutes before the target. The Liberator crews could see more fighters coming up at them, but no attacks were attempted until Truk's anti-aircraft gunners had their turn. The mission looked good, bomb bursts starting at the pale water's edge and thumping across the entire target area. Immediately after bombs away the Zekes and Tonys came in, lobbing five or six phosphorous bombs into the formation. About seventy-five fighters waded in eagerly from every direction, as the Liberators raced for home.

Over the target a fighter had punched a hole in Lieutenant William Francis's B-24 and cut a fuel line, and the ship was trailing a thin, transparent stream of gasoline across the target. As she passed through the smoky tentacles of phosphorous there was a muffled boom and the B-24 was engulfed by flames. The Liberator reared up and fell off to the right, five of the fighters following her almost all the way down to the water to make sure.

In another badly damaged aircraft Lieutenant Paul Rockas was struggling to get back as far as Nissan Island . . . he made it, but bringing in the wounded B-24 he swerved off the runway and hit a bulldozer. The Liberator somersaulted onto its back, killing everybody but the bombardier.

Gunners returning from the forty-five minute battle claimed thirty-one sure kills, and photos revealed that forty-nine aircraft were destroyed or damaged on the ground; the Long Rangers received a Presidential Unit Citation for their bloody flight.

Next day eleven Bomber Barons hit the runways and revetments at Moen, another Truk strongpoint, and in an hour-long running gunfight they lost three aircraft. The two groups teamed up three days later to make a very successful raid on Dublon town, despite murderous anti-aircraft fire and the challenge by fifty enemy fighters. The gunners were credited with thirty-nine kills, but four Liberators were lost, and Truk's toll was mounting. A night attack promised some respite, so with four 868th Squadron Snoopers in the lead, twenty-seven Long Rangers went back to Dublon on the black night of April 6, losing one aircraft.

The Truk strikes ended when the Long Rangers suspended operations to follow the Bomber Barons to their new bases on Los Negros.

* * * *

The Drive Through New Guinea

Hollandia in Netherlands New Guinea, promising sheltered anchorages and suitable locations for airfields, was chosen as the landing point for the next amphibious operation. The Flying Circus, to be based at Dobodura, would support the left flank of the Allied advance, but planning the Fifth's over-all role in the Hollandia operation made Major General Ennis C. Whitehead apprehensive about the status of his bombers. Ken's Men had forty-eight aircraft, counting their twelve Snoopers, the Jolly Rogers had forty, the still-converting Red Raiders thirty and the Flying Circus fifty-nine more at Darwin. Whitehead estimated he would have 117 aircraft available for day missions, excluding the Circus aircraft in Australia. It turned out to be four less, but the loan of a Navy PB4Y patrol squadron left all these available for offensive missions. Airfields around Wewak were attacked ahead of attempts to neutralize Hollandia, and these were tough targets; Whitehead planned for his Liberators to take out enough flak sites to open it up for his mediums. The B-24s ultimately developed such a disregard for the defenses that on March 21 they took individual four-minute runs over Wewak mission, receiving only twelve pitifully inaccurate bursts of flak in reply.

With Wewak down, Hollandia was next. Seven Liberators attacked before dawn on March 30, and just after sunrise seventy-five more, armed with twenty pound fragmentation bombs, were airborne. The crews came home with the conviction that Hollandia had really "been Wewaked." Strike photos revealed that the first day's missions had burned out and destroyed seventy-three Japanese aircraft, and a similar force attacking a day later made the total nearer two hundred. Six blue F-7 Liberators from the 20th Combat Mapping Squadron photographed the landing beaches at Hollandia on April 16, one taking flak hits which knocked out two engines. She cracked up on landing at Saidor and became the second Liberator loss of the entire operation. The troops went ashore six days later.

Lake Sentani in the Hollandia area being obviously inadequate, Wakde had been selected by Kenney and Whitehead as the area which would support the kind of heavy bomber base they wanted. Nearly a hundred miles up the coast, Wakde was to be attacked as soon as Hollandia was secure, and for five days before the landing Fifth Bomber Command would employ its heavy groups in concentrated attacks. Then they would hit areas where reinforcements might come from, and finally they would support ground operations. D-Day at Wakde would be May 17, and Z-Day, for the invasion of Biak Island, would be ten days later.

Daylight strikes began on April 28, when forty-seven Jolly Rogers and Ken's Men Liberators flew up from Nadzab to hit Biak. The weather closed in along the north coast of New Guinea, effectively blocking all but a few missions into the Wakde-Sarmi area for two weeks, but while the Fifth's B-24s were locked in the Markham Valley the Thirteenth Air Force took over the Biak job from the Admiralites during the first couple of weeks of May. Meanwhile the Flying Circus had been carrying out its private war, continuing a string of strikes against Noemfoor and the Vogelkop airfields. By linking the Liberators of the Fifth and Thirteenth, Whitehead was able to send ninety-nine bombers over Biak on May 17, ringing in an almost daily campaign against the island. The Biak campaign was officially terminated on August 20 after the last Japanese had been liquidated.

Noemfoor was required next, to facilitate fighter escort for bomber strikes to the Halmaheras and to effectively deter any Japanese efforts to reinforce Biak. Much of the aerial preparation for Noemfoor Island, lying in the northwestern limit of Geelvink Bay, had already been accomplished in support of Biak, confusing the enemy as to the next Allied objective.

Surprise enemy raids on forward airstrips were sometimes costly. This Jolly Roger was destroyed on Wakde on the night of June 5, *1944. Tail colors identified Jolly Roger squadrons, with red, blue, green and black for the 319th, 320th, 321st, and 400th respectively.*

* * * *

By late July the captured airfields on Biak, Owi, and Noemfoor were ready to receive the concentration of aircraft necessary for raids on the Halmaheras. A weather front over the target delayed the first mission until July 27, but early that morning the largest formation since Hollandia went out. The Jolly Rogers and two squadrons of Red Raiders took off from Wakde for rendezvous with the other two Raider squadrons at Owi. Over Japen Island they linked up with Ken's Men, who took the lead. Covered by Lightnings they flew directly to the target, then divided and dropped frag bombs on dispersal areas at Lolobata and Miti airdromes.

The close co-operation of the Fifth and Thirteenth gave emphasis to the great achievements after two hard years in the South and Southwest Pacific. The Allies now controlled the Solomons, the Bismarcks and new Guinea. The Philippines would soon be within reach.

While the plans for invading the Philippines were forming, the Liberators had been moving up to Netherlands New Guinea, from where they would be able to support the invasion of the northern Moluccas, the Palaus, and then the southern Philippines. The missions would be long and over water,

Patched Up Piece *was taken overseas by Lieutenant John Wooten, but Lieutenant Dave Ecoff flew her on her most memorable mission. On August 14, 1944, he was on a flight to secure photo coverage of Morotai from 25,000 feet in fine, clear weather. During the photo run the number 4 engine began losing oil pressure, so Ecoff feathered it and called his flight leader to let him know he was aborting. Slowly descending, the F-7 headed for Biak. Then oil pressure began ebbing in the number 3 engine, and Ecoff began worrying. Deciding to idle the engine rather than shut it down,* he took on the unenviable task of flying a Liberator with two engines out on one wing. Patched Up Piece *was sinking, so the pilot ordered the crew to throw out everything except the cameras and asked his navigator for a heading to Middelburg, recently invaded by the Allies. The radio operator was sending their position to air-sea rescue, and finally they came within voice range of Middelburg. Ecoff asked for radar vectors for the shortest route, still wondering whether he had enough altitude to get there.*

When the crew of Patched Up Piece *sighted Middelburg there was still equipment on the unfinished runway, so Ecoff made a low pass firing red flares and came around and lined the Liberator up. He had to put her down as close as possible to the beginning of the strip to* *have enough runway, and when he checked the next day he was pleased to find his tire marks about fifteen feet from the edge. A few days later the runway was complete enough for* Patched Up Piece *to get away again.*

and in July 1944 estimates indicated there were more than eight hundred Japanese aircraft to meet, over half of them in the Philippines and within striking distance of the invasion areas. Japanese carrier planes which could be expected brought the possible total to twelve hundred aircraft.

The Far East Air Force, combining the Fifth and Thirteenth, had over twice that number, but this strength was spread all the way back to Australia. Before air support for Morotai and the Palaus could reach effective strength, the center of airpower, now at Nadzab and Manus, would have to be moved up. By early August, Ken's Men were on Owi, where construction had outpaced other areas, along with PB4Ys from VB-115. Part of the Jolly Rogers, still headquartered at Nadzab, was based on the small island of Wakde, 180 miles east. Thirteenth Bomber Command was officially established at Wakde on August 22, and soon the Bomber Barons and Long

Nadzab still life: the cannibalized remains of a crash-landed Jolly Roger. (Boyd O'Donnell)

Rangers were bombing the Palaus nearly every day, demolishing Koror town. After September 7 the two groups almost exclusively bombed airfields in the northern Moluccas, and a little over a week later the important targets had been taken care of.

*   *   *   *

September 1944: The Ploesti of the Pacific

   The Japanese had long had uninterrupted use of the Balikpapan oil refineries, second only to Palembang on Sumatra in production. After the Flying Circus strikes in 1943 Kenney had noted that within two weeks the Japanese were "short of aviation fuel at all their fields from Ambon to Wewak and even at Palau and Truk."

   Such side effects were especially desirable during the forthcoming operations, and Kenney had tried to get some Superfortresses assigned to this choice target, but had been refused. So with Whitehead he made plans to use Liberators from Netherlands New Guinea; General St. Clair Streett of the Thirteenth also wanted to use his heavy bombers from Noemfoor against Balikpapan, so Whitehead offered to furnish the Fifth's groups, which flew as a support force on the first, third, and fourth missions.

When Lieutenant Charles Kleist's crew reached the replacement depot at Townsville they were given the choice of joining either the Fifth or the Thirteenth. They mulled it over and reasoned that they had never heard much about the Thirteenth, whereas the Fifth was always in trouble, and chose the former. They joined the Long Rangers on Los Negros and the green crew looked at the dirty, patched-up, well-holed B-24s and wondered what the hell they were getting into. Their only consolation was a B-24D called Frenisi, standing there with 110 bombs painted on her nose, ready for a flight back to the States to sell war bonds.

Lieutenant George Kubiskie originally called this B-24D San Jose Special after his home town, but in the Southwest Pacific she was more elaborately decorated. As Gone with the Wind she flew well over one hundred missions with the Jolly Rogers. (Vern Goettler)

The Bomber Barons had been working on the Ceram Islands when they and the Long Rangers were alerted for a quick move to Noemfoor Island . . .

While the Thirteenth was setting up, the Fifth stripped all excess weight from their B-24s, including armor plate and the ball turrets, and struck Celebes targets on the road to Balikpapan. Representatives from Convair and Pratt & Whitney worked with air force officers in setting up the flight plan, which included an intricate table for shifting weights to get the utmost from the cruising B-24s. After four hours the fuel in the bomb-bay tanks was to be transferred, after six and a half hours one crewman would move from the waist to the tail, after nine hours two crewmen would move up to the flight deck. Ninety minutes away from the target all remaining 50-caliber ammo was to be jettisoned.

General Matheny addressed the crews and told them that little was known about what they could expect at the target; he reminded them that Liberators had been loaded up with the same weight they were carrying and had been flown around until they were forced to land, so it could be done. The engineers in his audience knew fuel consumption *averaged out* at about two hundred gallons per hour, but could go forty gallons either way . . . in the Long Rangers the more skilled and experienced pilots would be given the known gas hogs.

The Jolly Rogers staged up from Biak to Noemfoor on September 29, and thirty-five minutes after midnight on September 30 the first Bomber Baron taxied onto the strip and the engines roared. Waiting for the green light the big Liberator was indicating around sixty or seventy miles an hour airspeed as the pilot ran up the engines.

Searchlights shot four beams straight into the sky, one at each corner of the long rectangle of runway.

Five minutes later the heavily laden bomber bounded along the mile and a half of airstrip and within a hundred feet of the runway's end she slowly lifted, her running lights joining the sprinkle of stars.

Nine hours later the twenty-three Bomber Barons which had made it to their rendezvous point were over Pandansari, number one target of Balikpapan. Five minutes behind them the Long Rangers arrived to find the refinery almost covered by drifting clouds and seven of their twenty-three aircraft bombed by radar while five bombed the paraffin point and the rest dropped blindly into the murk. When the Jolly Rogers reached the target they found solid cloud cover and only one squadron bombed. The crews had expected heavy flak, but not the experienced fighter response, and three Bomber Barons went down.

The Thirteenth went back alone on October 3, with the two groups briefed to bomb separately in twin two-squadron sections; each section was supposed to go over the target in javelin-down formation from 15,000 to 13,000 feet. The Long Rangers, leading for the day, got twenty aircraft over the target. About forty fighters intercepted them five minutes before they bombed and followed them all the way back to the coast of Celebes. Seven Long Rangers went down along the way, and in the seventy-minute battle most of the B-24s ran short of ammunition, and two were entirely out when the fight was over.

The Bomber Barons, contrary to briefing, joined their sections closely at the rendezvous and flew abreast, as close together as possible. The Japanese seemed to avoid this formation, and the nineteen blue-tailed Barons suffered no losses.

Some change in tactics was evidently necessary, for the Long Rangers had never taken such losses. Following the Barons' success, Streett introduced his Liberator groups to the combat box formation, proving the point with a couple of practice missions against P-47s.

Streett borrowed all three Fifth Air Force groups for the third mission, and they were to fly over at medium altitude while the Thirteenth went over high; the Fifth would draw the flak, the Thirteenth the fighters. Two Thunderbolt squadrons would sweep the sky above the target before the bombers arrived, and a Lightning squadron would escort. The 63rd Squadron Snoopers would harass the defenses and keep fighter pilots awake the preceding night, and shortly before the bombers were due to arrive an 868th Squadron aircraft would drop a thousand pounds of aluminum foil strips on a course leading in to less than 60 miles from Balikpapan, and bring the fighters up.

The first phases went roughly as planned. Seven 63rd Squadron Snoopers harassed Balikpapan on the night of October 8, and five more the next night. Between 8:30 and 9 in the morning of October 10 the other lone Snooper dropped its load, and between 10:10 and 10:45 sixteen P-47s appeared over the target at about 20,000 feet. Pouncing on twenty-five fighters they shot down a dozen for one of their own. According to plan the Thirteenth should have gone over the target immediately prior to the Fifth Air Force groups, all the Liberators completing their runs in ten minutes . . . but the Fifth had arrived at the rendezvous first, lingered as long as possible, then proceeded. The Jolly Rogers, twenty-one aircraft, divided their bombs between Pandansari and Edeleanu, under attack by a score of fighters. One Jolly Roger exploded in a brilliant swirl of fire as a phosphorous bomb connected with it, but in return the group claimed sixteen fighters. The Red Raiders' eighteen planes placed most of their bombs on Pandansari, although the Japanese fighters threw some aircraft off their mark. One 33rd Squadron ship was so badly damaged by cannon fire that it crash-landed on Batoedaka Island— after destroying six of its attackers on the way down. A Zeke rammed another

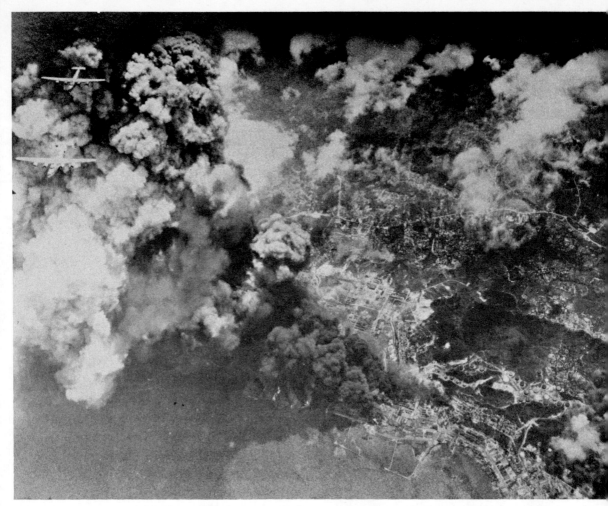

The Long Rangers come off Balikpapan on October 14, 1944, with Lieutenant Don Forke's aircraft in the lead. This group used a stylized LR in a dark blue ball as their group identification, while squadron identification was provided in several ways. For some unknown reason, each of the squadrons had its own card game . . . the 370th played poker, the 371st bridge, the 372nd Black Jack, the 424th an intricate species of Hearts, and it was strictly taboo for a bridge game to develop in the Black Jack squadron. Late in the war each squadron was also allocated a comic strip upon which to base its aircraft nicknames, and the 424th got Lil Abner, *resulting in aircraft like* Tobacco Rhoda. *But officially the squadrons were identified by a colored tip on their tails.*

Liberator, exploding it, and another was crippled, singled out and shot down. Nineteen of Ken's Men bombed without loss during a lull in the fighter attacks. but still claimed thirteen kills. When the Barons' twenty-four bombers arrived the Japanese were spent, and attacked half-heartedly. The Liberators plastered the paraffin plant and a few minutes later twenty-five Long Rangers hit the cracking plants.

The next mission went almost the same way; led by the Jolly Rogers, Fifth

Air Force's forty-nine Liberators, each carrying two 1,000-pound bombs and a single 500-pounder, arrived over Edeleanu precisely on schedule. Forty-nine Thirteenth Liberators arrived a little late, but plastered their targets.

This was the first truly successful attack, and MacArthur sent his commendation for another "magnificent" strike. It was also the last effective strike, because the next, by Thirteenth Air Force on October 18, was largely thwarted by weather.

In the five raids three hundred and twenty-one Liberators had gone over the target and dropped 433 tons of bombs; they had lost twenty-two Liberators, but not the entire crews because sixty fighter and bomber crewmen had been picked up. The raids had hardly crippled the target but the pilots were now experienced in long range missions, which would help them greatly in the Philippines, where their full strength was now required.

* * * *

Return to the Philippines

During early September Fifth Air Force Headquarters moved to Owi, and Whitehead was pressing to bring the Jolly Rogers and the Red Raiders up squadron by squadron as revetments were completed; by September 15 the 20th Combat Mapping Squadron's F-7s were on Biak, while Royal Australian Air Force Command, with the Flying Circus, would continue mauling Japanese airfields in the Ambon-Boeroe-Ceram islands and other islands in the Timor and Arafura Seas. The invasion of the Palaus would be accomplished in two stages, beginning with a heavy bomber base being built on Angaur, at the southern end, by D-Day plus thirty-five. Then air units would pin down the thousands of enemy troops remaining on nearby Babelthuap and the adjacent islands.

September 15 was the tentative date set for the beginning of the Palaus drive and the island of Morotai was the first target. Since it was desirable to have the Allied air base as far north as possible and to also avoid most of the thirty thousand enemy troops in the Moluccas, Morotai, an island just north of Halmahera, lightly held and with a seemingly abandoned airstrip site at its southeastern end, was the logical objective.

There had been no real change in targets in late September and October. In the Celebes the Japanese were tenaciously keeping their airfields open, and moved in more aircraft to attack Morotai during September. All components of the Allied air forces attacked fields in the Ambon-Boeroe-Ceram areas, and Vogelkop, to prevent night raids against the build-up of heavies

Corporal Al Merkling's artwork was unsurpassed in any theater of the war. Serving with the 20th Combat Mapping Squadron, he was responsible for such classics as American Beauty, Photo Queen, Cherokee Strip, Patched Up Piece, St. Louis Blues, and this one, soon to be The Rip Snorter. The squadron's F-7As were originally painted blue, making them conspicuous any time, and sore thumbs in regular Liberator formations. Finally the crews were given buckets and solvents and told to take the paint off. (E. P. Stevens)

One of Ken's Men from the 65th Bomb Squadron. The tail insignia, a pair of dice, shows six and five for the squadron on top, with four and three for the group below. Toward the end of the war many 43rd Group aircraft had KEN'S MEN painted in large red letters on the left side of the nose. (Dayt Blanchard)

in northwestern New Guinea. Enemy night sorties were centered on Morotai and Sansapor, but after September 9 there were no more raids against Allied airstrips at Geelvink Bay for the rest of the year. There was limited activity against the Philippines during late September . . . twenty-seven Liberators from Ken's Men and the Red Raiders bombed enemy barracks near Davao, while twenty-three Jolly Rogers bombed oil storage tanks nearby.

Major Joe Davis's 20th Combat Mapping Squadron had the job of providing photographs which would be the basis for the planning of the assault on the Philippines, and they received their Distinguished Unit Citation for their unescorted flights to Leyte in September 1944. On October 24 two of their silver F-7s left Morotai, piloted by Lieutenants John Wooten and Dave Ecoff. They were scheduled to fly a long-range photographic mapping mission to Luzon, but on the way they sighted a Japanese task force made up of a battleship, six cruisers, eight destroyers, three large transports and ten merchant vessels, obviously enroute to Leyte to relieve their troops, losing ground for the four days since the American invasion. The aircraft immediately sent a report back, then moved in to photograph the ships from nineteen thousand feet above the Sibuyan Sea. Some of the ships were hidden by clouds, so the F-7s caught them in oblique shots by setting their intervalometers at runaway speed and snatching the fleeting images as the clouds whisked by.

On the way home from their assigned target, the "Hawkeyes" came in again to get pictures of the convoy from a different angle; the force split into two elements and the F-7s recorded that too.

At 12:25 they sighted a second task force, this one with three battleships, two heavy cruisers and three destroyers, headed east in the Sulu Sea. They circled the ships, photographing them all, from the uncomfortable but necessary height of fourteen thousand feet. The Japanese filled the sky with smoke, fire and steel, but somehow none of it found the two Liberators.

The invaluable intelligence resulted in the largest Fifth Air Force strike up to that time, but Morotai had been in possession hardly more than a month and its facilities were barely adequate for one heavy squadron; distance and lack of co-ordination between naval and air forces added to the difficulties. Nonetheless, a squadron of the Bomber Barons was ordered to Morotai on October 24, and at Biak the Liberators crews of Ken's Men, the Jolly Rogers, and the Red Raiders were briefed on a "golden opportunity" to destroy enemy fleet units. After a hazardous predawn takeoff Fifth Bomber Command had all available heavies airborne on the morning of October 25, with wing rendezvous scheduled for a point on the northern coast of Mindanao at 0900. Towering cumulus blocked the assembly, necessitating movement to another area about 20 miles west of Tagolo Point. When the fifty-six Liberators converged from all directions the resulting confusion was compared to hide-and-go-seek. With no information on the location of Japanese fleet units, the leader hand-picked the new formation point in full view of the light cruiser *Kinu* and an escorting destroyer, both of which livened up the assembly with well-placed gunfire. The bombers could not effect a proper formation, and with nothing better to do the Liberators attempted to bomb the two speedy vessels. With the B-24s ten thousand feet above them the

Mechanics overhauling an Australian Spitfire on Morotai watch an all-black Snooper drive by. In the background is a blue-tailed Bomber Baron. (*RAAF*)

enemy ships had a full twenty-five seconds to evade while the bombs were on the way down, and only near misses were scored. Seven Bomber Barons arriving from Morotai had little luck, and the mission was "a dismal failure."

Next day the Thirteenth sent its two groups out from Noemfoor and twenty-two Fifth Air Force aircraft left Biak and Owi. A crippled light cruiser, the *Abukuma*, which had been spotted earlier with its escorting destroyer, was attacked by twenty-one Bomber Barons who scored one hit and set fires. A few minutes later three Red Raiders scored a couple more hits, spreading the fires and dooming the vessel. The destroyer took off survivors and the *Abukuma* sank off the northwest coast of Negros in the early afternoon.

Between 10:55 and 10:59 twenty-seven Long Rangers had met Admiral

Kurita's retreating force midway between Panay and the Cuyo islands and the group leader crossed the course of the column, causing them to engage in intricate evasion maneuvers, and putting the sun behind the bombers. Selecting the shortest runs and dropping to nine and a half thousand feet, the group chose the mammoth battleship *Yamato* and the *Kongo* and placed two squadrons over each. Neither scored direct hits, but fragments from the thousand pounders caused casualties on the *Yamato* and severely wounded Kurita's chief of staff. Three B-24s went down and fourteen were damaged by the huge guns of the ships, fired at them from eight miles away as they approached.

And so ended the organized fighting for Leyte Gulf, in which the Liberators played a minimal part; Kurita escaped to Brunei Bay with four battleships, and Admiral Jisaburo Ozawa withdrew to Empire waters with ten of his seventeen vessels, and Japan was no longer a great naval power. All told the enemy lost three battleships, four carriers, six heavy and four light cruisers, and eleven destroyers.

* * * *

October 1944: Mission to Halmahera

The Bomber Barons would be brought into Morotai with the Long Rangers, around October 20, 1944, and they would find their new base an interesting place. Just across a short stretch of water lay the big island of Halmahera, like most of Morotai still in Japanese hands. Morotai was raided eighty-two times between the unopposed invasion of September 15 and February 1945, and it may have been molested even more often had it not been for one of the shortest missions of the war . . . Visiting natives informed the Long Rangers that they had seen the Japanese on Halmahera building about half a dozen aircraft from parts of wrecks, and sure enough a few nights later engines could be heard running up in the distance.

So the next day three Liberators took off, raised their landing gear, opened their bomb bay doors, dropped their bombs, turned, lowered their landing gear, landed, and taxied to their revetments. Thirty minutes was all it took.

December 1944: Clark Field

By the end of November the Red Raiders were on Angaur, with the Seventh Air Force's 494th, and the two groups were within easy range of the Bicol

Clark Field, in the rolling plains of central Luzon, was first hit by the heavies on December 22, 1944. On the thirteen landing strips more than four hundred Japanese aircraft were destroyed. In this photo taken from a Red Raider more than sixty enemy aircraft dot the target area. (Roy Parker)

A Zero crashed headlong into this Long Ranger, returning from a mission to the Philippines. The fighter had been making an attack from the rear and crewmen in other bombers believe the pilot of the fighter was unable to pull out in time to avoid the collision.

Peninsula, the Visayas, and Mindanao. As soon as fighter cover was available they would be able to hit Manila and Clark Field.

Leyte's Tacloban airstrip was to become the major base when the island was secured, and the troops had been looking forward to the civilization of the Philippines after New Guinea, but they were soon dismayed . . . there was only mud which defied description, storms and floods, poor food, deadly whiskey, and a lousy mail service which was still processing Christmas packages as late as May 1945.

So the Jolly Rogers and Ken's Men were attacking targets on Mindanao and Celebes, the Raiders were flying from Angaur, and some Snoopers from the 63rd Squadron were staging through Tacloban from Angaur, heckling Luzon night after night. Whitehead had assumed his heavies would be on Leyte by December, and attacking Clark Field before Christmas, but other than small night attacks and unescorted raids into the Bicol provinces from Angaur, heavy bomber missions to Luzon had not been possible.

Fighter escort finally became available just before Christmas, and on December 22 the Red Raiders sent Liberators to Clark Field, but the attacks were limited to alternate days because of the necessity of staging home through crowded Tacloban.

As weather permitted the B-24s continued their strikes at Clark's six airdromes, but there was not enough available air power to neutralize Luzon. Tacloban was the problem, and only one heavy group at best could get over Clark each day. Snoopers were setting fires almost nightly, but the Thirteenth's two groups on Morotai could not reach Clark, nor could the Jolly Rogers from Biak. Except for the night flights by its 63rd Squadron and filler crews rotated to Angaur, Ken's Men on Leyte, having no base facilities, were out of action.

The Seventh Fleet had left Leyte for Lingayen Gulf, and was exposed to violent suicide air attacks which could only be stopped by vigorous air attacks directed at the source. Twenty-two Red Raiders hit Clark and thirty-four Long Rangers and Bomber Barons covered dispersals at Nichols and Nielson fields with frag clusters on January 6, but neither Admiral Halsey's carrier pilots nor the Liberators stopped the savage assault on the shipping in Lingayen Gulf.

To prevent a possible disaster the medium and light bombers flew the largest mission of the war and the kamikaze attacks declined as the Japanese at Clark Field were paralyzed. Only sporadic attacks continued after January 7 and the 40-mile invasion convoy from Leyte was virtually unhurt, though not unhindered.

Formosa had to be kept neutralized, and the campaign had begun in a small way when one of the 63rd Squadron's new black H2X B-24s climbed

An all-black B-24M from the 63rd Bomb Squadron, the Seahawks, at Clark Field in May 1945.

into the velvety darkness with two other aircraft on January 11. For the next few weeks Formosan airfields remained the primary targets.

Whitehead had planned to begin daylight attacks on Formosa as early as January 16, but had problems with weather and slow progress on airfield construction on Mindoro, plus the demands of ground support on Luzon. An attack was planned for January 21, to be flown by the Red Raiders from their new Samar base, but the B-24 portion was scratched when the aircraft carrying the group's twenty-six-year-old commander, redheaded Colonel Richard Robinson, hit a parked Corsair and crashed at the end of the runway, killing all on board. The Red Raiders went over the next day, strongly escorted by P-38s, and were successful. Still, the reduction of Corregidor kept heavy attacks on Formosa down to occasional strikes by one or two groups. On February 12 the "Seahawks" were returned to their favorite target, shipping; newly arrived radar Liberators flown by the Jolly Rogers took over the Formosa role, and toward the end of the month more came to fill the pathfinder role with Ken's Men, the Red Raiders, and later the Flying Circus.

Beginning a series of raids against Cavite on January 24 the Barons and Long Rangers pulverized the former American naval base lest its rehabilitated fortifications flank the route of advance toward Manila. After its February 3 strike the Thirteenth pronounced Cavite Island and Canacao Peninsula 96 percent destroyed, and Allied naval planners squirmed as their hopes to repossess and use the base went up in the boiling smoke of each successful strike.

After the airborne landing on Corregidor on February 17 the way was clear for an all-out assault on Formosa. The second daylight attack had been launched from McGuire Field on Mindoro by the newly entrenched Jolly Rogers, and the Flying Circus soon arrived from Darwin to be part of the four Fifth Bomber Command groups striking together on February 18.

The Quick and the Dead

On March 9 another of those inexplicable incidents occurred, when a force of Bomber Barons left Guiuan on Samar and headed for their target, Zamboanga on Mindanao. One of the aircraft was piloted by Lieutenant Ken

The Red Raiders hit Corregidor in February 1945. For squadron identification they used a colored rectangle on the fin: blue for the 2nd, *white for the 19th, yellow for the 33rd, and green for the 408th.*

Gutheil, and over the target, just after bombs away, he looked up to see a formation of Long Rangers about two thousand feet higher dropping their bombs.

At first sight it looked to Gutheil as if every bomb was going to come right into the cockpit. One tumbled into the wing root of the aircraft right in front of him, and there was a huge explosion. Three of the five survivors of the 394th Squadron's six-plane formation were damaged, but Gutheil's aircraft was hit hardest of all. Flying junk had cut seven holes in the wing leading edges and damaged the radio antenna, the left stabilizer and the number one engine, smashed both waist windows, cracked the nose turret glass, and burned off the left aileron and rudder. About two feet of the left wingtip was gone, and the number one engine was cocked up at an angle to the left.

Back at Samar the aircraft was towed off to the boneyard. Gutheil and his crew reported that there could have been no survivors of the Liberator that had exploded. The tremendous blast had torn the Liberator to pieces

Lieutenant Richard Benson's 531st Squadron Liberator racked up an enviable score. Several more in the Flying Circus flew over one hundred missions, among them Sandra Kay, Dottie's Double, Deanna's Dreamboat, Male Call *and* Sultan's Daughter. *(Jerry McLain)*

except for the forward part of the fuselage, which spiraled slowly into the sea near the shoreline.

The bombardier of the unfortunate aircraft, Lieutenant Pete Kanduros, had put on his flak helmet over the target, then checked his watch to note the time of impact of his bombs. He never knew what hit them. He heard and saw the explosion of the wing tank, and felt a great ball of flame rolling around him. Then the aircraft was in a violent spin, and the next thing he knew was that the nose section was separate from the rest of the aircraft, and he was pinned to the top of it. His head was right next to the astrodome, which had been blown out, and he thought it was the end. He could see the nose turret gunner in his shattered turret, before he was thrown out of the aircraft. Konduros did not know whether he had been alive or dead.

His parachute was hanging to his left, and he reached for it, taking care not to move his body in case he too was thrown out. He clutched the chute to his chest, but he still had his flak suit on . . . thinking how dumb he was he tightly held the chute and pulled the release on the flak suit and it slipped off. He snapped on the chute, then tried to get out through the astrodome opening, although there was absolutely nothing left of the airplane behind him. As soon as he moved he was whisked outside the wreckage, but his foot was caught up in an ammunition belt and he swung around a couple of turns with the wreckage before he could kick free.

Certain that he was clear he pulled the rip cord, the chute blossomed, and seconds later he smacked into the water.

He was only a couple of hundred yards from the shore, but rather than risk capture he began swimming for a group of ships three or four miles away. Soon a Kingfisher float plane was landing to pick him up, covered by a couple of strafing Corsairs, and he was soon drinking coffee aboard the USS *Phoenix*.

April 1945: Tying Off Loose Ends

Formosa's estimated air strength had been cut by over a third by April 1, but with the invasion of Okinawa scheduled for that date the Fifth Air Force continued the pounding day and night.

The Liberators of the Thirteenth, although heavily committed to the support of Southern Philippines operations and Australian landings in Borneo, carried out attacks against airfields throughout Borneo and even mounted extremely long range attacks against shipping and airfields at Soerabaja. The Fifth's B-24s hit shipping at Hong Kong, Hainan Island, and other areas, and by April 9 Whitehead reported that the Japanese sea lane from Hong Kong south was cut. Sea searches continued, but virtually all missions were briefed for a secondary target in China or Indochina. The takeout of Saigon began on April 19 when eight Thirteenth Air Force Liberators staged through Palawan and bombed the harbor, and three days later the Flying Circus went there, followed the next day by the Jolly Rogers.

May 1945: The Australians Take Borneo

Tarakan, a pear-shaped island a few miles off the northeast coast of Borneo, was invaded by Australian troops on May 1, and for the heavies preparation for the following landings was simply a continuation of their earlier support. The Fifth sent its planes down to southwest Borneo while the Thirteenth and the RAAF worked over the Brunei area, and to supplement this effort the Jolly Rogers and Flying Circus joined in the final assault, pouring nearly 3,500 tons of bombs on Borneo targets between May 13 and June 9. Over half the sorties had the tactical function of isolating the invasion areas by attacks on troop movements, railroads, barges, and roads to prevent any substantial number of Japanese moving inland, east coast to west coast, reaching Brunei in time to be effective.

With dawn on Z-Day, June 10, the naval bombardment began and thirty-five minutes before H-Hour aerial bombing by eight Thirteenth and two Australian squadrons commenced on the three beaches, lasting for twenty minutes. Australian 9th Division troops went ashore on Labuan Island, Muara Island and at Brunei Bluff at 9:15, unopposed. Muara was found to be deserted, the Brunei force captured Brooketon and advanced rapidly toward Brunei town, while the Labuan force reached the airfield by nightfall.

Next objective was Balikpapan, the last amphibious operation of the war. The date was set at July 1, and the Jolly Rogers, Flying Circus, Bomber Barons, and Long Rangers joined with the Australians in a sustained effort throughout the rest of June. On June 23 the Red Raiders moved to Morotai to further augment the aerial strength.

July 1 dawned with a red glow visible to the troops and men waiting in the ships. After a forty-minute precision attack by eighty-three Liberators the troops landed under a smoke screen five minutes ahead of schedule, and seventeen assault waves reached the tortured shore without a casualty. Over the beachhead a Liberator from No. 24 Squadron reported progress to the command ship, USS *Wasatch*, and strafed a retreating transport column. In the afternoon a second air observation Liberator was hit by flak and ditched off the beach, and two more Australian Liberators were shot down carrying out impromptu duty as artillery spotters, one hovering at two hundred feet when hit.

The first Australian Liberator squadron was No. 24, which had been with the Flying Circus. They were to take over the duties of the 380th, which for nearly two years had provided the main offensive strength in the Northwestern area, operating under Australian control with only minor friction. Although chagrined at being given what they considered a "mop up" operation, the Australian B-24s played their part in the pre-invasion softening of Tarakan, Labuan and Balidpapan, where seventeen assault waves were able to land without a casualty. This 24 Squadron Liberator is carrying observers over Brown Beach on Labuan on D-Day, June 10, 1945.

The Bomber Barons over the invasion fleet off the coast of Borneo. Late in the war this group began using geometric symbols for squadron identification—a square, a diamond, a triangle and a circle. Top o' the Mark is from the 23rd Squadron.

On Ie Shima, at the very end of the war, an artist named Bartigan began painting the most lavish murals of the war on the B-24s of the 43rd Bomb Group. Among them were The Dragon and His Tail, It Ain't So Funny, Last Horizon, Michigan, Cocktail Hour, and Mabel's Labels. (*J. R. Fleming, Larry Kleiger*)

Close up of The Dragon and His Tail (*Stewart Bolling*)

During the rest of July progress was slow as the enemy was rooted out of pockets, and the impending victory turned sour for the Bomber Barons. On a series of strikes against airfields in the Celebes and southwestern Borneo their group commander, Colonel Isaac J. Haviland, was missing in action. His aircraft had disappeared on July 4, 1945.

Around the middle of April 1970 newspapers around the world carried a story, datelined Djakarta, about "old bomber wreckage found in the jungle." The scattered Liberator was at the top of Mount Batu in Indonesia, and it was ascertained that the aircraft had been reported missing after a mission on July 4, 1945. An expedition trekked to the site, reaching it on April 9, just short of a quarter of a century after the aircraft had flown into the cloud-covered mountain. The plane had been flown by Colonel Isaac Haviland of the Bomber Barons.

* * * *

The Liberators were now needed northward, for the invasion of Japan. Whitehead had thought his command could "accomplish" the job of pre-invasion bombardment from the Ryukus, but that was the job in line for the Twentieth Air Force, and the Seventh was going to the Ryukus. When the capture of Okinawa dragged on the seizure of Ie Shima, desirable because of its three airstrips, was accelerated. It was captured in six days after the landings on April 16, while Okinawa was not secured until late June. Although Yontan and Kadena fields on Okinawa were problems, the strips on Ie Shima were restored and by May 12 an all-weather strip was there, and the following month two more were ready.

By the end of July, Ken's Men were flying from Ie Shima and attacking targets on Kyushu, southernmost of the Japanese home islands, and one hundred and one Liberators from the Red Raiders, the Jolly Rogers, and the Flying Circus were on Okinawa.

On August 4, Fifth Air Force pilots, flying against half a dozen targets including railroads, shipping, port areas and industrial and urban targets, reported that Japanese civilians were waving white flags from their fields and villages.

* * * *

The two Thirteenth Air Force groups finished their war flying missions against Formosa and Indochina. For seven consecutive days prior to the end of the war the Long Rangers heard rumors and trotted off to bed thinking combat was over, only to be rudely awakened for an impromptu mission. At that time crews were alternating between combat and cargo missions during the movement of the group to Clark Field, and bombs were replaced by loads like plumbing pipe, furniture, canned goods, tents, and cots. After three hard-drinking victory celebrations the supply of liquor was running low, and by the seventh celebration the Long Rangers were reduced to displaying their festive air by dying their clothing various colors, such as purple, orange, and green.

After VJ-Day Lieutenant Don Forke was in a B-24 on a surveillance mission over Indochina highways and railroads, because some of the Japanese weren't stopping with the rest. He reported and photographed small native military units south of a pretty town called Hue, and back at the debriefing the intelligence officer filled Forke in on the story. With the French out of the way, he said, and the Japanese defeated, certain groups were revolting in hopes of self rule, one of them calling itself the Viet-Minh. The intelligence officer said a lot more, warming to his subject, but the war was over and Forke just shrugged and wandered off to go to sleep.

Jammed onto Ie Shima, Liberators of the 43rd Bomb Group await the final assault of Japan. Lined up along the center are ships from the 65th Squadron, and behind them their sisters from the 64th, with black diagonals on their fins.

VIII

Air War: Italian Style

General Henry H. Arnold first submitted the plan to split the Twelfth Air Force into two in October 1943, and it was supported by the evidence. The surrender of Italy and the situation for the Allies at the time made the formation of a strategic air force a sound scheme; bombers flying from fields near the Adriatic coast could reach out and pound targets in the Balkans, Austria, Czechoslovakia, and Germany. Rich targets like the Ploesti oil fields and Wiener Neustadt's factories were within their reach, and a strategic air force based in Italy could complement the Eighth in England, fragmenting enemy air and ground defense, and exploiting every concession made by the weather. Arnold laid out the plan, whereby the Twelfth would become a tactical organization, and a completely new air force, the Fifteenth, would take over the strategic role.

While both forces would operate under the theater commander, the Fifteenth would be periodically directed by the Chiefs of Staff to take part in the Combined Bomber Offensive. The Twelfth's heavy bombers, which included two Liberator groups, the vastly experienced Liberandos and Pyramiders, would be the basis of the new air force; fifteen more heavy groups would be diverted from allocations to the Eighth.

Eaker, once bitten, objected loudly, having seen his force denuded before by the formation of the Twelfth. He saw the proposal as a real danger to the forthcoming operations against Germany, and he was convinced that neither the fields nor facilities could be provided to successfully operate such a force from Italy. He also expressed doubts about the weather aspect, considering more favorable weather for operations out of Italy a debatable point.

General James H. Doolittle sided with General Carl Spaatz against Eaker,

The Liberandos, like the Pyramiders, were unique in that they served with three air forces during World War II. When the Ninth moved to England to become a tactical force, these two groups were assigned to the Twelfth, then the new Fifteenth a couple of months later. The wading B-24D is from the 513th Bomb Squadron, revealed by the golden falcon swooping through the black diamond on the nose.

arguing that Foggia had a distinct advantage over England as a base for winter operations against southern and eastern Germany and the Balkans. He backed up his stand by pointing out that winter storm tracks were much worse in England than in Italy, that Foggia was better protected from weather, and that icing was a greater problem for the Eighth because they had to fly through cold fronts, whereas this new air force would usually be able to fly between them.

Eaker lost the battle, and Eisenhower was informed in late October that there would be a new air force under his command: at first it would be comprised of six heavy groups and two fighter groups, but by the end of March 1944 it would have been built up to twenty-one heavy bomb groups. In November General Spaatz was appointed commanding general of the Army Air Forces in the theater, and he named Doolittle as commander of the Fifteenth.

Headquarters staff was at Bari by the first week of December, but the movement of aircraft was not so easily effected. Enlarging old airfields was a slow process, as was building new ones, and the weather did not make the engineers' jobs any easier. It was the end of the month before the Fifteenth's heavies could leave their Tunisian bases, and after their movement to the north their old fields became staging areas for the new groups coming in. It had been planned to divert three Liberator groups to the Fifteenth each month from November 1943 through January 1944, then in March and April

The 449th was one of three brand-new B-24H groups which arrived in the Mediterranean Theater in the middle of December 1943.

The 450th was one of four Liberator groups making up the 47th Bombardment Wing; their tail symbolism was simple, the triangle indicating the wing, and the number in the other white ball denoting the group . . . 1 for the 98th, 2 for the 376th, 3 for the 449th, and 4 for the 450th. In addition the 450th had white rudders, occasioning their nickname, "the Cottontails." When the white rudder was abandoned later it was said to be because one of the group's B-24s had surrendered to enemy fighters by lowering its landing gear, then shot them down and escaped, making the 450th a marked group. This B-24H made it back for a belly landing after taking heavy flak damage.

another six groups would be sent. The 449th, 450th, 451st, 454th, 455th, and 456th Bomb Groups, each with sixty-two B-24Hs, were set to leave the States before the end of the year, but only the first three made it in December, followed by the others in mid-January.

Early in November the Combined Chiefs had called for co-operation between the Eighth and Fifteenth in order to speed up Pointblank, the Combined Bomber Offensive, and directed that a priority target list should be drawn up for the new force. So Generals Spaatz, Eaker, and Doolittle met with the British at Gibraltar to thrash it out. The Eighth's well-established list of target systems was not subject to change, and the conference was mainly concerned with the division of targets between the two air forces. A directive born of the meeting set out the main objectives, and they were firstly the destruction of the Luftwaffe, secondly the support of the Italian land campaign, thirdly participation in Pointblank against fighter factories, oil, ballbearings, rubber and munitions, and fourth to hound the German forces in the Balkans. The Fifteenth would be playing its part in all these operations, but its main role would be in the first and third categories. The fighter production centers at Wiener Neustadt and Regensburg produced some 500 of the 650 Messerschmitt 109s produced each month, and factories in Italy were turning out an additional couple of hundred fighters monthly. Other fighter plants at Brasov and Gyor, and jet factories around Augsburg, Schwechat, Budapest, Oberpfaffenhofen, and Friedrichshafen were also in the Fifteenth's domain, as well as ballbearing plants at Steyr, Klosterle, Fuerstein and Schweinfurt, and Turin and Villa Perosa in Italy. For Pointblank the Fifteenth was given seven specific targets in the last two months of 1944—aircraft factories at Augsburg, Wiener Neustadt, Steyr, Budapest, Regensburg, and bearings plants at Turin and Stuttgart.

The 1,400-mile diameter circle centered by Foggia contained twelve German or German-occupied countries, and a wide range of worthwhile targets. Intelligence came to the conclusion that the Fifteenth would have choicer targets than the Eighth, an example being the fact that thirty-one plants producing nearly half of the Germans' crude and synthetic oil were less than six hundred miles from Foggia, and twenty-one more producing another 30 percent were within 800 miles. Between the fifty-two plants 11,825,000 tons of fuel per year were produced, and it was to be the Fifteenth's campaign against German oil which made its indelible mark on the air war.

It was well into 1944 before the new strategic air force could devote much of its time to industrial targets, for obvious reasons. During November of 1943 operations had eased to less than a third of those of September, and maintenance was so poor during the upheaval that up to forty percent of the bombers were aborting missions. The weather was another villain waylaying formations planned for Pointblank targets, forcing them to be employed against communications targets in Italy. They did manage to hit their priority targets on several occasions, but their first blow for Pointblank was a necessarily light one. On November 2 thirty-eight Liberators and nearly twice that number of Fortresses hit Wiener Neustadt on a 1,600-mile trip from their Tunisian bases. The long flight gave the crews an idea of what they would face, because the Luftwaffe made it clear that these were targets they would fight for. Well over a hundred enemy planes swarmed all over the bombers, and heavy and accurate flak took its toll. Eleven bombers, five of them B-24s, were lost, but the mission was to be considered the outstanding Fifteenth operation during its first four months. They had destroyed a large assembly shop and two hangars in the Messerschmitt factory, damaged another assembly shop and a third hangar, and also damaged shops in the Henschel and Steyr-Daimler-Pusch works. The Fifteenth was credited with cutting fighter production at this target by thirty percent, and costing the enemy around two hundred and fifty fighters per month for several months.

Finally, on February 19, 1944, the weather began to clear again over the German fighter plants, and for six days the planned mass attacks by the two strategic air forces, the Eighth and Fifteenth, became possible. The plan, coded Argument, called for attacks against assembly, ballbearing and components plants, to cripple fighter production in several ways at once; so when the Messerschmitt assembly plant at Regensburg Obertraubling would be hit, so too would the component factory at Regensburg Prufening, in a one-two punch. Or the Junkers 88 factory at Bernberg would share its fate with the fuselage factory at Oschersleben and the wing factory at Halberstadt.

Argument had been scheduled repeatedly before, every time the weather forecasts made it seem feasible, but each time the elements had betrayed them. By February it was virtually imperative that the plan be carried out, regardless of the risks involved in operations in poor weather. In the first week of February, Spaatz had decided that Argument must be completed by March 1, and the gamble paid off. But the Fifteenth could not be pulled away from its Anzio commitments, General Mark W. Clark deciding that February 20 would be a critical day at the beachhead, so rather than harm future combined operations Eaker decided to go ahead with the Eighth alone. On February 21 the Fifteenth again could not participate in the Big Week, in fact the weather was so bad they could not even fly their scheduled ground support missions. The target weather reports still looked good for the following day, with clear weather moving southward in a way that indicated both Regensburg and Schweinfurt would be susceptible. The fine weather spread far north, adding the possibility of putting the Erkner ballbearing works near Berlin on the list, but this would spread the bombers perilously thin. Even

The Fifteenth had the most colorful identification system in the Army Air Forces, but occasionally it went awry. At the time this 460th Group Liberator, high over Capri, arrived, it had been intended to mark the new bomb wings similarly to the 47th Wing. Accordingly the 55th Wing was given a square to paint within a small white circle, along with the "1" indicating the 460th, or first, group. Then somebody changed the markings system and this was an interim result.

without Erkner there was a dangerous spread, and the news that the Fifteenth would be ready to add their weight by attacking Regensburg delighted the Eighth's planners. So it was decided that on February 22 the Fifteenth would hit Regensburg while the Eighth hammered Schweinfurt, Bernberg, Oschersleben, Halberstadt, Aschersleben, and Gotha. The Schweinfurt force had to abort because of bad weather at their bases, which left the Fifteenth to face stronger defenses in their southern target area, and they paid heavily.

The following day the Eighth stood down, but the Fifteenth sent a small force to Steyr in Austria, and on February 24 they headed out for the Steyr-Daimler-Pusch plant. Again they got trouble, but they were out again the next day, this time headed for the Messerschmitt components factory at Regensburg Prufening.

Big Week came to an end as the weather took a more usual turn, and during the month of March the Fifteenth made little contribution to the Pointblank operations, although they carried out the war of attrition against the Luftwaffe by attacks on Italian airfields. Three new groups, including the 459th and 460th flying Liberators, bolstered the air force, and although seldom able to vault the Alps to German targets, the heavies struck heavily at bridges, marshaling yards and airfields. The indecisive land campaign took much of their energy, and the weather was hardly compatible—missions were scrubbed on eighteen days of the month and the cloudy barrier separating the Fifteenth's bombers from southern Germany was solidly entrenched.

April 1944: Oil, the Achilles Heel

In April the Fifteenth began the campaign which was to be the most rewarding and glorious of all. Germany's oil production had been an Achilles Heel which the Allies were now ready to exploit; when Germany invaded Poland she had only enough fuel for six months of operations, but the rapid occupation of the European countries brought the resources of France, Hungary, Romania, and others under her control. The enemy had also developed

Over the deep blue Adriatic, this 460th Group Liberator limps home in April 1944; her identifying symbols are repeated on the upper surface of the tailplane. The Fifteenth had their own "Iwo Jima" in the Adriatic Sea, the tiny island of Vis, where as many as thirty-seven crippled aircraft landed in one day. It was an inadequate, primitive strip, surrounded by wrecked B-17s and B-24s, but it could look awfully good.

The story of Sunshine *is clouded. She flew with the* 449th Bomb Group, *from Grottaglie, until April 1944, when she mistakenly touched down at Venegono airport, twenty-five miles north of Milan. The Germans maintained that she surrendered, and pictures of Luftwaffe personnel warmly greeting an "American" crew were widely circulated. A close inspection of the photos indicates that the star-and-bar on her fuselage had been replaced with a black cross, and she was serving with* Kampfgruppe 200 *at the time of this elaborate stunt.*

a huge industry to produce synthetic oil from coal, and by 1943 these plants were turning out over 6,000,000 tons of petroleum products, while 2,000,000 tons of crude oil were brought in from Romania and Hungary. By early in 1944 synthetic production was increasing and the German position was becoming sound.

Until May of 1944 only a little more than one percent of all Allied bombs had been loosed on oil targets, mainly because the Allies did not have sufficient air forces for the job. Oil refineries were excellent targets for the heavy bombers, because of their rambling structures and the difficulties involved in camouflaging smokestacks and distillation equipment. The surrounding tank farms also boldly identified such targets, and synthetic plants were also large and easily identified by distillation, carbonization, compression, conversion, catalysis, and purification plants, along with oven houses, gas generators, tanks, injector plants, and other specialized equipment.

Oil production centers were scattered throughout the German territories in over eighty different locations, many of which had been out of reach prior to the Fifteenth's formation. This factor, coupled with the other demands on the heavy bombers caused by the preparation for the invasion of Europe, led to oil targets receiving no priority in the strategic air war; however, in

The Cottontails grind through flak to hit Toulon, France on April 29, 1944.

March, General Arnold informed General Spaatz that the Combined Chiefs had no objections to attacks on Ploesti, although it was deemed wise to begin under the cloak of a directive which called for the bombing of transportation targets which aided the Germans fighting the Russian forces surging into Romania.

In the vicinity of Ploesti's fabulous oilfields were these transportation targets, and on April 5, 1944, the Fifteenth sent two hundred and thirty-six Liberators and Fortresses to them. This, the first high-level raid on Ploesti, was led by Major Corwin C. Grimes of the 454th Bomb Group, and he recalls that "shortly after passing Sofia, Albania, the group lead ship indicated that he was having mechanical trouble and was returning home, so I immediately took over the lead and we continued on to the Initial Point. We had several targets in the area that were going to be hit by the different groups, but since we knew the refinery was very heavily protected with guns as well as fighters, all the groups departed from the same I.P. My group was assigned the railroad yards in Bucharest and we hoped this would draw enough fire from the Ploesti guns that they would have used up a goodly portion of their ammo prior to the next group arriving over Ploesti. This was supposed to give the group that was to bomb the Ploesti refinery a better chance to knock it out, but of course we never did completely knock it out.

"Fighter aircraft, Me-109s and Ju-88s, hit us shortly after I took over the lead and were on us continually until about half way between the I.P. and the railroad yards. As soon as they left the 88-mm guns began to pound us. The Me-109s would make head-on passes. Some of them flew straight through the group while others would do a half roll and head for the deck. In the meantime the Ju-88s would sit just out of range of our guns and lob rockets into our midst. Our group lost six or seven aircraft and when we returned home we counted thirty-odd holes, flak and bullets, in our aircraft."

Most of the 550 tons of bombs struck the Astra group of refineries, but the Americans did not "admit" to opening the oil offensive, even in secret reports. On April 15 heavies again attacked the Ploesti transportation targets, and once more on April 24, both producing encouraging "incidental" damage to the oil refineries.

In May the oil missions took on a more positive air, when Mediterranean Allied Air Forces granted permission to carry out such attacks when the tactical position allowed. The Eighth had got around the problem by the obvious fact that missions against oil brought the Luftwaffe up, and decimation of the Luftwaffe, in battle or elsewhere, was the chief goal. With the Eighth tied to Overlord, the forthcoming invasion, the Fifteenth took the lead against oil, concentrating on the nineteen square miles of targets at Ploesti, still the source of perhaps a quarter of the enemy's petroleum.

Hit by flak over Porto Santo Stefano, this Cottontail stayed in formation for seven minutes with the entire left tail section shot off. The aircraft stood on one wing a couple of times, but the pilot fought it and managed to get her level again long enough for the crew to bail out.

This Liberando caught a flak shell over Toulon on June 8; the French targets were far from easy.

The 465th Bomb Group flew from Pantanella in Italy as part of the 55th Wing; the aircraft crossing the Alps is from the 781st Bomb Squadron. The color of the large aircraft letter on the fuselage indicated the squadron in 55th Wing's four groups—red, yellow, white, and blue in order of ascendancy for the 465th and 485th, red, yellow, white, and, black for the 464th, and blue, red, white, and, yellow for the 460th.

The Fifteenth was hitting smaller oil targets in Austria, Yugoslavia, and Hungary at the same time, while the Liberators of the British 205 Group were regularly mining the Danube and disrupting shipments of oil to Germany.

On May 5 the enemy sent up more than one hundred fighters against nearly five hundred heavies. A fortnight later, on May 18, seven hundred more B-17s and B-24s ranged over the Romanian target. Two thirds were thwarted by poor visibility, but good results came from the next mission, on the last day of the month, and on June 6, when three hundred Liberators hit Ploesti hard.

On June 8, only two days after the troops were ashore in Normandy, General Spaatz informed both the Eighth and Fifteenth that from then on, they were to deny oil to the enemy. In the division of targets the Fifteenth drew their old enemy, Ploesti, and Vienna and Budapest, and the synthetic

When oil became the primary target after D-Day, the Fifteenth drew the crude oil refineries around Ploesti, Budapest, and Vienna; *this red-tailed 451st Bomb Group Liberator was chewed by fighters over Austria.*

Enemy smoke drifts across Ploesti, veiling the Romanian target as the Cottontails cruise past. *The rudder numbers on* Boobie Trap, *52, tell that she is from the 722nd Squadron.*

The yellow-tailed 460th Bomb Group over Vienna on June 16, at the beginning of the all-out campaign to erase Germany's oil centers. One of the crew of the blazing aircraft is lifting himself out through the top hatch in front of the upper turret. Cuddles *is an early aircraft, with the original 55th Wing markings beneath her new ones. The unmarked aircraft in front is a recent replacement.*

plants at Brux, Oswiecim, Blechhammer North, Blechhammer South, and Odertal. In effect, the Fifteenth would merely keep doing what it had been doing. They had already hit twenty-nine of the more than sixty refineries within their reach, and within a week after the new order the Fifteenth took large forces to the major Hungarian refineries, all the Yugoslav refineries, and all but one of those in Italy. And Ploesti.

Since the attacks of April and May the Germans had introduced a new and effective defense at the sprawling Romanian target; as soon as they received reports that a bomber force was heading for them they used the forty-odd minutes they had to ignite hundreds of smoke pots. Precision attacks were not possible as the streams of chemical smoke jetted out to form a thick, murky blanket.

Ploesti was also thought to be the third most defended target in Europe, and in second place was Vienna . . . both were high up, and frequently on, the Fifteenth's target list. The Fifteenth suffered noticably higher losses than their English-based associates, and often the whitewashed clubs around the Foggia fields resounded to a bitter parody of an evergreen song: *It's still the same old story, the Eighth gets all the glory, while we go out to die . . . the fundamental things apply, as flak goes by.*

Five crude oil refineries were attacked at Vienna on June 16, and a week later 761 bombers hit Ploesti, but the smoke pots forced them to bomb blind and the effects were not observed. The next day the heavies were back in Romania, and again the bombs were swallowed by the clinging smoke. On June 25 the Fifteenth went to oil storage areas in southern France, and a day later five hundred and fifty Liberators and B-17s hit marshaling yards and aircraft factories in Hungary, as well as the Moosbierbaum, Lobau, and Florisdorf refineries around Vienna. On June 27 and June 28 the bombers worked over Hungarian and Yugoslav marshaling yards and oil refineries at Bucharest. The German position was bad, and Hitler and Speer gave Edmund Geilenberg full and far-reaching powers to carry out a mammoth dispersal and reconstruction program to keep fuel flowing to the Reich. With 350,000 workers, mostly slaves from occupied countries, and priorities in materials, Geilenberg's force repaired damage as soon as the bombers left and busily went about building smaller units in out-of-the way places. The program was so well executed that intelligence officers were often led a merry chase, and bombers were compelled to keep hitting targets again and again as the individual plants became more resilient and the actual number of targets kept growing.

Preparations for the invasion of southern France and support of the ground forces in Italy took much of the Fifteenth's time in July, but its strategic work was reflected in their highest ever losses, 318 heavy bombers. During the opening days of July the Fifteenth ranged over a wide variety of targets from France to Romania; reinforced by Fortresses temporarily based in Italy after an Eighth shuttle mission to Russia, they sent almost a thousand aircraft over the Balkans on July 3, hitting oil and transportation targets in Bucharest and Belgrade. A day later small refineries in Yugoslavia and Romania were hit, and the day after that the largest mission of the week softened up southern France, firing the inactive French battleship *Dunquerque* and smothering the submarine pens at Toulon. Italy suffered their wrath on July 6, and on July 7 the synthetic plants at Blechhammer North and South and Odertal were hit, but with rather disappointing results. Vienna was the target for July 8, and successful blows were struck at oil refineries, airfields, and oil storage depots. It was the average Vienna mission, with interception by one hundred-plus fighters and savage flak.

The next day the Fifteenth was over Ploesti again, using H2X "Mickey" methods to beat the smoke screen, but results were still not comparable to the effort. One of the Pyramiders' B-24s that day was piloted by Lieutenant Donald Puckett, and just after the bombs had tumbled from the Liberator flak slammed into her. One crewman was killed, six were severely wounded, two engines were dead, the control cables were cut, there was a fire in the oxygen system, and the bomb bay was awash with gasoline and hydraulic fluid. Puckett gave what controls he had to the co-pilot and looked after the wounded crew members as best he could. Inspecting the damage he found the bomb-bay doors jammed, but managed to crack them by using the manual crank and drain the fuel out. He threw out guns and equipment, but the plane was going down quickly, and he ordered the crew to jump. Three would not go out, and Puckett would not leave them. He fought to regain control of the aircraft as the three men cowered in the mutilated aircraft, but the burning Liberator crashed into a mountainside and exploded. Puckett received the Medal of Honor, the last of seven to be awarded for actions over the bloody Romanian target.

Following four days of poor weather and tactical work the heavies went back to their task on July 14, heavily damaging four oil refineries and a marshaling yard in Budapest. Six hundred bombers were over Ploesti the

The high-level bombardment of Ploesti began in April 1944 and was kept up until the Russians captured the area four months later.   *The 451st's* Screamin' Meemie II *was part of the force above smoke which boiled up to 23,000 feet on July 15, 1944.*

next day, and subsequent investigation revealed a very successful Mickey mission which damaged most of the refineries. Their third successive day of strategic operations took them to Vienna's oil storage areas, aircraft engine works and marshaling yards. Half of the ninety fighters sent up to meet them fell to the American guns. Nine bombers were lost.

Railways in France were the target for July 17, and the 459th Bomb Group drew Avignon. Although the bombers were trying radar jamming it did not work for the Liberators of the 759th Bomb Squadron. A group of four 88-mm shells burst in the formation, the first neatly clipping the entire left wing from one B-24. The second, third and fourth hit the plane flown by Lieutenant William Zoerb, knocking out the left inboard and right outboard engines, peppering the entire aircraft and all but flipping it over onto its back. Zoerb was down to 10,000 feet before a friendly P-51 came by and escorted the battered plane to Corsica. Zoerb made several Ploesti trips but to him the French targets were always the roughest.

Jet aircraft installations at Friedrichshafen were the target on July 18, and three hundred fighters came up to stop the five hundred bombers. Two hundred and twenty-two heavies hit Munich the next day, and the greatly increased flak defenses scarred many of the bombers. The Friedrichshafen job was completed for the time being on July 20, when two hundred Liberators struck again, and post war investigation concluded that the bombings had cost the Germans nearly a thousand jets.

Oil again took first place, with Brux the target on July 21, and Ploesti once more on July 22. Tactical targets in southern France and Italy took up a large proportion of the effort in late July, but on July 23 the 450th Bomb Group flew what gunner Richard Clark recalls as the "Smallest Heavy Bomber Strike of the War": as part of the day's effort the 450th sent four 717th Squadron Liberators, escorted by two P-38s, to bomb the Berat Encove oil refinery in Albania. The flak was thick and accurate, and one B-24 took a direct hit over the target which blew it into small pieces before anybody could bail out. Good results were had on July 28, again at Ploesti, when a weather ship sent in advance of the bomber stream reported on the smoke screen's consistency at various points. On the last day of the month the scheme worked again, and three refineries were hit.

Gradually Ploesti was being worn down. A score of daylight missions denied the Germans nearly 2,000,000 tons of crude oil, and although individual attacks by hundreds of bombers never seemed to do what was intended, this, plus the strikes against oil in Poland, Hungary, Austria, Yugoslavia, Czechoslovakia, and Germany, was draining away the enemy's fuel. Ploesti was rested in favor of aircraft factories on August 3, when over four hundred Fifteenth Air Force heavies bombed aircraft factories in Germany. After some tactical

Ploesti was always a tough target ... this 451st Bomb Group aircraft, one of the first uncamouflaged B-24Hs, collected some flak hits and crash-landed successfully at Castelluccio.

work the Fifteenth attacked the great Silesian Blechhammer refineries on August 7, temporarily halting production. Two days later Hungary was the target, and Ploesti was hammered by three hundred heavies. The fighter defense ebbed suddenly and the bombers paraded over the target in a long, dawdling stream which took so long to go over that the smoke screen thinned out and five refineries were heavily damaged. Every one of Ploesti's refineries had been damaged to some degree, the region was cut off from Germany by the desolation of railways and the mining of the Danube, and the Red Army was moving closer. Ploesti was finished. There was more to be done to make sure that the enemy could salvage nothing as they moved out, and the successful invasion of southern France gave the Fifteenth the chance to keep the pressure on. For three days from August 17 they plastered Ploesti, and by August 24 all work had ceased at the target.

Germany was next on the list with her remaining oil resources; five hundred Liberators and Fortresses droned over oil targets in Poland and Czechoslovakia on August 20, losing only four bombers. Two days later a larger force attacked targets which included both Blechhammers and Odertal, and the next day Vienna's transportation, oil and aircraft targets were hit. On August 24 a combined assault from Italy and England spread over targets in Czechoslovakia and western Germany with pleasing results; the six hundred Fifteenth Air Force bombers met only slight resistance.

Heavy attacks on the Blechhammers and Austria's Moosbierbaum, Schwechat and Lobau refineries closed the Fifteenth's summer oil campaign, while the Fifteenth also loaned its weight to hastening the collapse of the stubborn Balkan front.

January 1944: Anzio, Prelude to Anvil

Rome had not been occupied until July 4, putting the invasion of southern France back a couple of months; it had been hoped that the assault would nearly coincide with the Normandy invasion, but that was not to be. Shingle, the invasion of Anzio, had been designed to cut around the right flank of the German's Winter and Gustav lines and break the stalemate which was so dangerous to the Allied timetable. If Anvil, the invasion of southern France,

Another face of the air war: a seriously wounded gunner is removed from the mangled wreckage of this B-24H, shot up over southern France.

was to begin anywhere near on time, this was imperative. The strategists had been convinced that the Anzio landings would force Field Marshal Albert Kesselring to withdraw troops from the Gustav line to protect his rear, and General Mark Clark's Fifth Army could then break through into the Liri Valley which, with Cassino, was the gateway for the advance. If Kesselring did not follow this projected strategy, the Anzio force could cut him off and trap him—either way the Allies could get moving again. Twenty-seven 449th Group Liberators played a most important part on January 19, dropping sixty-five tons of bombs on the Perugia long-range reconnaissance base and effectively blinding the Germans for four days; the tactical surprise at Anzio was largely due to their demolition of this key airfield. Anzio was a risky operation, and when the Fifth Army offensive failed to break through in Italy it became even more risky. German air defenses were surprisingly effective, and the Mediterranean Allied Air Forces swiftly ordered a series of attacks to squash the threat by enemy bombers. After small raids on January 23 the Fifteenth blasted fighter strips in the Udine area in northeast Italy on January 30, using a clever new approach. Fortresses, with Liberators from the 449th and 450th Bomb Groups and strong P-38 escort, flew along normally, allowing themselves to be plotted on enemy radar. Thunderbolts took off after the bombers and went out over the Adriatic at wave-top height, climbing high and streaking ahead to the target area as soon as they overtook the bombers. They found the enemy fighters in the midst of taking off to meet the heavies, and the P-47s minced them. There was almost no opposition left for the bombers, who rained down 29,000 frag bombs.

The Fifteenth flew tactical-type missions which were beyond the range of the mediums, flying seven successful missions in five days at the end of March. During that month the Fifteenth flew its first "thousand ton" raid, with Fortresses and Liberators from the 376th, 449th, 450th, 451st, 454th, 455th, 456th, and 459th Groups. The targets of the seven attacks were marshaling yards and nearby industrial targets at Verona, Mestre, Turin, Bolzano, Milan, Bologna, and Rimini. The Fifteenth soon returned to its primary role, but until the fall of Rome it was on call to aid the tactical air forces in their attacks on transportation and communications. Liberators of the 98th, 376th, 450th, 451st, 460th, 461st, 464th, 465th, 484th, and 485th Bomb Groups hit Piaombino, San Stefano, and Porto Ferraio harbors on May 17, and between May 22 and May 26 supported the Anzio breakout by pounding troops, communications, and other targets. Attacks on communications in southern France began late in the month, and these attacks, with others in the first week of June, were helpful to both Overlord and the later Anvil.

Missions flown in preparation for Anvil involved the strategic bombers throughout July, and six of these were particularly fruitful; on July 5 For-

Colonel William Keese's 484th Bomb Group was originally intended to be the Fifteenth's Pathfinder unit, but General Nathan Twining decided to use them as a regular bomb group, *much to their relief. Assigned to the 49th Bomb Wing they carried the wing's red upper tail plus their own symbol, the "bow tie." (Bill Keese)*

tresses with 319 B-24s hit marshaling yards at Montpellier and Dizier and submarine pens at Toulon, then the Liberators went back to Toulon Harbor six days later. On July 12 some 315 Liberators bombed marshaling yards at Nimes and Miramas, while a hundred more hit bridges across the Var River and at Theole-sur-Mer. Bridges at Arles, Tarascon, and Avignon were targets for 162 Liberators on July 17, and a week later Liberators dropped thirty thousand 20-pound frag bombs over airfields at Chanoines and Valence. That night twenty-two Royal Air Force Liberators, led by Halifax Path-finders, repeated the dose at the bases at Valence and la Tresorerie. The last heavy bomber mission, flown on August 2, cut the railway lines ten times between Lyons and the mouth of the Rhône.

The limited aerial offensive against southern France prior to the invasion had been possible largely because of the effectiveness of the French resistance forces. The Maquis were blowing up bridges and trains, picking off German troops, and blasting installations, and for this work they had the support of Fifteenth B-24s in an unusual way. When Eaker had moved from the European Theater he had given a great deal of thought to American participation in supply operations in the Mediterranean, and the 122nd Liaison Squadron, which had flown special operations since November 1943, was chosen to be

Lieutenant Bernard Ball brought this 449th Group aircraft in to Bari after taking a direct hit in the waist from an 88-mm shell. Two gunners were killed as the shell exploded on contact with the roof inside the bomber, and all the controls were severed; Ball got her home by using engine power to control pitch and yaw. The wreck had served with the 717th Bomb Squadron, and was on a mission to Yugoslavia in August 1944.

reorganized as a heavy bomber squadron with the primary mission of supporting the Maquis. Arnold approved the move in 1944, and in June the 122nd was redesignated the 885th Bomb Squadron, under the command of Colonel Monro MacCloskey. Based near Algiers at Blida, the squadron was fully operational by May 1944, and that month completed forty-five of the seventy-two missions it began. The weather and navigation shortcomings were responsible for some of the misses, but failure to make contact with the "reception committees" on the ground was the main reason.

Just a few days before the invasion of General Alexander M. Patch's Seventh Army, on the night of August 12, 1944, the squadron was sent out to deliver supplies and drop leaflets over French cities to alert the resistance forces. Eleven black Liberators took off that night and made their separate ways to their dropping points, loosing 67,000 pounds of ammunition and supplies, eighteen parachutists, and 225,000 leaflets. The squadron received a Presidential Unit Citation for that job.

Operation Reunion

In August there was another highly successful operation, one which gave Fifteenth morale a tremendous boost. It was codenamed Reunion, and it began when Lieutenant Colonel James A. Gunn III of the 454th Bomb Group was shot down over Ploesti. The 454th had been briefed for Ploesti for twelve or thirteen days straight, and Major Pat Grimes was scheduled to lead the mission. Pappy Gunn was acting group commander, and Grimes had taken a few of his flight leaders out into the country to drive around and ease the tension, so when an early briefing was called, Gunn decided to take the mission.

The 461st Bomb Group was unloading ferried gasoline in southern France when a spark ignited a load of fuel and flames consumed this aircraft. Crewmen strain to swing another Liberator around and out of danger.

Warrior's Maiden *of the 454th Bomb Group streaks away from the burning target in Czechoslovakia; the 454th was part of the 304th Wing, which used a diamond and a color on* *the lower half of the tail to identify its groups. The 454th had white, the 455th yellow, the 456th red, and the 459th stood out with black and yellow checks. (Sam Asquith)*

Over the target the flak had zeroed in right on the 454th, and Pappy Gunn and his crew were forced to bail out, landing right next to the refinery. Gunn was immediately captured, and as ranking officer he became commander of the prison camp in Bucharest. When Romania shifted sides in the war in August, he took advantage of the confusion and set out to find a Romanian pilot willing to fly him to Italy. He found one who wanted to trade his Me-109 for a Mustang, so Gunn agreed and they took off . . . with the American lying in the belly of the fighter without oxygen or parachute. Upon reaching the 454th's base at San Giovanni they caused some consternation, but they had judiciously painted a rough Stars and Stripes on the Me-109's fuselage. The men meeting the aircraft were still somewhat surprised, particularly when the Romanian officer began opening the small hatch in the aircraft's fuselage and informed them that, "I have someone here I think you will be interested in seeing."

A crewman who had flown to Italy in an air-craft called Extra Joker approached Sergeant Leo Stoutsenberger a few minutes before the Initial Point during the mission to Markers-dorf's FW-190 plant on August 20, 1944. He wanted Stoutsenberger to get a picture of the ship for him, so the photographer moved to the port waist window and cocked his K-20 camera. Suddenly the interphones came alive with fighter calls as Focke-Wulfs swept in out of the sun, and with shaking hands Stout-senberger clicked the shutter, watching cannon holes puncture Extra Joker's wings and fuse-lage, and a vaporous stream of fuel spill from the left wing. Stoutsenberger kept taking pictures as the fire took hold.

The 451st Bomb Group photographer thought she looked like "a burning piece of tinfoil" as Extra Joker became enveloped in the flames. The doomed plane circled and slowly fell. There were no chutes as an FW190 followed closely to survey their work. Stoutsenberger remembered seeing the crew at chow that morning. On the photographer's aircraft they had taken hits, but the crew was uninjured. (Leo Stoutsenberger)

The captain got his Mustang, the 454th kept the Me-109, and when Gunn explained the situation fifty-six Fortresses were modified as transports and flown to Popesti airport near Bucharest. To the uncomfortably audible accompaniment of artillery fire, 1,162 American prisoners were evacuated in three days.

August 1944: Flak Shak III and Pardubice

Intelligence reports indicated that for a short period in September 1944 no German oil installations of any type were operating, and at the end of the month only three of the more than ninety were in full production and twenty-eight in partial production. One of the missions flown the preceding month was to Pardubice in Czechoslovakia on August 24, and one of the aircraft from the 485th Bomb Group that day was Lieutenant James Mulligan's *Flak Shak III,* Blue Mike of the 831st Squadron. For the crew the mission began at 2.45 A.M., in the flicker of matches lighting candles and cigarettes. Sergeant Leonard Little, the tail turret man, dressed, washed in a helmet, picked up his mess kit and wandered off to breakfast. The group was flying its fourth consecutive day of combat, and the mess hall was quiet.

Back in his tent, Little picked up his dogtags, pocket compass, watch, a picture of his wife, a ring, and a copy of the New Testament his father had given him. His money and wallet went into a metal ammo box, along with his other possessions and a letter in case he didn't get back.

The trucks took them to the briefing room, where they hunched on bomb fin cases before the stage and the large, covered map of Europe. The briefing officer stepped onto the creaking boards and turned flood lights onto the map, and there was silence. As the cover came off the chart like a shroud the crewmen saw the red line taking them from Venosa to Pardubice on the Elbe River. Then they were prepared by the various officers for every contingency . . . route, weather, target, flak, and death.

They passed their officers, yet to be briefed, as they hurried toward the trucks going down to the flight line. At the hardstand *Flak Shak III* waited, a dull sheen on her silvery body, and in a heap near her were the crew's flying suits, parachutes, Mae Wests, oxygen masks, flak suits, and helmets. When the officers arrived the gunners had completed their preflight checks, and Lieutenant Sam Giaimo, the navigator, passed out the escape kits containing silk maps, small compasses, and fifty dollars in fives and tens. There was plenty of time that morning for a bull session.

When the time for start engines drew near the crew donned their heavy gear and began boarding. The crew chief always rubbed Little's close-cropped

The 485th Bomb Group was the last of the Fifteenth's fifteen B-24 groups. Like all 55th Wing units they used the yellow upper half of the tail, with a square cut out of it and painted black; beneath that this group had a yellow cross, against a black background on fully marked uncamouflaged aircraft.

She flew with the 484th Bomb Group. (Gerald Maddux)

hair for luck before a mission, but somehow that had been forgotten. The gunner bounded out through the camera hatch and ran to the crew chief, standing fire guard by the number 2 engine, and had him rub his greasy hands through his hair. As he got back into the plane she was moving out.

As soon as they were airborne Little settled himself down on the deck beneath the right waist window and lit a cigarette; opposite him Sergeant Leo Gagne, the ball turret gunner, was listening in on the flight deck conversation through his headset. He reached over and grabbed Little's arm and shouted something in his ear. Little stood up and looked out the waist window and saw the burning wreckage of a B-24 on the field below. So that was it—*Flak Shak III,* the "spare" that day, would be going to Pardubice, whether others aborted along the way or not.

The group assembled and droned over the southeastern coast of Italy and north over the Adriatic. The gunners squeezed off a few rounds and checked out the power turrets. Soon after, the co-pilot told them to go on oxygen.

Flak Shak III left the Adriatic near Trieste, the crew silent except for the necessary periodic checks. Little was in his tail turret, enjoying the sun beating down through the glass. When the navigator called that they were approaching the Initial Point they turned off their heated suits and Little turned on the power to his turret and guns. He took off his goggles and draped them over his sight and reached back out of the turret to grab his flak helmet.

"Bomb-bay doors open," he heard bombardier Francis Nardi call.

Little thought there should have been flak by now, but the sky was clear.

"Bombs away", Nardi called.

The bombs nosed down and by the time the Liberators had rallied and set course for home two big black pillars of smoke were climbing to twenty thousand feet from the target.

Little switched his heated suit on again, took off his flak helmet and tossed it back into the fuselage. Above *Flak Shak III* the Mustang escort weaved an intricate pattern over the formation. The intercom was alive with happy talk after the four and a half hour flight. Seitz, the co-pilot, was commenting on the beauty of the Mustangs, and Sergeant Sam Nenadich in the top turret was reading the not-too-personal parts of the latest letter from his wife over the intercom. It had been eight hours since breakfast and Little was hungry. He had a canteen of lemonade and some K-rations within reach, but he had to wait until they got down from altitude and he could remove his oxygen mask. So he contented himself with dreaming of the weekly ration of cigarettes, beer, Coca-Cola, and candy that he could buy at the base when they got back.

One Liberator had slipped out of position in the formation and was cruising a little below and to the rear of *Flak Shak III.* All four motors were working but for some reason she couldn't hold formation. Then there were two Me-109s on her tail. Little squeezed off a short burst as they overshot their target and slid in underneath the tail of *Flak Shak III*. The straggling Liberator seemed undamaged.

Little yelled into his mike: "Get the hell off the intercom, there are Jerry fighters out here!"

Their eyes were darting all over their portions of sky, but no fighters were in sight. Then without warning the trailing Liberator went down. Another two fell out of formation. Little could not see German fighters and the intercom was silent.

A group of twelve or fifteen Focke-Wulfs came into view on the horizon, rapidly closing the gap. Little punched his intercom switch and called their position. As they grew larger he watched them through his optical gun sight, waiting for them to get within range. About twelve hundred yards out the fighters split into three-plane flights and each latched onto a bomber. The three heading for *Flak Shak III* were coming right at Little's turret, wing to wing. The center man was set up on their fuselage, the other two aimed for the wings and engines.

Little aimed for the central fighter and at eight hundred yards he let go, several short bursts. At five hundred yards he fired continuously into the German. At three hundred yards pieces of the cowling and maybe the canopy shredded from the Focke-Wulf. The enemy plane lost power, stopped firing, and began a horizontal slow roll that took it under the Liberator, uncomfortably close.

Little was already firing at the left wing man. He could hear cannon shells exploding as they hit *Flak Shak III*, above the sound of the engines and the rattle of the machine guns. The sounds grew louder as the shells exploded nearer and nearer to his turret.

Little reasoned that the shells hitting near him could not be from the two fighters closing from the rear, because those two were firing into the engines and wings. The plane hitting them was shooting from four o'clock high, and Little glimpsed him through the top of his turret and swung his guns up to stop him. Too late. The fighter had raked *Flak Shak III* from the bomb bay to the tail and now the tail turret. Little felt as if he was being torn into a million pieces as the blast threw him from his turret into the rear fuselage.

The four fighters had managed to set both left engines on fire and the command deck over the bomb bay was a mass of flame from the ruptured fuel transfer system and punctured oxygen bottles. A large panel had been blown from the fuselage beneath the right waist position and Little's turret was a crumpled mass of broken Plexiglas and burning hydraulic fluid.

The six men forward of the bomb bay had not been injured, but the left waist gunner and ball turret man both had shrapnel wounds in their legs. The right waist gunner was unscathed although a cannon shell blew out a piece of the fuselage at his feet and a machine-gun bullet passed through the metal eyeglass case he carried in the leg pocket of his flying suit.

Nenadich in the top turret had exploded the aircraft Little had tried for. When Little regained consciousness and opened his eyes he could not see properly. He rubbed his glove across his eyes and it came away smeared with blood. His eyes cleared and he realized with relief that it was only glass cuts in his forehead. He thought he was allright, but he was numb all over.

The first thing he had to do was put out the fire in his turret, so he rolled onto his back and began crawling toward the fire extinguisher at the aft end of the bomb bay. He began realizing how badly *Flak Shak III* had been hit, and saw the waist and ball turret gunners had their chutes on. He crawled to the camera hatch, where he and a waist gunner cleared away the empty shell cases and ammo boxes so it could be opened. Little grabbed the handle to open the hatch and stood up on his left leg, then stepped on his right leg. Pain wracked him and he clutched at the handrail to keep from falling. Looking down he saw his shin bone sticking through a rip in the leg of his pants, and his booted foot twisted behind him.

Easing back onto his knees Little knelt by the open hatch and took off his flying helmet and oxygen mask, looked below to see that he could jump clearly and then, with his head almost on his knees, he dove head first through the camera hatch.

Out in the clear sky he watched *Flak Shak III* still headed for home, trailing smoke and flame and crewmen. After the last man was out she executed a partial chandelle and tumbled down.

October 1944: Oil and Ordnance

The oil campaign went on in October with as much weight as other operations permitted, because the victory could slip away if the pressure was eased for any length of time. October was good for the Fifteenth, which bombed Brux, and Blechhammer South, Blechhammer North, Odertal, and Austrian targets. It had become standard procedure to keep up attacks on targets regardless of reconnaissance data.

If October was good, November was better. The Fifteenth rang in the month's oil campaign with one of its biggest efforts, 1,100 tons of bombs on the Florisdorf refinery, followed the next day by 400 tons on Moosbierbaum.

Burma Bound *from the 451st's 727th Squad-* *as two missions for Fifteenth crews, as were* *ron took a flak hit in number 1 over Munich,* *Bucharest, Ploesti, Brux, Vienna, Graz, and* *but struggled home on the remaining three.* *other long, tough ones.* *Munich was a "double credit sortie," counting*

The Liberator at her most majestic: the 465th Bomb Group near Vienna, September 10, 1944.

Because of hazardous conditions over the Alps no further missions were possible until November 17, when Blechhammer South and Florisdorf were hit. Then a day later Florisdorf and Korneuberg were bombed, and the following day Vienna, Lobau, and Linz. The last oil mission of the month was a combined visual and blind-bombing attack on Blechhammer South.

In December the Eighth was tied up with bad weather, the ground offensive, and the German offensive, but the Fifteenth was able to keep up the pressure. On December 2 they sent four hundred and fifty bombers against Blechhammer North, Blechhammer South, Odertal, and Florisdorf. For one 464th Bomb Group crew, formed in May at Lincoln, Nebraska, December 2 was a memorable day. The crew, led by pilot Lieutenant August Lechner, had flown their first mission against Blechhammer on August 27, and in accordance with Fifteenth policy Lechner and his co-pilot, Lieutenant Don Baker, had flown on separate aircraft as observers. On December 2 they were again separated, Baker flying as a fill-in co-pilot on another crew.

Over the target the aircraft carrying Baker and piloted by Lieutenant Charles Stanley took flak hits. The fuel lines were punctured and gasoline was sloshing into the bomb bay as they came off the target, so they left the bomb doors open, opened the nose wheel door, the cockpit windows and vents, the flight deck escape hatch, the camera hatch and anything else that would open. The fuel poured in and the wind swirled it back through the plane; after about ninety minutes of this harrowing flying the crew bailed out over Yugoslavia and walked out . . . Stanley's crew were old hands, having already been shot down once over Blechhammer, on October 13.

That same day Lechner's original bombardier and navigator, Lieutenant Sidney Watson and Lieutenant Leo Kennedy, were flying with George Maheu's crew in Yellow How. Their ship was hit heavily by flak and Watson was wounded in the knee. Past the target Kennedy gave him a shot of morphine, and with the intercom shot out they never received the signal to bail out. Kennedy noticed the rest of the crew was gone, and started dragging the wounded bombardier toward the nose wheel doors. By that time they were practically in the tree tops and Kennedy sat down, ready to die.

Yellow How crashed and started to burn, as German soldiers rushed to the wreckage. They cut through the mangled metal and got Kennedy out, but Watson was pinned there and they left him, fearing an explosion any minute. Kennedy broke away from his captors and rushed back to the wreckage, and the Germans began helping him to pry Watson loose. Both men became prisoners and survived the war.

Meanwhile, Lieutenant August Lechner and the rest of the crew were still flying missions. They were finally shot down over northern Italy, bailing out near the enemy lines. The engineer was shot twice through the back by rifle fire, and was captured with some of the crew, but Lechner and one or two others got back through the lines to safety.

Luck was with the ten men moulded into a crew at Lincoln in May 1944; shot down in three separate aircraft, all ten survived the war.

Moosbierbaum on December 11, Blechhammer South December 12, Brux and Linz on December 16; the Fifteenth's oil war ground on.

On December 20, as the afternoon faded into overcast and fine rain, a yellow-tailed cripple from the 455th Bomb Group was struggling across the Adriatic. That day she was little different to any other Liberator in trouble on the way home. The big silver aircraft was named the *Dakota Queen* . . .

She had taken off from San Giovanni to attack the Skoda works at Pilsen, and at her controls sat her twenty-two year old pilot, Lt. George McGovern from Mitchell, South Dakota. Nothing out of the ordinary happened until the *Dakota Queen* was perhaps an hour from her target. Then the #2 engine quit. The pilot feathered the propellor and balanced the ship with the other three engines. The B-24 was almost at the target, and McGovern decided against leaving the formation and returning to base.

There was flak at the target, and slivers nicked *Dakota Queen's* silver skin as she struggled through. There was less than a minute to go before bombs-away when the #3 engine stopped. *Dakota Queen* was suspended solely by her two outboard engines. The oil pressure had ebbed away before McGovern was able to feather his second useless engine, and the big propellor windmilled uselessly in the frigid air.

When the bombs left their shackles the airplane responded better, but there was a six hundred mile journey back to Italy, and the rest of the 455th's formation was already pulling away from the *Dakota Queen*. McGovern's B-24 was losing precious altitude every minute as they raced across Yugoslavia toward the Adriatic Sea.

By the time they were over the water the *Dakota Queen* was flying at six thousand feet, and the crew was throwing everything overboard in their fight for time.

It looked as if the race was lost when flames burst from the #3 engine and hungrily licked at the Liberator's wing, but then the tiny island of Vis was in front of them.

McGovern set up the crippled *Dakota Queen* for the landing on the tiny strip as his co-pilot talked to the ground controllers.

The big tires touched the edge of the runway and screeched and smoked as McGovern used everything to stop the *Dakota Queen* in time. He made it. As the crew left the aircraft the red-hot engine was already smothering under a blanket of chemical foam.

The crew were flown out by transport, leaving the *Dakota Queen* to be patched-up, stripped-down and eventually flown out by a repair crew.

Lt. George McGovern received the Distinguished Flying Cross for that mission, which was just one part of a rather disappointing offensive against enemy ordnance depots, tank factories and motor vehicle plants; the campaign had been begun in August with the goal of denying equipment to the German armies.

*　　*　　*　　*

Between August and November there had been a rather disappointing offensive against enemy ordnance depots, tank factories, and motor vehicle plants, with the goal of denying equipment to the German armies. Obviously, the Germans would have guns and ammunition to defend their homeland, but it was supposed that heavy and continuous bombing of these targets would mean no tanks, self-propelled guns or trucks. In August Spaatz had ordered the bombing of twelve ordnance depots, eight tank factories, and seven truck works whenever it was possible, and in September this target system took second place on the priority list. That month the Fifteenth hit Saint Valentin, and in October the effort, seeming to have good effect, was increased. On October 16 the Fifteenth bombed Saint Valentin and Steyr and Pilsen's Skoda works on October 23; smaller forces struck at Vienna, Graz, Linz, and Milan. At the end of the month it was obvious that the campaign was not having the desired effect, and German tank output rose in December.

Weather and blind bombing techniques always had a marked effect on strategic operations by both the Eighth and Fifteenth Air Forces. The Eighth's approach was to assign two Mickey Liberators to each group, but the Fifteenth divided its groups into Red and Blue Forces. The Red Force had four pathfinder aircraft and flew all missions against major German targets, and

The final 49th Wing markings were bold; this 450th Bomb Group Mickey ship carries a portion of her old markings with the new black and yellow stripes on the diagonally halved fin and rudder. The H2X equipment in her belly radome gave the operator a radar map of the ground below, and was particularly effective against coastal targets because of the good contrast between land and water. The Fifteenth had greater success with the device than the Eighth. (Max Schuette)

were given all fighter escort. The Blue Force usually bombed by visual methods without escort, and hit objectives close to the Italian bases. The Fifteenth continued getting better results from Mickey bombings than the Eighth, which had an average circular probable error of two miles on blind bombing missions, which called for saturation bombing. The Fifteenth was doing "twice as well or half as poorly."

Later in 1944 the Fifteenth began flying small missions using their Mickey aircraft alone, and the 464th Bomb Group was typical. Their first mission of this type was flown on November 3, 1944, by three aircraft. Their target was a marshaling yard at Munich, and one of the aircraft was piloted by Lt. Lechner; a crew from each squadron had been training for night flying since October, and been made familiar with radar bombing. The briefing for November 3 was almost the same as usual, except that the weather was terrible, and the aircraft were to take off at ten-minute intervals and maintain that spacing throughout the flight, which meant they would be perhaps thirty miles apart, or alone. The crews were instructed not to bomb if the weather was clear. The three gray aircraft took off at 8 A.M. in driving rain, flew through two weather fronts and broke into clear sky at 22,000 feet. As the frosting of ice cleared from the windshields the pilots looked anxiously for fighters, but they were alone. Leveling off before the Initial Point Lechner's crew was waiting for the Munich reception, but nothing happened. They dropped their bombs and there was still no reaction, and co-pilot Don Baker wondered if the navigator had brought them to the right place. Then they realized they must have been first there and taken the enemy by surprise, because about a mile behind them the sky turned black with antiaircraft fire. After six and a half hours they were back home, having seen only one other aircraft; the ground had not been visible at any time. On November 15 Mickey B-24s from the 464th hit Linz, and ten days later three more flew a night mission to Munich; the group flew a half dozen more similar missions before the end of the war.

There was no rest for the oil installations during the German offensive in the Ardennes, the Fifteenth flying mission after mission in one of the great aerial operations of the war. They crippled the major refineries and knocked out all the synthetic plants on their target list. Both Blechhammers, Oswiecim, Brux, Odertal, and Austrian targets were heavily bombed, with excellent results and light losses. The results were outstanding in this campaign, but the bombings of vehicle plants and ordnance depots seemed wasted. Weather in the latter part of January 1945 tied the Fifteenth down, allowing them only eight operational days in the whole month. On January 20 they hit Regensburg, and on the last day of the month four hundred Liberators and a force of B-17s hit Moosbierbaum. Flying conditions did not improve during

Dogpatch Express *from the 459th's 756th Bomb Squadron. This group introduced a unique "squadron code" which was made up of the last numeral of the squadron number and the aircraft's individual letter, placed in a black rectangle on the fuselage.*

the first half of February and were the worst they had met, with 80 percent of the missions by blind bombing, but the results were very good. Nearly 25,000 tons of Allied bombs were aimed at oil during that month, and the enemy was beaten. All that was left to the Germans were synthetic plants in central Germany and Austria and some crude sources and benzol plants in the Rühr, as the Russians conquered large pieces of Poland, Silesia, and Hungary.

The Fifteenth was also involved in supporting the Anglo-American and Russian land forces, and this meant strikes at transportation, particularly marshaling yards in Vienna and railways in Hungary, Italy, and Yugoslavia. Ground fog over the bases and violent weather over the Alps kept the Fifteenth in Italy until February 5, when the heavies got through and plastered oil storage at Regensburg. Weather pinned them down again the next day, but on February 7 the Vienna oil refineries were bombed, along with Moosbierbaum. More attacks on Moosbierbaum on February 9 and February 14 left the target half destroyed, and railway targets in Austria were hit on February 8 and February 9. Weather again intervened, but on February 13 837 heavy bombers rose up and streamed over Vienna, crippling marshaling yards and freight stations and blocking all railway lines in parts of the city. Although the damage could be repaired, Vienna was temporarily paralyzed, and on February 16 the Fifteenth turned its attention to German jets. Eaker had been waiting to "crack the jets," and 700 bombers flew to southern Germany. The weather was poor, and the most effective attack was made by 263 Liberators which hit the airfield and Me-262 plant at Regensburg.

February 1945: the Silver Queen at Vienna

If the air war seemed to have eased in the Allies favor, individual crews could still find that things were as grim as ever. On February 19 the 98th Bomb Group, the old Pyramiders, were briefed for Vienna; it looked like a fairly easy mission. Ken Scroggins was top turret gunner on a B-24 called the *Silver Queen:* flying south of Klagenfurt thirty Me-109s attacked the 98th, knocking one of their ships down before passing on to the following group. Their heading changed toward Vienna and the 550 flak guns they had been briefed about, mostly the superb 88-mms.

The 98th had put up twenty-eight Liberators, seven from each squadron, but one had blown a tire on takeoff and lay in three pieces on the runway at Lecce. Two more had lost engines and aborted over northern Yugoslavia. Another dropped down to seek a secondary target after the oxygen system failed. As the bomb run began two of the three aircraft left in the 344th Squadron already had engines feathered due to flak damage and a strong headwind at 28,000 feet was buffeting the Liberators and the gunners below were getting good targets. The red centered eighty-eights began bursting around the *Silver Queen* and chunks of flak smashed through Scroggins's turret and cut the oxygen lines to four stations. Other pieces slashed into the head and stomach of the painted *Silver Queen* on the nose and clipped a piece out of the co-pilot's parachute harness, tore through the tail turret, zipped between the navigator's legs and clunked off the armor plate behind the pilots' seats. More flying steel bounced off the ball turret, blew out the right tire, hit a fuel cell, tore a four-inch hole in the command deck above the bomb bay and hit the right outboard engine, setting it afire. The pilots managed to feather it before it tore itself from the wing, and the fire was extinguished; the *Silver Queen* had over one hundred flak holes, but the painted lady's mute smile never faded.

The pilots got her down to 12,000 feet as quickly as they could, and wondered how close they would get to home. They slipped into some overcast when they spotted three fighters near Graz, but they had a worse problem with three engines and the climb over the Alps ahead of them . . . they made it as far as Zara in Yugoslavia, three hundred miles from Vienna and three hundred miles from home. Fuel was too low to fly on out across the Adriatic, and the ship was going down.

The *Silver Queen* landed on rough ground just south of Zara, the flat tire wrapping itself around the wheel and spinning the aircraft around 90 degrees at 120 miles an hour. She finally stopped, scraping her belly but with her crew intact.

The dazed crewmen saw some horsemen coming in their direction and the pilot ordered his gunners into their turrets. The riders paused about three hundred yards away and one horseman and one crewman moved out slowly toward the neutral ground between the aircraft and the mounted strangers.

They were Yugoslav partisans, and on February 21, after a couple of C-47s had flown in the necessary equipment, the crew of the *Silver Queen* took their patched up lady home. *Silver Queen* went on to become one of the legends of the Fifteenth Air Force, with more than one hundred and ten missions to her credit.

*   *   *   *

The Greater Areas of Hell

Oil refineries and railways in Vienna were the target on February 20, and the next day another five-hundred bomber attack on the rail system finished Vienna; her oil, transportation, and industrial installations were all but demolished. The Fifteenth would go back before the Russians moved in, but for the present Vienna was eliminated. Fine weather during the last days of February at the bases and along the routes let the Fifteenth fly tactical missions against railways in northern Italy, Austria, and southern Germany. There were no longer any fighters, but a shrunken Germany meant a greater concentration of flak guns, although countermeasures were more effective than they had been before. Two thirds of Fifteenth effort was now directed at

This old B-24H was flying with the 485th against Neuberg in Austria in March 1945. She looks to have originally flown with the Eighth, as markings have been painted out on her fuselage and she carries the armor slab which protected the pilot and co-pilot, an in-the-field modification in the European Theater.

transportation, and the other third at oil. In the second week of March the Fifteenth flew largely in support of the Russians, hitting railways, bridges, airfields, and troop concentrations in Hungary, Austria, and Yugoslavia. The most memorable Fifteenth mission of the period was the March 12 attack on Florisdorf, when B-17s and 522 Liberators plastered the target in their largest single operation. On March 21, as the Fifteenth's strategic war was nearing an end, 366 Liberators carried off one of the most effective missions of the war, a visual attack on Neuberg's jet factory and airfield. The plant was almost obliterated and three days later another 271 Liberators returned to finish the job, destroying an estimated twenty-five jets on the airfield. The good weather aided the Fifteenth in the completion of their work; 124 B-24s put a Czech refinery at Kralupy out of operation, and, on March 23, 157 Liberators were over the crumbling Saint-Valentin tank works in Austria.

The day began badly for the 456th Bomb Group; Saint Valentin was undesirable at best due to its proximity to Linz, a "flak hole." Lieutenant Robert Carlin was piloting G for George that day, and he says that "the brakes hissed like those on a Greyhound bus as we waddled nose to tail toward the runway. The taxi strip was narrow, and high in the middle. We watched Q for Queen carelessly taxi near the edge. The plane listed heavily with its five-ton bomb load. Our squadron pet dog, Tracer, playfully running along the line of Liberators, was suddenly bisected by the propeller of Number 4 engine, dipped low by the preoccupied pilot. No one said anything."

Carlin was in Able Box of Blue Force, twenty-one Liberators flying one half hour behind a similar number in Red Force. The takeoff and assembly went as planned, and the 456th began the climb to altitude as they passed over the Adriatic. Time passed and the target drew near.

"We could see the target clearly as we turned to start the bomb run," Carlin remembers. "It was a biting clear day, and intensely cold at 26,000, all making for flawless visibility. Black boiling curls appeared at once. We were eleven minutes from the target and already the shells were exploding around us. They were huge, meaning they were close. The flak these days was so bad that we were being forced to split the mission. The first wave would suppress the gunners, hopefully allowing the second wave to approach and bomb with greater accuracy.

One of the most famous and horrifying photos of World War II: Black Nan of the 464th Bomb Group. She was a new, all gray path-finder aircraft called Stevonovitch II, *named by the 779th Squadron Commander, Colonel James Gilson, for his son. Supporting ground troops near Lugo, Italy on April 10, 1945, Gilson and nine others were killed in the blazing wreck, but one waist gunner was thrown clear and survived. The mission was supposed to be a milk run, and in the target area there was only one four-gun flak battery, so men who were about to finish their tours were sent along. After bombs-away four flak shells burst near the 464th, and the fourth hit Black Nan between the #2 engine and the fuselage.*

The 459th's Judith Ann *lands at the Poltava shuttle base in Russia on April 12, 1945.*

The 461st Bomb Group's last operation was to supply the Spittal POW camp near Villach, Austria, on May 9, 1945. Lieutenant John Stegeman's number 33 is from the 765th Bomb Squadron. (Stan Staples)

"Like roll-top desks the doors went up the sides of the swollen Liberators. Able Three was already hit; oil smoke poured back. He stayed in close formation. Loud, close flak, bursts overlapping, continued. Looking ahead we could see what was being prepared for us. A rectangle of flak was laid out directly in our path. All gunners would now merely keep filling it. And we would go through it.

"Our fear of going so close to Linz, one of the greater areas of hell, turned out to be correct. Somebody in Able Box broke radio silence to report wounded aboard, a futile gesture born of panic.

"Nine full minutes to bombs away. We heard the ting-tong of metal fragments resonating in the metallic hollow of the fuselage. Seven minutes to go.

"One minute to go. But Able One dropped his bombs right now. So did we, and so did everybody else. Radio silence ended as we broke into a hard right turn. Down steep, hard right. We leveled off only to find more flak awaiting us. Hard left, and dive. Able Box dropped beneath my vision. The horror of sliding into them gripped me in sudden panic. They appeared again, but it was an effort to release the steel grip I had on the yoke.

"The Alps came into view dead ahead. B-24s began to appear from above, from far out. They joined us for protection. Some had feathered engines, others streamed oil. One was trailing the gummed rubber of his self-sealing tanks. Able Box was minus a ship that had been hit early. Baker was hurt but incredibly intact. Charlie Box was asked to report in, wherever they had scattered. There was no response. It dawned on us that Charlie Box had been eliminated. Able Seven had moved up for the downhill ride home. We could see the red smear of blood from our dog, Tracer. It sparkled in frozen crystals near the name *Agony Wagon* on the nose."

A day after Saint Valentin the Fifteenth hit Berlin for the first time, with Fortresses, and by the end of the month the strategic air offensive was practically over. On April 9 and April 10 the Fifteenth sent eight hundred bomber formations to attack positions before the ground forces crossed the Senio River, and on April 15 the largest Fifteenth operation of all, Wowser, took place. Every airplane that could fly, 1,235 heavies, hit troops, gun positions, and strongpoints which faced the ground forces breaking through at Bologna. After this huge operation the heavies were sent out to stop German troops escaping from Italy, and marshaling yards in Austria and the Brenner Pass line received repeated attacks. When the Germans finally surrendered in Italy on May 2 the Fifteenth occupied itself with dropping supplies and evacuating prisoners of war.

Never glorified, the Fifteenth's Liberators flew a hard and bloody war, and won it.

IX

Pacific Tramps

The Battle of Midway had been won. How it had been won, how much of a part good fortune had played, all these things were lost in the waves of relief and exuberance which swept over the American forces and the tiny Seventh Air Force, a threadbare phoenix which had risen from the ashes of the old Hawaiian Air Force and Pearl Harbor. And on Midway, in the Seventh Air Force headquarters tent, five men were arguing about the best way to get a maximum-load Liberator from Midway to Wake Island—and back again.

Lieutenant Sugar Hinton, a fighter pilot turned to bombers, was arguing the merits of flying a B-24 to Wake Island at 140 miles an hour. Truman Landon, Robert L. Waldron, Roger Ramey, and Art Meehan were trying to convince him that 160 would get him there with gas to spare: you just didn't fly fully loaded Liberators at stalling speed . . . unlike some gentler aircraft, once a Liberator fell away with a full load you might never pull it out.

Hinton was pilot for Major General Clarence L. Tinker, commander of the Seventh Air Force, and Tinker wanted Liberators in the Pacific. On the line at lonely Midway were four LB-30s, and the mission was scheduled for that evening, June 6, 1942. All five men wanted Tinker to get a good mission, but they differed in their ways of guaranteeing it. To Wake Island and back was 2,500 miles, and the others heaved a sigh of relief when Hinton gave in and agreed to fly it their way.

Tinker knew the Flying Fortresses would be going to Europe, but the flamboyant, part-Indian commander hoped for a good chunk of the B-24 Liberator production for his air force. Nobody seemed to want the boxy Liberators, but their range made up for many things, and Tinker believed

The 307th spent less than five months as a Seventh Air Force Bomb Group, and their most successful mission was to Wake Island on December 22, 1942, when twenty-six aircraft swept over the target and the total cost was *patching up two bullet holes in group commander William Matheny's aircraft. The crew* of Bundles for Japan *are relaxing on Midway, staging point for the Hawaii-based Liberators.*

that if his pilots flew the aircraft the way they wanted to be flown the problems would disappear. Convinced that he would have to do something spectacular to sell Hap Arnold on his plans, he felt a counterattack on Wake, which had fallen to the Japanese six months ago and become a symbol, was one way to get his story across.

Tinker saw his opportunity when Major Robert Waldron brought a flight of four LB-30s from the mainland to Hickam Field on Hawaii. He got permission to carry out his plan, which was essentially that the four aircraft should fly to Midway from Hawaii, refuel, and hit Wake at dawn.

Waldron and the Hawaiian Air Depot prepared the aircraft as the Midway battle ran its course, and on the night of June 5 the four bombers slipped away from Hawaii.

The flight to Midway was teeth-gritting agony for the more experienced pilots as Hinton, flying Ramey's plane and calling the shots, cut their speed to a breath above a stall. The others left him behind, feeling it was too damned dangerous, and spent agonizing minutes on Midway's airstrip until their leader's aircraft finally appeared over the horizon.

That night an overcast at about 6,000 feet shrouded the four aircraft as they wheeled down the runway on Midway's Eastern Island, took off, and rendezvoused above.

To their dismay, the other three aircraft commanders saw Hinton was again holding his B-24, loaded like the others with every pint of gasoline she would hold and six 500-pound bombs, down to that final degree. They couldn't understand why he would not believe that fully loaded and hanging on that slim Davis wing, a stalled Liberator glided like a rock.

Their consternation was bolstered by Hinton's prompt deviation from the planned course, which he did not soon correct. Dutifully and in grim silence, the other three followed their commander's meandering aircraft.

After about thirty minutes of ambling around, Hinton's aircraft nosed forward into the overcast; neither falling off on a wing nor spinning, the LB-30 just mushed into the clouds and fell from view. His voice edged with worry, Ramey, commanding in Landon's plane, flipped on the intercom. "What do you make of it, Ted?" Landon answered that he wasn't sure, but maybe it was engine trouble and they had gone back to Midway. "Should we go on?" was the next question, and Landon decided that would be what Tinker would want.

Setting the correct course, the three bombers droned into the darkness. Tinker had hoped to find damaged Japanese ships which had retired to Wake after the Midway engagements, and as first light filtered into the cockpits and flickered over the weary faces of the pilots, they searched for the island. There was no sign of Wake, and nor could they find it. Without a star shot for four hours due to heavy weather, even experienced overwater flyers could fail, and they had. There was little time to search for the elusive island, and when that was used up and their point of no return glared back at them from their fuel gauges, they turned back.

Over Midway that evening, Landon noticed the general's plane was nowhere in sight. He wondered if perhaps Tinker had already started back to Hawaii . . .

General Clarence Tinker was never seen again. Not a single trace of the aircraft ever turned up, and Landon and the rest decided that it must have fallen like a stone and sunk with all on board.

Determined and saddened, Landon, Waldron, Meehan, and Ramey decided to carry out Tinker's wish, and on June 26 they climbed back into their cockpits and pointed their Liberators' stubby noses toward Wake again. This time, led by Ramey, they arrived over the island at midnight, finding their overcast target by radar. Coming out of a dive and gliding down a farther 500 feet they went in on their bomb run.

Wake blazed with fire as every enemy gun pointed in the direction of the three aircraft, but the pilots had chosen 4,000 feet so as to be too high for

When the tide of war turned in the Pacific there was more time for cultural pursuits, such as decorating aircraft. Nipponese Clipper *flew with the 38th Squadron of the 30th Group.*

small-arms and machine-gun fire, and too fast past the heavier weapons. They crossed over Wake's fury at the cost of one small flak hole in the left wing of Ramey's plane. Behind them their eighteen bombs had plowed through hangars, runways, and part of the fleet of aircraft Japan had been planning to move to Midway when they captured it.

There would be Liberators in the Seventh Air Force.

* * * *

Eight months later, as Flying Fortresses plowed into the Rühr Valley, as Guadalcanal in the South Pacific was secured, the Seventh was still a forgotten air force. Nothing much happened at their Hawaiian headquarters, but General Willis H. Hale had his problems. Tinker's affection for the Liberator had not been shared by many of the men, and the changeover period was full of pitfalls. To the Seventh's bomber crews, here was another example that they were second-class citizens, a bastard outfit which might be useful if there was nobody else around to do the job. As their beloved B-17s brought crews home from European targets in mangled, unflyable aircraft, their tirade grew more bitter. Hale eventually relieved one of his group commanders for echoing the men's disapproval so loudly it was heard in Washington.

The Liberators had proved something when Colonel William A. Matheny, commander of the 307th Bomb Group, led twenty-six on another mission to Wake on December 22, 1942. Bombing from 8,000 feet down to 2,500 feet, the Liberators ran Wake's fiery gauntlet. The cost: two holes in Matheny's lead plane. This brought a few shrugs and mumbles from the B-24 haters, but there was still a solid core of resentment.

March 1943: A Triangle Named Tarawa

In March 1943, the Seventh was given a job; Admiral Chester W. Nimitz wanted them in on the invasion of the Gilberts in the Central Pacific. At first they would hit the Gilberts and Nauru on a regular basis, feeling out the enemy there. Then they would begin applying the pressure until finally mounting an all-out bombardment in November.

They were to fly from Funafuti in the Ellice Islands, and on April 18 General Hale took the Seventh down: twenty-four Liberators from the 307th Bomb Group. Among them were veterans of the earlier Wake strikes, like Lieutenant Jesse Stay and Lieutenant Colonel Jay Rutledge, men who would grow with the Seventh Air Force.

Their first target was Nauru, a lonely island lying over a thousand miles from Funafuti. Tarawa, 800 miles to the north, was second. The targets on Nauru were the phosphate works, but behind this there was a grander purpose: combat training for the new crews. It was a morale builder which would shake out the boredom of Hawaii and give the men a sense of achievement, it provided a testing ground for logistic support in the upcoming island-hopping campaigns, and it tested the enemy's strength. It was almost a bonus that it would also do some damage to the Japanese.

After their first strike at Nauru, the crews were exuberant—Japs weren't tough. The next day, April 21, Tarawa was scheduled and about seventeen aircraft were ready to go. Then at 3:30 in the morning the Japanese returned their compliment and the Seventh Air Force jumped out of bed and scurried under whatever offered shelter. The first bombs gouged the runway and after regrouping the enemy began their second attack. They hounded Funafuti for several hours, making five separate attacks in all, and worked well. Two B-24s were destroyed, and only twelve were in good enough condition for the Tarawa mission. Hale killed the plan for a daylight raid, and the dozen machines took off from their battered base at midnight.

Tarawa's teeth weren't too sharp, and the crews were still elated when they flew back to Hawaii that afternoon in what Hale called "the quickest and farthest retreat in military history."

*   *   *   *

The Seventh still considered itself a short-changed outfit; the 307th moved to the Thirteenth Air Force, but seemed to leave their worst planes for the re-equipping of the 11th Bomb Group. The peace of Hawaii was shattered by curses as the crews inspected the bullet holes in their "new" B-24s . . . old stagers like *Green Hornet, Brunnhilda, Thumper,* and the *Gremlin* wheezed and clanked in on May 18, and the crews growled. Those maudlin months of preparation were marked by isolated missions like the run to Wake on July 26, 1943. Staged through Midway, the mission hardly rates a mention in the history books . . . except the 42nd Bomb Squadron history book.

Sexy Sue II screeches along Makin's airstrip on one wheel, while the ambulance waits to race to her aid. Piloted by Lieutenant Lewis Cartwright, she was shot up over Mille on December 18, 1943. The first Sexy Sue *had been lost during the Gilberts campaign, Lieutenant Charles Hopkins landed* Sexy Sue III *at Nanomea and she was destroyed when another landing aircraft taxied into her, and Hopkins then took over* Sexy Sue IV, *lost over Wotje during a night mission in January of 1944.*

Whenever a plane was junked, the Seventh cannibalized her and called her "Miss Tech Supply," but she was still Sexy Sue II, *Mother of Ten, deep down. Out in the taro patch her hollowing body lay, until one line chief could confidently say that "every B-24 flying in the Central Pacific has something off* Sexy Sue."

The 42nd's five B-24s took off from Midway in driving rain; Lieutenant Jesse Stay was leading in *Doity Goity,* and behind him trailed *Daisy Mae, Cabin in the Sky,* the *Wicked Witch,* and the *Sky Demon.*

Over Wake a Zero rammed into *Cabin in the Sky's* rear stabilizer and she spiraled down, shooting all the way at a sky full of Japanese fighters. *Daisy Mae* trudged through the air, braked by the jagged metal ringing two hundred holes; on *Sky Demon* the crew had two engines left and were throwing everything they could pick up or unbolt out of the plane. Thirty Zeros had minced the 42nd before they were free of them, and *Daisy Mae* only just made it to Midway for a harrowing crash landing. *Wicked Witch* staggered in with a dead crewman, and only one of the five, *Doity Goity,* was fit to return to Oahu.

* * * *

While the Seventh teetered on the brink of lethargy, what had been an idea now had a name: Operation Galvanic. The Gilbert Islands were an obvious first step. Just over 2,000 miles from Hawaii the chain of sixteen barren atolls, cast over five hundred miles of deep blue ocean, had been in Japanese hands since December 27 of 1941. Tarawa, the big atoll, was composed of a chain of long, narrow islets on a reef shaped like a triangle. The Japanese had an airfield on the atoll named Betio, and Makin had a seaplane base and an airfield on its four large islets; it was number two target. The third objective was Apemama, a minor base and lightly fortified.

The Seventh's part in Galvanic was specific: denying the Japanese use of their airfields on Tarawa and Makin, and also Nauru to the west, and Mille, Jaluit, and Maloelap in the Marshalls to the north. The Marshalls targets meant grueling, dangerous missions. Jaluit was a major seaplane base and supply center, Mille had two runways and numerous installations. If the invasion was to proceed without devastation by Japanese air forces, the Seventh had to knock these targets out.

General Hale, commander of all land-based planes, needed to keep one heavy bomber squadron in the Hawaii defense role, which left him with seven squadrons of Liberators from his 11th and 30th Bomb Groups. These were virtually new units, so the hard training for the long, overwater flights was intensified. The brand-new 30th Group did not reach Oahu until October 11, which left just six weeks to teach them the rules of the Central Pacific war, and their crews were more experienced than some of the replacements in the 11th. But somehow, along with the mountains of men and supplies, they all were ready for D-Day: November 20.

For the Seventh, Operation Galvanic began a week early. General Hale was at Funafuti with two squadrons, two more were at Nanomea, one was on Nukufetau, and two on Canton; seven B-24 squadrons had been assigned the brunt of the battle to neutralize the Japanese air forces within reach of the Gilberts. At dawn on November 14 nine B-24s screamed over Tarawa's gentle palms, pouring out a shower of 30-pound frag bombs and scooting 70 miles away before the fires they set disappeared from their view.

Three days later eleven planes from the 11th Group attacked Taroa Island in the Maloelap Atoll. One of them, flown by Lieutenant John Lieb, was under fighter attack and flying on three engines when fire broke out in the waist section. Heading back for Canton with a dozen enemy fighters after him, Lieb's aircraft was slowly being devoured from the waist back by flames. It was not until the enemy turned for home that the crew could start fighting the fire. His engineer, Sergeant Lewis Horton, then proceeded to open cans of fruit juice and pass them out among the crew. Luckily they had more fruit juice than fire, and finally Horton was able to go back to the steaming, sticky metal and repair the mutilated control cables.

November 21, 1943, was finally selected as D-Day, chosen by planners who had worked for months on the scheme to give the right tide to carry the landing craft across Tarawa's shallow lagoon to the shores of Betio. In the landing craft and the transports everybody watched as the guns of the fleet pounded the beaches and swarms of Navy carrier planes zoomed over the tortured land. There was American air supremacy over Tarawa but the story of the Second Division's Marines is a bloody one. Tarawa exploded with fire from Japanese guns so well protected by concrete that the thousands of tons of explosives rained around them were ineffectual. Five hundred pillboxes waited for the Marines who waded through chest-deep water to fight and die for every inch of the bloody little island.

Tarawa was a hard lesson, well learned.

The Seventh's job was to keep the enemy out of the sky, and on the four days after the landing they dropped their bombs throughout the Marshalls and Nauru. Operation Galvanic ended on December 6, and the cost to the Seventh was seven aircraft in their twenty-nine strikes.

*   *   *   *

January 1944: Flintlock, the Conquest of Kwajalein

Then there was Flintlock. The code names were full of the sense of power which pervaded the American forces. Flintlock meant Kwajalein, the largest atoll in the world. In the Japanese mandate, they had had twenty-four years

Two days before Christmas, 1943, the Kansas Cyclone *took off to bomb Wotje atoll. Flying right wing in the last of three formations, she was about to unload when the target was obscured by cloud. So the pilot decided to hit Taroa in the Maloelap atoll; out of the cloud bank, the Liberators encountered thirty to forty Zeros.* Kansas Cyclone, Galvanized Goose *and* The Dirty Woman *pressed on into flak over the target, taking a few hits, then rejoined* *battle with the fighters.* Kansas Cyclone's *gunners got five of the fighters, but she was shot to pieces. One crewman was killed, two were wounded, the hydraulics were shot out, one engine was gone, the emergency life raft had been hit and had ballooned out and broken free, crippling the rudder as it slid back in the slipstream. For more than seven hours the pilot nursed her home to safety at Funafuti.*

to fortify it . . . on Tarawa they had had but two. The men saw the arithmetic and wondered.

D-Day for Kwajalein was set as January 31, 1944, and for the Seventh it was the same route over again, except Flintlock called for a seventy-day pre-invasion assault which had actually begun before the end of Galvanic and which would cease exactly one quarter of an hour before the first soggy American boot touched the shore.

Tarawa would become headquarters for the Seventh Bomber Command and the 11th Bomb Group. Up to D-Day minus three, the Seventh was to deny the enemy their airbases on Mille and Jaluit and to plaster Maloelap,

Brigadier General Truman H. Landon prepares to move forward to Kwajalein; looking over his right shoulder is his 11th Bomb Group navigator, Captain Louis Schauer.

The Tropic Knight, at left, was one of the leading contenders in the race for the 100 missions in the 30th Bomb Group. Within a year after this picture was taken on Tarawa she had flown eighty-six missions, running just a breath behind Come Closer with ninety-one and Punjab and Kontagious Katie. both on ninety. She flew seventy-seven missions without aborting, and was finally turned back by three bad spark plugs. But she did have the biggest single flak hole of them all, an award she collected over Iwo Jima.

Walt Disney, Al Capp, Milt Caniff, and other cartoonists were favorites among the artists decorating the bombers. Warner Brothers' Bugs Bunny featured in squadron insignia and on the noses of aircraft like the 11th's Wabbit Twansit and the 30th's Bugs Bomby.

Wotje, Roi Namur, and Kwajalein. While Flintlock was in progress they would also have to keep Nauru neutralized and pave the way for the next Central Pacific invasion.

Maloelap, in the center of the four islands of the Marshalls, was the toughest target. On their first strike at the 30-mile chain of islands the 30th Bomb Group brought up more than thirty fighters. Next time it was worse. Forty interceptors rushed into their formation, dropping aerial phosphorous bombs as too-accurate flak chased the B-24s from the target. The long white tentacles unnerved the crews, two aircraft never returned, and every Liberator was damaged.

As Flintlock moved into high gear in the early weeks of January the attacks had been stepped up in the face of increasingly punishing resistance. One B-24 which barely made it back from Maloelap was the *Belle of Texas*. Chased from the target by thirty Zeros, the *Belle* was in bad shape. Lieutenant Charles Pratte, the pilot, had four hundred miles to fly back to the Gilberts; he had no hydraulics and one of Tarawa's strips was his only chance. The strip he chose had only been adequate for fighter aircraft. A little crowd had gathered to watch the first landing by a Navy fighter and then the *Belle of Texas* loomed on the horizon. As Pratte leveled out his approach he could see a field which was too short even if he had had the luxury of brakes, and at the end of it there was a solid heap of coral. If he swerved around that he could carry on down as far as the sea.

While Pratte was worrying about this, an engine died. He managed to grapple the B-24 back up and proceeded to come around again on three engines. Necessity then made him mother to an invention. He ordered his crew to get three parachutes, and the waist gunners were instructed to rig a chute to each gun mount in such a way that they would pop open in the slipstream, and the tail gunner similarly rigged the third parachute in his position. Touching down at well over a hundred miles an hour, Pratte barked his orders and the three parachutes bloomed simultaneously. The *Belle* dragged along to a stop, fifteen feet from the water's edge.

Flintlock ultimately cost eighteen B-24s, and among them was the *Galvanized Goose,* an aircraft which became a bitter memory in the 11th Bomb Group. She turned up on the control tower's radar passing over Tarawa at 3,000 feet in the overcast and, obviously lost, flew on and on into an area where there was no land for half a million square miles except tiny Nauru and Ocean islands. Flak over Kwajalein had knocked out the *Goose*'s radio, weather had scattered the formation, and the lone B-24 was trying to find Tarawa alone at night. The navigator brought the aircraft directly over Tarawa by shooting stars and telling the pilot which way to go; their compass had been shot out along with every other instrument.

With the overcast extending to 11,000 feet they never knew when Tarawa passed beneath them, only that they should have been there and that they were running out of gas. Throwing out everything they could unbolt or rip out of the plane, they were finally forced to ditch with no lights and no altimeter, into waves they estimated were thirty feet high.

The *Galvanized Goose* hit a swell and just broke up. Navigator Dan Norris recovered consciousness in the water, miraculously thrown free of the disintegrating ship, which was in four separate parts. Fighting out mouthfuls of nauseating sea water, the dazed man struggled to climb onto the waist section, the largest area, and see if anyone was trapped. He saw the bombardier, almost decapitated by the flak helmet which had been jammed down onto his neck, and the top turret had torn free and crushed another crewman. The ball turret gunner, Sergeant Glenn Howell, had been lying in the camera hatch by the tail with several others when the aircraft ditched. The hatch sprang open and he found himself in the water. Altogether eight of the crew had survived somehow, but as they groped around for life rafts they found themselves in a school of sharks. Terrified, Norris watched the pilot, co-pilot, and a gunner go screaming beneath the sea.

Somebody had some rope and they tied themselves together, the five of them doing their best to find a life raft. All injured, Norris with a broken leg, they finally found one and managed to get aboard. After that they found four more, and Norris had time to vomit up his stomach of sea water.

With dawn the real terror returned. The sea was alive with sharks and the rafts began leaking from the small rips made by the sharks skimming under them as they zipped after fish. The survival kit aboard the raft informed them that they could scare off the sharks by thumping them on the nose with a paddle, but these sharks were made of sterner stuff. Howell took charge of the shark fighting, but they got angrier and angrier, so he broke off the engagement.

Norris glumly announced that they had been short-changed on their emergency equipment; there was only a pint and a half of water, the rations were soaked by sea water and they were unable to use the Gibson Girl emergency radio because the aerial would not rise. On the third day they heard a plane, but didn't stir because they recognized the sound as Japanese. On the seventh day a New Zealand Catalina, 160 miles off its regular patrol, stumbled upon them. It was a week before they could eat, and two before they could travel, but they had survived.

Three days before H-Hour for Kwajalein, the Liberators began nightly harassment missions against Roi, Kwajalein, Maloelap, and Wotje. On the night of January 28 eleven B-24s lingered over Kwajalein from dusk to dawn, dropping one or two delayed action bombs on each pass over the island. Nine more aircraft were keeping Wotje's garrison awake the same way.

Madame Pele, *bought for the 11th Bomb Group by Honolulu school children, was named for the Hawaiian Goddess of Fire; she put* the heat on the airstrip on Moen at Truk on this mission.

Fifteen minutes before the Seventh Division went ashore on January 31, six Liberators swept in low over Kwajalein carrying 1,000-pound bombs and 2,000 pound "atoll busters" to crack open the kind of installations which had survived on Tarawa. One heavy coastal gun was blown completely out of its mount and hurled end over end into the water. As the B-24s drove on by, the gunners opened up with everything they had at nearly treetop level. They moved off and swung around so they could see the landing craft heading for the beach; as they lingered they could tell this was no Tarawa. Kwajalein, Majuro, Roi, and Namur were ours by the afternoon of D-plus-one.

* * * *

Eniwetok, Truk . . . One Damned Island After Another

Eniwetok, most northerly of the Marshalls, lay five hundred miles to the northwest of Kwajalein, and was so well defended it was treated as a separate entity in the plan to capture the Marshalls; the success at Kwajalein meant the second part of the plan could be moved up in time, and on February 4 Operation Catchpole was planned for the new schedule.

Eniwetok had been under continuous attack during the Kwajalein assault, and Navy Liberators had brought back pictures that revealed negligible fortifications above ground, but developing foxhole and trench systems. Accordingly, landing operations began on February 17, and heavy air strikes simultaneously hit Saipan and Tinian in the Marianas, Truk, Ponape, and Kusiae in the Carolines, Wake, and Jaluit in the Marshalls.

It was then that the neutralizing of bypassed islands became a prime Seventh Air Force task. The Japanese had occupied every Pacific island they thought they could use, and it was clear that capturing each one would lengthen the war by months or years and cost thousands more lives. So they leapfrogged over them. Nauru and Ocean were to the rear of the Americans and were occupied by the Japanese; in the Marshalls the enemy still held Wotje, Maloelap, Mille, and Jaluit on the eastern flank, and Rongelap on the northern. To the west the Carolines bases such as Truk, Ponape, Woleai, Yap, Kusiae, Hall, Oroluk, Puluvat, Mokil, Pingelap, Pulawat, and Namonuito were in Japanese hands, and Wake and Marcus lay to the north.

Aerial bombardment could nullify their worth in two ways: by cutting off their supplies, of necessity brought by sea, or by destroying their installations as they were rebuilt. The Seventh Air Force and Navy Liberators proved particularly adept at this work, and neutralization worked like a charm.

In addition there was the job of softening up the Marianas, the next stage

While the first troops were struggling for a foothold in Europe, planes like the 11th's Dual Sack *were hammering away at resistance in the Marianas.*

Stepped up behind Gun Site *is the* Merry Boozer, *on one of her twenty sorties against the Truk bastion. Lieutenant Tucker White, her pilot, was a teetotaler . . .*

of the Central Pacific campaign, but neutralization meant a series of never-ending missions, some long, some short. Ocean was 240 miles to the southwest of Tarawa, Nauru 380 miles to the southwest, and the Japanese Marshall islands even closer. The Carolines, to the west, had the most powerful enemy bases, at Truk, Kusiae, Ponape and Palaus, Yap, Ulithi, and Woleai . . . these islands would be the steppingstones to the Philippines.

Truk, 1,400 miles from Tarawa and nearly one thousand from Kwajalein, presented the greatest problem. The Gibraltar of the Pacific, it was considered the center of Japanese resistance in the mid-Pacific and the primary supply base for the entire mandated area. Consisting of 118 islands and islets, about fifty of them in a great encircling reef, Truk had an enclosed lagoon some thirty-three miles in diameter and containing the larger islands of Moen, Dublon, Tol, Fefan, Uman, Udot, and Falabeguete. Overlooking the lagoon were 5- and 6-inch gun positions, on hills which gave Truk more natural defenses than Pearl Harbor. At one time there were seventy fleet repair shops in operation, with supporting facilities such as small marine railways, and a 2,500-ton floating drydock and crane-equipped repair ship. There was a seaplane anchorage and Japanese surface craft were often there, although the main fleet cautiously fell back to Palau after the Marshalls were invaded.

After February 16, 1944, when carrier planes sank more than thirty ships, Truk's value diminished in the eyes of the Japanese Navy. The mission of their air forces there was protection of the base, and no offensive flights ever emanated from Truk.

In the week ending February 22, Liberators hit Ponape four times with incendiaries and high explosives; there was no aerial opposition, and the antiaircraft gunners were eager but inexperienced. The 176 Ponape sorties cost no planes and no lives. Four days later Ponape received the *coup de grâce*, smothered under twenty-five tons of bombs and incendiaries. It had taken eleven days to "neutralize" Ponape, at the cost of what was dropped onto it. Kusiae was the same story.

*   *   *   *

The Japanese expected their next fight would be in the Carolines, but the Marianas, 1,200 miles ahead, was to be the next target. By early March 1944, Liberators were based on Kwajalein, and from there they began their attacks on Truk. The first mission was on March 15, when twenty-two 30th Bomb Group B-24s took off on a night attack. Flying through lousy weather those that got through arrived over their target in darkness, finding every light burning and workers going merrily about their business. As the Liberators moved in, searchlights reached out for them with long fingers, and red tracer cascaded around them. They had two targets, and Dublon and Eten islands' fuel tanks and ammunition dumps provided spectacular explosions as the Liberators skittered off into the night without a loss.

Truk became a regular Seventh Air Force excursion.

*   *   *   *

One of the pilots of the 11th Bomb Group's neutralization team, paying a cursory visit to Maloelap to hit a portion of the runway, came over the island to find a black-out so complete that he couldn't find his target. Circling low, Captain Al Taflinger expected to draw antiaircraft fire which would reveal his aiming point, but the Japanese refused to play that game. So Taflinger flew off out to sea and made a long, large circle, then turned back. Coming in low for what he figured was the runway, he was almost on the ground before he switched on his landing lights. The Japanese courteously turned on the runway lights for their returning aircraft, and Taflinger dumped his load squarely on his target and was lost in the darkness before the enemy could work out exactly what they had done wrong.

Taflinger's luck didn't quite match his courage, and he went down over Truk in April.

By April the Seventh's two B-24 groups, the 11th and 30th, were side by side on Kwajalein, and the next act began. In the closing days of March they had teamed with the Navy in attacking the westernmost Carolines: Palau, Yap, and Woleai. This thrust had carried the fast carriers 1,200 miles west of Truk and only 550 miles short of the Philippines. Part of the over-all plan was the destruction of every Japanese air force east of the Philippines, and this meant the neutralization of every air base for hundreds of miles to the south and east. The Seventh hit Truk from the east, and the Fifth and Thirteenth Air Forces from the south, while the Seventh also kept a heavy boot firmly planted on Ponape and Kusiae. The Thirteenth knocked out Kapingamangari to Truk's south, and the Fifth hit Hollandia in New Guinea. At dawn on March 30 the Navy had hit Palau, Yap, and Woleai. The Japanese fleet did not respond, and the thread of supply lines to the enemy's mid-Pacific garrisons grew more tenuous.

Truk was pounded without respite during April, and *Heaven Can Wait*, piloted by Lieutenant Arthur Suojanen from the 11th Bomb Group, was one of the pounders. Assigned to hit the Param airstrip from 8,000 feet as part of a night force going after individual targets, she entered the lagoon through Otta pass, and a searchlight on Fefan began to move up on her from behind. Turning west for Param, she was caught in the beam. Two other lights on Dublon clicked on immediately and swung toward her as *Heaven Can Wait* lurched into a half circle to lose the lights, only to be picked up by two more.

Trapped in the web of five lights, Suojanen pushed her into a 70 degree dive, riding down the cone of light. Nearly blinded by the glare, the bombardier was dropping his bombs as fast as he could. As they exploded on a built-up area of Fefan, two of the lights went out and the pilots cut the engines and held the plane in the dive. At 4,000 feet, still at the end of three searchlight beams, they began pulling her out. They switched on the engines and nothing happened for what seemed a rather long while, but finally they caught and *Heaven Can Wait* nosed up violently, shook off the lights and bounded for home.

The Japanese hadn't seen her pull out, and the next night Tokyo Rose announced the shooting down of an American Liberator over Truk. *Heaven Can Wait*'s crew were greatly amused, but they had a short lease on life . . . on May 4 they headed for Ponape and were never heard of again.

Truk was tough. *A-Vailable* from the 30th Bomb Group was over Fefan at 10,000 feet when searchlights and flak picked her up. Dodging and diving, Lieutenant Woodrow Waterous piloted the ship through a steep bomb run and headed out to sea at 6,000 feet. Again trapped by searchlights, they were almost out when the tail gunner spotted a shadowy outline. "Zero coming in fast at 4:30," he called from his exposed turret. All Waterous needed was night fighters. The right waist gunner missed with a snap burst as the fighter dived under the B-24 and the ball turret man couldn't pick the fighter out through the fogged windows of his turret. The Zero got in five cannon hits. One exploded just above the co-pilot's seat, killing him and blinding Waterous. The navigator was wounded in the leg. Then one of the bomber's gunners got a damaging burst off at the Zero and the top-turret's fire sent him flaming into the sea. The co-pilot's shattered body had slumped over his control column, jamming the controls, and Waterous was down to 3,000 feet before he could drag the ship back onto a level course.

The hits had knocked out all the trim tab controls, the co-pilot's junction box, and large pieces of the greenhouse. The radio was dead, and the automatic pilot was useless. Waterous, dazed, bleeding, and seeing only blurs, had to stay in his place. His engineer, Sergeant Paul Regusa, took over the co-pilot's seat and read off the instruments.

It was a five-hour trip back to their base, with a blind pilot and an unconscious navigator. In front, black clouds were gathering as Sergeant Bill Shelton relieved Regusa while he went back to try to repair the interphone at least. On the catwalk through the bomb bay Regusa glanced down and saw a 500-pound bomb dangling from its rack. He yelled for Young, the right waist gunner, and together they lay on the catwalk and cranked open the bomb-bay doors. Beneath them was a narrow strip of metal and the ocean, as they struggled to dislodge the bomb. They got it released, but then it caught and dangled halfway out of the aircraft. Sweating and cursing they got what handholds they could and lifted the nose of the bomb back inside. Finally they had it secured again and they cranked the doors shut.

Gas was running low and Waterous told them to get everything they could overboard. Ammunition, guns, flak suits, and the Sperry ball turret all went sailing down as they fought for time. Regusa kept thinking of the 500-pound bomb they were stuck with and groaned inwardly.

Daylight came, and all that was ahead of them was more ocean. Waterous reluctantly decided they would have to ditch soon and they did not even

A formidable lineup from the 11th Bomb Group, on Eniwetok in April 1944. Soon over Truk will be Censored, *on her right the* Wabbit Twansit, *and* The Sunsetter.

Secrut Weapin's *only secret was how she managed to survive so long. Once her crew was relaxing over a completely socked-in target when they sailed over the one tiny break in the clouds; the B-24 was pelted by flak which knocked out one engine and peppered the whole right side of the ship. She landed with the very last of her hydraulic pressure braking her to a stop — the departing crew had to chock her wheels with rocks to keep her from rolling away.*

know for sure if they were on the correct course for Eniwetok. A few minutes before they would have had to head for the water they sighted land—Eniwetok. Waterous brought her in, using the eyes of his bombardier, Lieutenant Bob Irizarry, sitting beside him in the torn and bloodstained co-pilot's seat.

June 1944: Springboard to Japan

On April 15 General Hale moved up to Kwajalein under the imposing title of Comairforward, directing all land-based planes in the forward area. Two days after that the 30th Bomb Group's 392nd Squadron, known as the "Pathfinders" because of their record of firsts over various targets, made their initial attack on Tinian and Saipan when *Bugs Bomby* and four others took off with Navy PB4Ys for a photo-recon and bombing mission.

It was a fourteen and one half hour flight, involving what General Truman H. Landon of the National War College in Washington calls "the longest combat bomb run in the history of aerial warfare." The Liberators were glued to the rails for a full ten minutes at low speed so the pictures could be just right. With flaps extended and engines throttled back to 140 miles an hour they soared across Saipan like giant hawks. They nervously watched the Japanese fighters coming up to meet them and that ten minutes over the lush-looking island seemed like ten years, but the run was well over before the fighters could reach 20,000 feet to get at them. As they left the area the formation tightened up and the Japanese fighters performed pretty aerobatics around them, trying to find a weak spot in the force and following for ninety minutes before they tired of it.

The 30th set another record in April with a shuttle bombing mission of more than 4,000 miles, when seven of their B-24s joined Navy PB-4Ys on a triangular route which included bombing Guam in the Marianas and the Carolines. Staging out of Eniwetok, the crews knew they were embarking on something new and foreboding; there were two full days ahead flying the longest route ever flown on a combat mission, with two targets to hit. One on Guam, which was new and an unknown quantity, long occupied by the enemy. There was also the problem of weather: a tropical storm could brew and upset everything.

When they finally came in sight of Guam it was a beautiful scene after all the water and all the shrapnel-shaved atolls. White cliffs ran along the coast and the land was carpeted in rich green. Then from out of the verdant island came more than a score of maroon, brown and silver Oscars and Zekes, spoiling their sightseeing.

First the fighters launched an attack with phosphorous bombs, which did

K Lucy II *from the 26th Bomb Squadron, immortalized by photographer Robert Meiborg during a practice mission.* (*Barry Gilkes*)

not cause the Liberators a great deal of concern. Then as they completed their bomb and photo run the fighters attacked from all sides. The fight lasted forty minutes and the beat-up Liberators dragged on to Los Negros in the Admiralties, where they were refueled and rearmed while the crews rested. The next day the force was airborne again, bound for Ponape; that was easier and everybody got home.

On May 15 a round-the-clock combined operation involving the Seventh's B-24s and Mitchells and Marine Corps Dauntlesses, Hellcats, and Corsairs poured 240 tons of bombs on Jaluit. A week later it got a second dose, and six days after that Wotje and Ponape caught it. General Hale was able to report that "the Marshalls no longer represent worthwhile targets for heavy bombardment."

*   *   *   *

In May 1944 the Fifth Fleet, the greatest long-range task force in the history of warfare, was forming in the waters around Hawaii. The roads and docks

This beached hulk provided a good target for 11th Bomb Group gunners. (*Barry Gilkes*)

General Landon of 7th Bomber Command had several aircraft at his disposal, including Pacific Tramp III *and a B-24D, complete with silvered nose glass and named* Pacific Vamp (Mrs. Pacific Tramp).

were clogged with trucks and jeeps and tanks and huge guns, and at Bellows Field the Seventh Air Force was planning a little sortie into the Navy's realm. There the P-47 Thunderbolts of the 318th Fighter Group were parked wing tip to wing tip; seventy-three of them would be loaded on the light carriers *Manila Bay* and *Natoma Bay* and while at sea catapulted on a one-way flight to Saipan.

When it was all provisioned and fueled, Task Force 58 steamed out. It gathered more pieces as it passed Kwajalein and Eniwetok until it spread out into a huge sea full of ships, at least fifty miles long.

That February, Admiral Marc Mitscher had taken his carriers to the Marianas to probe the defenses, and his aircraft had hit Saipan, Rota, Tinian, and Guam. They had been successful, and now the payoff was due. The Marianas invasion was the most complicated to that point of the war; on

Bolivar *flew eighty-one missions with the 30th Group, so they decided to send her home on a War Bond tour. Flown back to the States, she cracked up on a runway near the Consolidated factory in San Diego; Consolidated employees subscribed to over $200,000 worth of bonds to put a replacement in the field.*

August 1944, and the 30th flies through one
of Truk's treats, aerial phosphorous bombs.

The wispy finders were deadly but seldom
found their targets.

June 14 Mitscher dispatched three of his carriers, *Essex, Yorktown,* and *Hornet,*
to strike Iwo Jima and neutralize it the day before the toops went ashore
on Saipan. In the shadow of the 1,500-foot Mount Tapotchau, with Tinian
visible three miles across the channel, the Marines moved in under an umbrella of naval gunfire.

In the two-day air battle covering the landing, and called the "Marianas
Turkey Shoot," carrier planes knocked down over four hundred Japanese

Artwork like this 11th Bomb Group classic
did not come cheap. Seabees on the island bases
did some of the best art, and a billboard like
this could cost around $200.

aircraft. On the morning of the third day the Marines had captured Aslito airfield, but the enemy counterattacked and took it back. Out on the carriers the Thunderbolt pilots stood by their fat, waiting aircraft, until on June 22 they came ashore from the *Natoma Bay,* followed by the others the next day.

At the same time as the Navy hit Iwo Jima, the 11th Bomb Group had reneutralized Truk, cutting off the second avenue for relieving the pressure on the Marianas. Tinian fell on July 31, Guam was secured ten days later, and though the B-24 had taken a back seat in the Marianas operation, there was as yet no real rest for them in sight.

*   *   *   *

October 1944: Kelly's Cobras

Coral and jungle, the Palau islands lie four hundred miles from the Philippines. They could not be bypassed on MacArthur's road, and on September 15 the Marines went ashore on Peleliu, the smallest and southernmost of the group. Not a shot had answered the preinvasion bombardment, and the troops landed optimistically.

When they reached the beach the Japanese opened up, surging from the depths of dugouts and caves. They had to be rooted out with napalm and grenades and lives. Two days later the Army went ashore on Angaur to the north, capturing it in forty-eight hours, and the Palau islands slipped back into obscurity.

MacArthur had borrowed a Seventh Air Force group, the 494th, to support him in the Philippines, first putting them under the command of the Marine Corps general running the neutralization of the northern Palaus, then Bomber Command of the Fifth Air Force and finally Thirteenth Bomber Command. The 494th was the last B-24 group formed for World War II.

The weather in the Palaus was possibly worse than in the rest of the Pacific. Six typhoons came their way, including a three-day blast which snapped off four-foot thick trees and took the 494th's huts and tents. And there were fleas and flying insects and huge land crabs. Flying from their strip on Angaur, with the nearby islands of Koror and Babelthuap visible on a clear day and garrisoned by around 30,000 enemy soldiers, they were in an unenviable position.

On October 24, 1944 the group's Liberators, led by Colonel Laurence Kelly, had let down over Angaur and landed after flying the five thousand miles from Hawaii in formation. Seventy-two hours later Kelly's Cobras took off again to bomb nearby Koror, and Yap in the Carolines. They came back

Barren Johnston Island meant a brief stopover for Kelly's Cobras of the 494th Bomb Group on their way from Hawaii to Angaur.

Kelly's Cobras had the least complicated markings of the Pacific B-24 groups: Ben Sheldon's 864th Squadron was recognized by this black delta, the 865th by a narrow black diagonal, the 866th by two vertical black stripes and the 867th by black "squares" on the upper rear and lower forward quarters of the tail. Kuuipo is being readied for a mission to the Palaus, only twenty-two hours after arriving at Angaur; the bulky object in the foreground is a bomb-bay fuel tank.

in driving rain, in groups of one and two and three; they had struck heavy flak, but their first combat mission had not been as grim as they had expected. No fighters, and no losses.

The Cobras were a lucky group. In 5,565 combat hours they flew strikes against radio stations, bridges, bivouac areas, and storage dumps, usually well below 10,000 feet and in the hornet's nest where automatic weapons and anti-aircraft fire overlap, before their first loss.

Intelligence officers had been poring over a series of recon photos which showed a building on Koror where there was always much activity; ah, they reasoned, Jap high command in the Palaus. So Major Duncan McKinnon drew the several storied building as his target and put a 500-pounder squarely through the roof. Weeks later they learned it wasn't the command center after all; but it was the biggest brothel in the Palaus.

Early in December, with the Palaus firmly under control, the Cobras were ordered into the Philippines campaign. Their list of targets expanded . . . Clark Field, Grace Park Airdrome, Bataan, Manila, Corregidor. Legaspi, an airstrip on southeast Luzon, was their first target in the Philippines, and the predawn takeoff was full of expectation for the crews. They had never encountered an enemy fighter; Koror and Babelthuap were little pinprick targets compared to the Philippines. The new objective would have to be hot, hotter probably than any other target of the Pacific war. As they had racked up mission after mission without a loss each crew had wondered whose luck would run out first . . . it would happen sometime, and this mission was a likely time. When they landed again in the miserable rain they counted heads just to be sure they really had all come back. The anti-aircraft fire had been heavy and well aimed, but they flew through it without a scratch. And there were still no fighters. Their luck held for three weeks of strikes against the aircraft and airfields which could threaten MacArthur's troops on Leyte. These were usually fourteen-hour, 2,300 to 2,500 mile flights.

The Bull had struck the target, Luhag, and was plowing homeward when it happened, four hundred feet above the water in a blinding rainstorm. Two engines suddenly died. The pilot, Captain Earl Richards, had no time to even think about ditching properly. He just tried to straighten up and hit the bell. The B-24 met a huge swell head-on and fell to pieces. Richards, trapped by his safety belt, went under with the nose section. He fought his way free and clawed to the surface, where he managed to get two wounded crewmen aboard a life raft. Sergeant Bill Devlin, the ball turret gunner, had been making coffee in the waist area when the ditching bell rang, and his next conscious moment was when he was clinging to a piece of *The Bull*. Finding two damaged and useless life rafts, he was carried away from the wreckage. He grabbed the unsinkable Gibson Girl emergency radio and one of the useless rafts and tried to paddle back to Captain Richards's raft, but the ten-foot swell kept whisking him farther away. Soon it was dark, and all night Devlin floated around, until a destroyer picked him up the next day. A Dumbo had picked up Richards too, but the rest of the crew, and *The Bull,* became the 494th's first losses.

On Christmas Eve, 1944, during their first attack on Clark Field, the Cobras met their first enemy fighter . . . but after a few shots scorched across his bow the lone Zero decided to keep out of their way.

Escorted by Lightnings, twenty-five Cobras droned over Maclabat, an

Their target dimly visible through fleecy clouds, the Cobras wing toward Cebu on December 6, 1944.

airbase outside Manila, on Christmas Day. Eighty Zeros rose to meet them, but were jumped by the P-38s. About fifteen more Zeros managed to get through into the bomber formation. The Cobras got seven of them and plowed through a wall of flak, but not a single bullet hole was found in any of the B-24s. A couple had been nicked by flak from the nearly one hundred guns known to be in the target area, so the Cobras had been right . . . the Philippines were the hottest spot for anti-aircraft to this point in the Pacific war. Clark Field was one of the most bitterly defended targets: more than eighty flak guns, four hundred medium caliber weapons and nearly two hundred machine guns. Prevailing winds frequently forced the formation to make their run over Manila, where there were also too many guns. But it was at Clark that the Cobras' run of luck was interrupted.

On a visual bombing run, they were below 10,000 feet and flying into an ugly brown barrier of flak, thicker than they had ever seen before. It was their first mission since Christmas, and as the leaders went in, holding fast on their bomb run, three hundred bursts of flak blossomed in and around them.

Lieutenant Colonel Lyle Halstead, deputy commander of the Cobras, was flying as a co-pilot and saw a small black puff of smoke emerge from the leading edge of the wing on the plane ahead of his, between the two right engines. Then the entire wing parted from the fuselage and the explosion showered the trailing planes with debris. Engine parts slammed into one, clanging and denting. As the tailgunners rode away they could see three parachutes far below; two were furled, and a third, which had opened, seemed to be afire. It was a day of sadness for the Cobras. On the same mission Captain Ray Yeoman's plane had been under such close attack by one Zero that the enemy's propeller clipped a foot and a half from his B-24's right wing. He got home, but the Japanese were getting closer now.

The next day, again over Clark, the B-24 called the *Black Cat* was sieved by thirty-six holes from a single flak burst. In another Liberator nineteen hunks of flak ripped through the plane, knocking the controls from the top turret gunner's hands. In the aircraft directly behind, a waist gunner was looking out at the bomb pattern of the lead planes, holding a jug of water in his hand. The next thing he knew he was holding a handle and his coveralls were soaked. A two-inch hunk of sizzling spent shrapnel clattered to his feet after coming through the floor and bouncing off the ceiling of the plane.

Corregidor became the 494th's prime target when MacArthur's troops landed at Lingayen Gulf, Luzon, on January 9, 1945, and moved toward Manila. The planes that flew over the fortress in Manila Bay again expected hell, but the defenses were only half-hearted and scattered. On January 23 the Cobras teamed up with the Fifth and Thirteenth Air Forces in a one-day

The Cobras leave the target, enemy installations in the small village of Ising on Mindanao, on February 24, 1945.

Short Run, *carrying the blatant black tail markings of the Cobra's 867th Squadron, heads back to base after hitting Corregidor.*

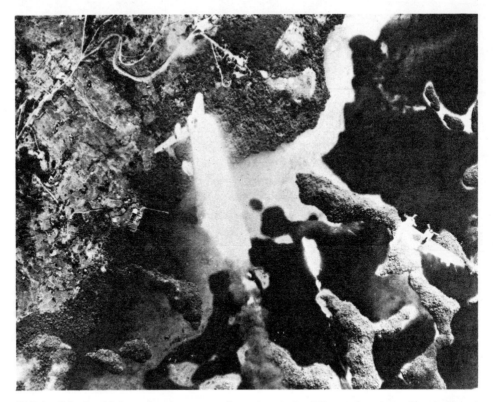

Kelly's Cobra's third combat loss, over the bypassed island of Koror. A direct flak hit ripped the Liberator's wing off and flipped the blazing wreckage over onto its back.

assault which involved single squadrons being briefed for specific gun emplacements, and after that, real return fire from Corregidor ceased to be a problem at all.

D-Day on Corregidor was to be the Cobras' own finest hour. MacArthur's headquarters had radioed that hundreds of wrecked Japanese aircraft had been found on Clark Field, where the 494th's pounding had left many of them. As a reward the Cobras were to fly in on Corregidor a few minutes ahead of the invading troops who would spill from the transport planes.

But on D-Day, February 16, an impenetrable storm front built up between the Cobras and the Philippines. Forgetfully cursing their stinking luck, the lousy Pacific weather and that God-forsaken Angaur, the Cobras gathered around their radios to try to hear the story.

February's weather continued to keep the Cobras at home, where they flew shakedown missions against the northern Palaus. After twenty strikes against Koror, the Palaus claimed their first 494th victim. A B-24 took a direct flak

Lady Kaye *carries the manual ventral guns in place of the Sperry ball turret as she heads* *out on a mission to the Gulf of Davao in February 1945.*

The Cobras head for Cebu City on March 25, 1945. Both built by Consolidated at San Diego, *#056 is a B-24M with fully enclosed waist position, and #561 is a late model B-24J.*

hit which blasted off the right wing and sent the rest hurtling down, the crew trapped inside.

The Philippines were ours, but there was still work to be done. Through March and April the Cobras flew in support of the guerrilla army, routine missions with no fighters. On a mission to Ising Town, near Davao Penal Colony, the Cobras blew up an enemy encampment and killed an estimated three hundred troops; over Cebu City they had 97 percent of their bombs on target and most of Cebu crumbled. At times it was even boring, and one Cobra pilot, on a photo run over Mindanao, spotted two trucks on a road below. Unable to resist, he put the B-24 into a steep dive and drove along the road with his forward turret and upper turret firing. The Japanese never knew what hit them, and disappeared in a cloud of dust and smoke.

September 1944: Toll on the High Road

Back in the Central Pacific, the other two Seventh Air Force Liberator groups were carrying on business as usual, and a couple of 30th Bomb Group Liberators became symbols of just how much the aircraft could withstand. One of them was called *Bombs Lullaby:* she had been in the Pathfinders for a while before Lieutenant Bob Nelson and his crew got her. The fact was that nobody else wanted the ship—she was heavy in one wing and almost impossible to trim. They said that firing the guns or even shifting a wad of gum to the other side of your mouth would knock off the trim, but after a while they got "kind of fond" of the old girl. Her first crew had named her and taken her on ten missions, and although Nelson's crew was unhappy with the title they left it for luck. From her twenty-eighth mission with her new crew, on Sunday, September 10 1944, she brought back over four hundred bullet and shrapnel holes, a dead engine and two dead crewmen.

The target was Iwo Jima, and *Bombs Lullaby* was flying through a curtain of flak, about a thousand feet below a veil of light cloud. Suddenly the clouds expelled a hail of cannon and machine-gun fire. Bob Nelson from Brooklyn, a little fellow who had trouble reaching the control pedals of the B-24 without a cushion under him, saw the tracer fire but not the fighter.

As the shells thumped into *Bombs Lullaby* the tail area became a shambles. Danny Keyes, the gunner, was killed. An incendiary bullet hit one of the tail guns and burned through, another hit an ammo rack and set off 150 rounds of .50-caliber. The crew's beer ration, stowed over the gunner's position to cool it, was shattered into broken glass and foam.

Photographer Milo Hackett, who had traded places with another to fly with *Bombs Lullaby*'s crew, crumpled with a machine-gun bullet through his heart. Wash Warshavsky, the waist gunner, was squirming on the bloody floor of the aircraft, badly wounded in the head and shoulder. Next to him Joe Scaro, the other gunner, had somehow survived the stream of gunfire. A cannon shell had exploded above his head, but the heavy waist window frame fell down in front of him and probably saved his life. Another Zero streaked in on Scaro's side and he held the window up with one hand and fired his gun with the other, scaring off the attacker. By then bombardier Mike Bartow and navigator Chuck Hall had made their way back through the ship to help.

Bartow thought Hackett didn't look dead, maybe shocked. There was no blood and he didn't see the small hole through the heavy sheepskin jacket. Keyes had obviously been killed, a six-inch black hole in his chest, and fragments of incendiary shell still burning inside.

There was no oxygen supply, Hackett's lifeless body having disengaged the lines when it fell. A dozen fighters were ganging up on the B-24 and the three turrets still working were roaring at them. Up front Bob Nelson and his co-pilot, Lieutenant Clem Claflin, were trying to keep up with the formation. The control surfaces of the elevator were shredded and the throttle control on the number 4 engine had been shot away, jamming it at high speed.

When the fighters finally broke off, Nelson was able to drop down to solve his oxygen problem, and Mike Bartow was attending to Warshavsky, attention which saved the gunner's life. Administering sulfa and oxygen, Bartow kept the gunner out of shock by talking to him. Joe Scaro remembers that "every time it looked like he would go unconscious, Lieutenant Bartow would find something else to talk about. I can't remember now anything he said but the doctors told us that if he had gone unconscious shock would probably have developed and he might have died in a few minutes."

As Bartow talked Nelson was listening to pieces of the elevator flapping in the slipstream, and counting the miles to home. He had been controlling the speed of his right outboard engine with the supercharger blast at high altitude, but that wouldn't work for a landing. He says he was "trying to jockey the plane in when suddenly she went into a P-38 climb—pieces of the elevator finally flew off and Claflin and I were able to fight the nose down."

Nelson thought he might have to ditch, but somehow he made Saipan. Tenderly lowering his lumbering plane, he felt the wheels touch and then the right one dug in. Tire shot out. Nelson revved his remaining right engine and somehow kept the speeding bomber straight.

A few days later Nelson and his crew were in another Liberator over Iwo while *Bombs Lullaby,* holed and smelling like a brewery, was patched and prepared to fly again.

The other aircraft was the *Chambermaid,* from the 38th Squadron of the

The Chambermaid *taunts her nemesis, the bloody island of Iwo Jima. The white ball is the trademark of the 38th Squadron.*

30th; she took off from Saipan early in the morning of September 20, 1944, and headed north to Iwo Jima.

In private her crew called her the *House of Bourbon,* after their mascot, and she was on her thirty-fifth mission. She had seen one crew through their quota of flights, and this second crew was flying their sixth.

Along the way to Iwo their only problem was weather, but they kept the formation tight and ground through. Fifteen minutes before they sighted ugly Iwo and "Mount Sunovabitchi," *Chambermaid*'s crew saw a group of eight Japanese fighters far below them. Pilot Bill Core thought that this was "unusual, but Iwo had the reputation for being the most unpredictable target in the Pacific anyhow."

More unusual was the fact that the Japanese began making long passes from below. Usually they held off until the aircraft came out of the bombing run and broke their formation to evade flak. One Zero was hit by .50-caliber fire and blew up before the enemy dropped back rather than be caught in

their own antiaircraft fire as the bombers went over the target. Core had been
to Iwo three times, but hadn't seen much of it. Turning over control to his
co-pilot, Lieutenant Glen Beatty, he leaned forward in his seat and watched
red and white flashes sparkling all over the island. He felt every gun was
firing at him and wished he had never bothered to look. The bombardier
released his load over the installations and storage areas around the airstrip
and back in the bomb bay Lieutenant Doscher, an Intelligence Officer who
had come along for the ride to observe, watched the big bombs tumble down
toward their target. He and the navigator, Lieutenant Clarence Wasser,
moved up to the flight deck and Wasser was leaning with one hand on the
pilot's seat and the other on the co-pilot's when it happened.

Less than half a minute after bombs away, Core was calling out Japanese
fighter positions to the gunners and Sergeant Mil Howard, in the nose, broke
in on interphone, asking why his turret had stopped. A few seconds later
Sergeant George Shahein said something was leaking into his ball turret, and
it was so damned thick he couldn't see a thing.

Core realized *Chambermaid* had been hit. Bombardier Melvin Harms left
his post to investigate and found that they had taken a flak hit on the nose;
some hydraulic lines had been severed and the fluid had spread quickly
through the plane and leaked into the ball turret.

"It was a hell of a mess," recalls Core. "I knew then that we were in a bad
way. One turret wasn't working and the other was useless because the gunner
couldn't see anything."

Two fighters sniffed around the stricken plane, and Core watched both
nervously. One out to the right at two o'clock half-rolled and dropped a
phosphorous bomb, then came in on the B-24, his wing guns trailing wisps
of smoke.

There was a dull explosion behind the co-pilot's head and Core looked
up to see a hole in the roof above them. Bits of aluminum and glass tinkled
over the flight deck. Core did not know Richards had been standing behind
him a few inches from the blast, and, seeing no visible damage, figured they
were allright.

The second fighter was still coming in from the left, and Core kept calling
him for the gunners. The co-pilot, dazed by the explosion, reached around
to feel his back because it had started to hurt. He looked surprised when
his hand came back covered with a red smear. He twisted in his seat so Core
could look him over and the pilot saw that Beatty's shirt was pretty torn
up and there was a lot of blood, but he couldn't have guessed that a sliver
of aluminum had been driven into his back. Even so, he realized things were
worse than he had thought. The throttle control for the left outboard engine
was loose and waggled back and forth; number two throttle was jammed,

and as the engines were running at a very high speed they would be drinking gas. The right outboard engine was spewing out oil, so Core knew that that engine was gone.

Summing it all up, he didn't expect to get home. He mused about his chances of ditching and was disheartened. He called his flight leader to ask for protection from the fighters, who now knew they had some easy meat. Four Liberators throttled back and boxed the cripple in, one on each side and one above and below, giving a tremendous boost to *Chambermaid*'s firepower.

Core was in for more bad news. Harms, coming back from his position in the nose, found Wasser and Sergeant Richards, the top turret gunner, lying on the flight deck in a pool of blood. A cold wind lashed through the aircraft, and where the top turret had been there was just a big round hole. A second shell had hit there, blowing the glass bowl away into the slipstream, where it managed to punch a hole in the leading edge of the right stabilizer on the way through.

Both wounded men were in bad condition. Forty pieces of shrapnel had punctured Wasser's right arm and shoulder, and he had also been hit by machine-gun fire. Three bullets had passed through his right hand, and two through his shoulders. He could bleed to death in far less time that it took to get to Saipan, if they got as far as Saipan.

That Richards was still even alive was incredible, because the direct hit on his turret exploded about three feet from his head. His face was laid open, his windpipe severed, and his left knee, right leg, neck and shoulders peppered with glass and metal.

Harms dragged Wasser to his feet and lurched along the catwalk with him, praying he wouldn't lose balance and drop the wounded man into the bomb bay. The catwalk was awash with hydraulic fluid and added to his consternation. Safely through, Harms laid Wasser down in the waist as gently as he could and ripped the leather sleeve from his mangled arm and rigged a tourniquet around it.

The waist gunner, Sergeant Mike Verescak, made his way forward to where Richards lay, shot him with morphine and began bandaging his wounds.

All the crew which could be there were in the waist section of the aircraft. The ball turret and nose gunners, without the use of their guns anyway, were helping the wounded. Lieutenant Doscher made his way over the catwalk, grabbed a bottle of iodine, took off his pants and dressed a deep wound in his own thigh. Harms, back in the waist bandaging Wasser, saw Verescak come sliding across the catwalk, bound to a gun and open up. Harms thought this must be the end, but Verescak, shocked, was angrily firing the gun into space . . . the Zeros had gone.

The co-pilot took his turn to come back to the waist and have his wounds cleaned up, and Core called for the other waist gunner, Sergeant Robert Martin. Martin was a frustrated pilot; he had washed out of flying school after 150 hours and Core knew his ability might come in handy one day. The time had come. Martin slipped into the co-pilot's seat.

With the fighters out of the picture, Core could now concern himself with his mechanical problems. All he really had was one engine, the right inboard, number 3. He had no throttle control over either left engine, and the left inboard would start to falter, go wild and speed up, causing the *Chambermaid* to shake like she was going to fall apart in the air. The right outboard was still throwing oil and smoking.

Promptly every hour, the right outboard would burst into flames, blaze for about thirty seconds until the coating of oil was consumed, then go out. Core wondered why the engine hadn't gone, but he wasn't complaining. He knew that unless he could get the engine speeds down on his two left motors, they were going to run out of fuel over the ocean. After a lot of experimenting he found that he could slow down number 1 by feeding it air from the turbocharger, which was usually used to feed oxygen to engines in the thin air of the stratosphere. He slowed down the left inboard by a rather novel use of the feathering button. He hit the button, waited until the propeller slowed almost to a stop, then pulled out the button again. He kept juggling supercharger settings to keep left and right side working somewhere near the same speed.

Every time things looked good Core turned and winked at Richards, lying on the flight deck behind him. Richards, unable to speak with his throat injuries, flashed bloody teeth as best he could.

While Core was working on engines, Martin was steering the *Chambermaid* for Saipan. They were making 140 miles an hour, and still eating up gas at an alarming rate. They were also descending toward the ocean at the rate of 40 feet per minute.

Back in the waist the able crew members began throwing stuff out. The waist machine guns, each weighing 60 pounds, went first. Then ammo belts, flak suits, extra radio coils. They were in the process of unbolting the Sperry ball turret when their special wrench, slippery from hydraulic fluid, fell overboard.

Except for Harms and Shahein, who stayed in the waist with Wasser, the crew moved forward to the flight deck area to help balance the aircraft, which was now in rough air and bucking violently.

Core had been concerned solely with keeping *Chambermaid* in the air; the possibility of reaching Saipan had been too remote to consider. But as the hours passed he found a grain of hope, and with that came other considerations—he had no brakes, for one thing. The wounded aboard cut out the safer solution of bailing out over Saipan.

Verescak worked his way to the *Chambermaid*'s smashed nose and tried to repair the hydraulic lines. He patched up one, taped the hole in another, and poured hydraulic fluid from the emergency tanks into the system. The tape gave and most of the precious fluid spurted out and was lost.

Core called his flight leader, Captain Valentine, and Valentine suggested he try the parachute rig which had worked for the *Belle of Texas* and several more.

When Saipan appeared on the horizon, five hours had passed since the first shells had thumped into *Chambermaid*. Dusk was moving in on the Marianas as three of the four escorting Liberators broke away to head for other fields. Valentine stayed with the cripple, leading her toward the strip.

Core could not raise the tower with his damaged equipment, so Valentine relayed the messages. Sergeant Martin took the controls as Core went back into the ship to prepare it for landing.

The emergency hand crank was all that was left to get the gear down. The right wheel went down and locked, but the cable controlling the left wheel snapped, and the huge wheel remained locked in its well under the wing. That was it. *Chambermaid*'s pilot felt like a condemned man whose final appeal has been denied; if they got down there would be a serious crash. Ditching or a belly landing now looked good to what faced them. Core vainly tried to dislodge the wheel by skidding the B-24 around the sky, but it was no use.

Two of the crew managed to kick the nose wheel into place, Valentine called the tower and they cleared the right side of the runway for a crash landing. Core moved everybody back into the waist except Martin, who remained up front with him.

On board the aircraft, the crewmen arranged themselves around the four wounded on the floor and waited. Two men braced themselves against the parachutes they had rigged to the gun mounts.

Core called Valentine: "Coming in."

Martin pumped the flaps down by hand. Core switched on his landing lights . . . he found he only had one. He wryly recalls that everything a B-24 had two of, *Chambermaid* had only one of. Martin cut the number 1 engine, and Core put his full weight on the left rudder pedal. The *Chambermaid*'s wheels touched the ground.

Every inch of the airplane screamed as they rolled along the crushed coral at 105 miles an hour. The big plane swerved to the right. Martin chopped all power. The chutes popped and slowed her a little, but not enough to stop her plunging off the runway.

Chambermaid stayed level for a moment, then tipped. The right wing hit the ground and a propeller snapped off and skidded down the runway. *Chambermaid* headed for a jeep trailer carrying a rack of floodlights and showered them into the air. Core watched the left side of the instrument panel caving in toward him. He was almost out of his seat but his safety belt held him in. With a final grinding, horrible moan the *Chambermaid* plowed a hundred yards of dirt and gravel, crashed sideways into a revetment, and subsided.

Number 1 engine was burning. The aircraft's back was broken. Core couldn't believe they were down, and alive. Men were crawling out through the multitude of available holes in the aircraft—every one was cut, bruised, and dazed, but not seriously hurt. The wounded were no worse than they had been. Beatty, the co-pilot, saw *Chambermaid*'s crew chief in the crowd around the aircraft. From his stretcher he croaked, "I'm sorry we wrecked your plane, Sergeant."

Battered almost beyond recognition, The *most spectacular crash-landing of the Pacific*
Chambermaid *got home to Saipan for the* *War.*

Iwo

From the first raid in August 1944 until the invasion on February 19, 1945, Iwo Jima and the surrounding islands took up all the two Seventh Air Force B-24 group's flying hours. Iwo was a dirty target anytime. One day the mission might be easy, then the next day the Japanese might fight for every inch of sky. Day after day the crews gathered on the ground outside the A-2 tent, heard their commander give a general outline of the mission, heard operations explain the formations and crew positions, then intelligence would give them the typical Iwo story. And the weary crews would trudge out to weary aircraft like *Lil' Audrey, Bombs Lullaby, Madame Pele, Rapid Robin, Merry Boozer,* or *Consolidated Mess* and do it all again.

By October 1944 the pounding had been stepped up. One hundred and fifty miles north of Iwo Jima was Chichi Jima, once under consideration for a major amphibious operation. The strategists chose Iwo, but Chichi, main island of the Bonins, was also a prime seventh Air Force target. The Japanese were in desperate trouble as Liberators mercilessly blasted shipping in the two groups of islands.

And during October the 30th was briefed and prepared for the mission that never was. The Battle of Leyte Gulf began on October 24 in Surigao Strait, and though the American fleet was successful, they exhausted most of their ammunition. As the next phase of the battle began, off Samar Island, things looked desperate for the escort carrier fleet, caught at close range by heavy units of the enemy fleet. On Saipan the 30th was told that the outcome was in doubt, and with thousands of troops ashore on Leyte they were told to expect a mission against the Japanese fleet because victory was imperative. They were briefed to attack the enemy fleet in the vicinity of the Philippines on October 25; ground crews had worked through the night of October 24 installing two auxiliary tanks in the front bomb bays of the Liberators, but even with this the 30th only had fuel for a one-way trip.

The crews were instructed to bomb at masthead height and continue on to Luzon, bail out over the jungle and link up with Filipino guerrilla units, who would be alerted to look for them. *Night Mission* and the other aircraft were loaded with four five hundred pounders, and the crews began to realize they were about to fly a genuine "suicide mission." They awaited daylight with serious misgivings. *Night Mission*'s ball turret gunner, six-footer Malcolm Wiley, had a brother in the invasion force on Leyte and to him there was no question but to go.

On the morning of October 25 the crews stood by their aircraft at daylight, the banter between air and ground crews subdued and stilted. Takeoff time

Two stalwarts from the 30th Bomb Group, the Curly Bird *and* The Jeeter Bug, *grind toward Iwo Jima in October 1944. The black* horizontal bar says they are from the 819th Squadron. Jeeter Bug *went to the 11th after fifty-three missions.*

She was almost the Silver Lady. *Lieutenant Winton Newcomb's crew had been flying to Iwo or Chichi every other day for nearly three weeks, and hadn't had time to get a name or picture on their plane. Newcomb asked for a night mission to ease the pressure, but no luck. So they named the aircraft* Night Mission *and never did get one in forty-two missions.*

was set and postponed several times, until at around 9:15 word came that the fleet had won a conclusive victory and the mission was cancelled. Wiley remembers that "everyone quietly thanked God."

*   *   *   *

Lieutenant Woodrow Waterous, who had flown home from Truk blinded, was still flying B-24s. On September 11 his ship had taken flak damage over Iwo, and on September 25 a 20-mm shell killed his navigator and ripped Waterous's cap to pieces. Six days later his airplane took more hits. On November 5 they sent him home.

The 11th Group hit Iwo Jima on November 11; little note was taken that it was the twenty-sixth anniversary of Armistice Day in the war to end all wars. Fifteen B-24s went after the runways and dispersal areas, and on one plane piloted by Lieutenant Leland Bates, fate stepped in on the bomb bay run. A 75-mm shell screamed through the open bomb-bay doors, whipped past the ball turret and continued on out the right waist window. The ball turret and waist gunners were dazed, but still alive.

By late November the 11th was involved in a top-secret project. As part of the campaign to keep troops and supplies from reaching the Bonins and Volcanoes area, a new one thousand pound aerial mine was brought into use and the assignment of placing these generously throughout the waters around the islands fell to the old 11th.

Mike missions, as they were called, were risky, needing a wave-top approach within range of deadly shore batteries. In the morning of November 29 three Liberators headed out for Chichi, and sixty minutes from the target they let down close to the water and moved in.

Passing Haha Jima they climbed to a thousand feet and headed between the two hills of the island. The Japanese guns opened up, and from six hundred feet the muzzle flash from the guns bracketing the valley was too close. The B-24 gunners fired back.

They were in tight formation, with Captain Phil Kroh's aircraft in the lead. Lieutenant Bob Strong was flying twenty-five feet out and seventy-five feet to the rear, and Lieutenant Herb Robinson was about a hundred feet above Strong and fifty feet behind him. As they plunged downward just before the bank that marked their target area, Robinson's ship suddenly lurched and brushed the wing tip of Strong's ship. This dented the nose compartment and threw bombardier Ernest Miles just as he released his mine.

As the two planes broke away one of the mines sailed into Strong's plane, and lodged between the waist hatch and the tail, tearing a hole in the fuselage six feet long and three feet wide.

TARFU, the abbreviation for circumstances even worse than Snafu, heads home after hitting shipping in Chichi Jima's harbor on November 19, 1944. She flew with the 26th Squadron.

Madame Pele and Hellcat Belle grind over Chichi Jima, the largest of some twenty rugged, unfriendly islands forming the Bonin group. Futami Ko, the primary target of many Seventh Air Force and Navy missions, is the large harbor encircled by the main island.

Strong thought they'd taken a direct flak hit and could not believe it when his waist gunner called in that they had a mine back there. The gunners had been strafing when the thing burst in, and they were a little incredulous too. Corporal Vince Sutter kept firing and looked at the mine several times out of the corner of his eye, hoping it would go away. They suddenly realized it might explode at any second, and started trying to get the thing out, but they could not do anything by hand, so they wrenched the barrels from the waist guns and used them as levers. It worked.

After that, all they had to do was fly back to Saipan with a fluttering tail section which might have sheared off at any time. They got there.

Iwo was on the defensive, but it wasn't finished yet. On December 7 eighty-nine Liberators teamed with P-38s, the Navy and B-29s and P-47s, to hit the volcanic outcrop. The overcast was heavy but the aircraft rained 600 tons of explosives onto the island, answered by but two flak bursts.

The Japanese gunners were getting trained, the hard way, and the *Patriotic Patty* and her crew were caught. Just after bombs away three flak bursts hit, knocking out the hydraulic system, puncturing the fuel lines and cutting forty electric plugs . . . meaning no heated flying suits and no power gun turrets. Overhead enemy fighters were dropping phosphorous bombs, one engine was out and the supercharger on a second badly damaged. The crew was desper-

Lieutenant Bob Strong's #377, back from a harrowing mine-laying mission at Chichi Jima. (11th Bomb Group Association)

*Fifty-five gallon drums of napalm spill from
30th Bomb Group Liberators over Iwo on
February 1, 1945.*

ately trying to plug the fuel leaks with broken pencils, plugs they cut from
a tail section banister, handkerchiefs, and anything else they could jam into
the holes. Five hundred gallons of high-octane fuel swamped the plane and
one of the gunners passed out, overcome by the fumes. The tail gunner was
drenched in gasoline but managed to breath through shrapnel holes in his
turret glass.

Japanese fighters followed them for thirty minutes but failed to attack, not
knowing that nobody aboard *Patriotic Patty* could chance firing a gun at them.
She made it home, using parachutes for brakes.

Even in the Pacific ice was one of the curses visited upon B-24 men. On
the average of three times a month the northwesterly monsoons moved a polar
front down from the Bonins and Volcanoes, and freezing level was about
10,000 feet. Lieutenant James Graham, leading a strike over Chichi at 18,000
feet, found that the bomb sight on his aircraft had frozen up. The lead planes

had been forced to turn back by ice and his ship's nose turret and leading edges were icing up. Graham dropped down to 9,000 but the bomb sight couldn't be used, so bombardier Robert Graham casually sighted over the big toe of his right foot and hit the target.

Later in December the Liberators took on the job of spotting for the Navy, whose fire control officers would ride in the B-24s, co-ordinating the shelling by direct plane-to-ship communication.

As the preinvasion bombardment of sulphurous Iwo Jima reached its peak, the Liberators were taking a beating overhead, but on February 1 every aircraft in the Pacific that could get there was assigned to hit the island, the 30th's 819th Squadron dropping fifty-five gallon drums of napalm.

The Seventh joined the Navy on February 16 to begin the final pounding and six battleships and supporting cruisers and destroyers drew up to the island and lobbed shells on positions revealed by the Seventh's planes.

Yet when the Marines landed it was Tarawa all over again. They had not given the Japanese credit for learning too, and what should have been already a graveyard was the costliest piece of volcanic rock in the history of the world.

Lil' Audrey, Queen of the Pacific

On February 5, 1945, *Lil'Audrey* returned from Iwo Jima and became the first Seventh Air Force Liberator to hit the 100-mission mark. In fifteen months she had dropped 416,900 pounds of bombs over Tarawa, Kwajalein, Truk, the Marianas, the Bonins, and other damned islands. She narrowly beat *Tired Tessie, Come Closer,* and *Miss Behavin'* in the four-way race to the century.

A lot of credit went to her crew chief, twenty-four-year-old Master Sergeant Lloyd Whyrick from Nebraska; before the war he had no mechanical background, and yet the final responsibility for every second of *Lil' Audrey*'s 1,200 combat hours, every inch of her 225,000 combat miles rested with him. After she topped the hundred Whyrick said simply that "if I have my way, I'll never take another job as a crew chief."

Whyrick sweated most during that final mission. *Lil'Audrey*'s second crew had completed their tour of forty on her ninety-seventh mission, and a new crew was flying her on the final three, a nightmare for any proud crew chief. On that last mission she had run into heavy overcast and storms on the way back, and as the last of the others in the formation landed there was no sign of *Audrey*.

On Guam everyone was as worried as Whyrick; the second crew, all ready to take the bomber back home for a tour, looked grayer and grayer as an

The queen of the Seventh Air Force was Lil' Audrey *from the 11th Group. She was the first in the Seventh to hit the 100 mission mark, on February 5, 1945, narrowly beating her sister,* Tired Tessie, *and the 30th's* Come Closer. *They spruced her up for a War Bond tour, but back in the States somebody insisted Audrey had to wear a bra, and she was covered up accordingly. The ball-joint for a 30-caliber machine gun in place of the astrodome between the cockpit and nose turret is unusual, but was shared by many Seventh Air Force B-24s.*

hour passed. Then about two hours after she should have arrived, *Lil' Audrey* was in radio contact. The crew had got lost, thrown everything out of the aircraft, and finally brought the stripped ship in, 160 nail-biting minutes late.

Whyrick should have been used to all this. Months before he had almost given up hope when his charge was on a night mission over Truk. Her job was to stay over the target and drop flares, and when the other pilots got back they reported that she had taken a flak hit in an engine which set it afire, and she was last seen going down. They all reported her lost except one who said, "Hell, she's not down, she'll be back."

A little forlornly, Whyrick and the optimistic pilot hung around the radio shack for two hours. The crew chief was just wandering off into the silent, soft darkness when he heard the call, and raced back. Captain Warren Rowe, the pilot, reported that she was still afire and he couldn't feather the burning engine. He was expecting a ditching and wanted a Dumbo out there. But he got back, the engine still blazing when he got down.

That broke *Audrey*'s record of consecutive missions at thirty-six, and Truk provided Whyrick's hardest job too, when the ship came back to Guam with no hydraulics after wandering into two flak bursts. The flight engineer patched up one line and the crew poured all the liquid in the plane—drinking water, extra hydraulic fluid, fruit juice and, according to legend, urine—into the lines to keep the pressure up. They pumped down the flaps by hand and cranked down the landing gear to leave them as much braking power as possible, then rigged parachutes, but their improvised hydraulics worked. Whyrick was not amused: "We had to rip out the whole system. It was all rusted inside and the worst part about it all was that we were already trying to keep up with some other planes on numbers of missions, and we missed seven gravy runs over Yap. That damned grapefruit juice!"

Lil' Audrey had a tendency to gulp fuel at high altitudes, but otherwise she was the perfect lady, and only aborted twice in her hundred missions. She was a sort of test-bed for any modifications thought up in the 11th Group—she carried the first flexible tail gun mounting after they had found the standard turret too heavy and limited in its field of fire, and there were a dozen more major modifications on her.

Lil' Audrey was spruced up for her homegoing, with ten neat rows of freshly painted bombs, four decals for her gunners' victories, and an enticing interpretation of Audrey . . . which unfortunately had to be given a brassiere for the homefront.

Her flight crews had always been superstitious, entering the plane from the lucky side, tapping a piece of wood on takeoff, and even nominating one man to serve the food on the way back from a mission, but Whyrick's only superstition was about the name. "I never wanted to have that name put on. My assistant crew chief kept pestering me to call the plane Audrey after his wife, but I was damned if I was going to allow it. Then on the morning she took off from Funafuti for her third, she swung onto the line and I saw the name painted on the nose. I hadn't noticed it before and I was sore as hell." He cast his eyes down and shook his head, then said through a lame smile, "I still don't think it was a very good idea."

*   *   *   *

Victory in the Pacific

After the Iwo job was over the 30th began disbanding, taking some of the 11th's older planes to Hawaii and swapping some of their better aircraft for them. It was the B-29's war now.

Okinawa, final stepping stone to Japan, would be invaded on April 1, then after Okinawa Operation Olympic, the invasion of Japan, would begin in November. Lieutenant General James H. Doolittle arrived at the new home of the mighty Eighth Air Force, and back in England the victorious Fortresses and Liberators were preparing to fly across the world to a new kind of war.

The Seventh moved onto the springboard. Kelly's Cobras came up from

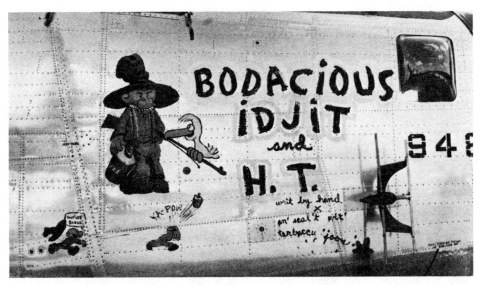

As the war moved toward its obvious end, their aircraft. Bodacious Idjit flew with the there was plenty of time for the bomber crews 11th. to compete with one another in personalising

Palau to Yontan, the aged 11th Bomb Group, the Fifth and Thirteenth Air Forces moved up. They were talking about five-thousand plane raids on Tokyo; they were talking about the use of the word "sir," and saluting. The earthy Seventh Air Force continued in their old ways, albeit tactfully.

The Cobras won the privilege of putting the first Army Air Force Liberators over Japan, to strike Omura airfield on Kyushu. Forty-eight of their Liberators took off in as many minutes and at the target they left an 8,000-foot column of smoke behind them.

The Seventh had never experienced missions like those that followed; old war-weary Liberators like *Dragon Lady* and *The Jeeter Bug* were surrounded by brand-new Liberators belonging to other groups with romantic names like Ken's Men and the Jolly Rogers. The early missions against Japan fell into the old deceptive pattern, getting harder as more bombs fell, but there was no turning back now.

* * * *

Captain Charles McKnight and the crew of *Top Secret*, sitting just off Iwo Jima's airstrip in their long, shimmering B-29, relaxed. They were not needed. Somewhere on the way to Japan the *Enola Gay*, along with *The Great Artiste* and a camera plane, were headed for Hiroshima. *Straight Flush, Jabbitt III,*

Bolivar Jr., *piloted by Fred Jacobs and Stan Winchester and watched by Colonel Lawrence Carr, commanding Seventh Bomb Command, and Major General Robert W. Douglass, Jr.,* head of the Seventh Air Force, taxies to her hardstand on Saipan in May 1945. A replacement for the 30th's old *Bolivar*, she went to the 431st Squadron of the 11th Group.

Okinawa, July 1945. *Against a background of Privateers, the 494th's* Riot Call *leaves* Yontan *for what remains of the Japanese Empire.*

The 11th's Dragon Lady *soars across Guam's swaying palms. The big black square is the 42nd Bomb Squadron's identification.*

The spectacularly decorated Dragon Lady *managed to survive the war, and joined the 11th on Okinawa for the final assault on Japan.*

and *Full House,* the photo-recon and weather Superfortresses sent to cover Hiroshima, Kokura, and Nagasaki, were rolling back to their fields on Tinian.

At 9:15 A.M., August 6, 1945, a single bomb slipped from *Enola Gay* and in Tokyo the Japanese Broadcasting Corporation noticed that the Hiroshima station had gone off the air.

Ready for an air war in another world, Eighth Air Force Liberators line up at Bradley Field in Connecticut prior to moving to *the Pacific Theater. They were never needed.* (*Barry Gilkes*)

Appendix

LIBERATOR PRODUCTION

The list which follows includes all 18,482 Liberators which were built between 1939 and 1945, designated as they were built at the five factories. Many of the aircraft were redesignated as PB4Ys, F-7s, C-109s, or one-of-a-kind experiments like the XB-41, which started out as B-24D 41-11822.

When a change was made in a model which did not justify a new model designation, there was a change of "block number" for the aircraft production batch effected by the change or changes. Many of the modifications had filtered back to the production line as a result of combat experience, but there

Michigan, *44-40429, and* Cocktail Hour, *44-40428, both B-24J-161-COs from the 43rd Bomb Group. Their billboard decorations* *were painted by the greatest combat artist of the war. (Stewart N. Bolling)*

were always more, and these were handled by modification centers both in the United States and overseas. Typical of these was the slab of armor fitted to all Eighth Air Force B-24s, on each side of the cockpit, and armament modifications were widespread, from Halpro's installation of twin fixed nose guns fired by the pilot to the Seventh Air Force's installation of a .30-caliber in place of the astrodome.

To facilitate the identification of the various airplanes, the factories assigned block numbers in multiples of five, leaving the intervening numbers for later assignment by modification centers; thus a B-24J like *Michigan* began as a B-24J-160-CO at San Diego, but was a B-24J-161-CO by the time she reached the combat zone.

CONSOLIDATED, SAN DIEGO

Model	Serial Numbers	Quantity	Model	Serial Numbers	Quantity
XB-24	39-680	1		41-11909—41-11938	30
(XB-24B)			B-24D-1	41-23640—41-23668	29
RB-24	40-702	1		41-23671—41-23693	23
LB-30A	AM258—AM263	6		41-23697—41-23724	28
Liberator I	AM910—AM929	20		41-23728—41-23750	23
Liberator II	AL503—AL641, FP685	140	B-24D-5	41-23751—41-23755	5
RB-24A	40-2369—40-2377	9		41-23759—41-23790	32
RB-24C	40-2378—40-2386	9		41-23794—41-23824	31
B-24D	40-696—40-701	6	B-24D-7	41-23825—41-23849	25
	40-2349—40-2368	20		41-23853—41-23858	6
	41-1087—41-1142	56	B-24D-10	41-23864—41-23902	39
	41-11587	1		41-23906—41-23919	14
	41-11590—41-11603	14	B-24D-13	41-23920—41-23958	39
	41-11606	1		41-23960—41-23969	10
	41-11609—41-11626	18	B-24D-15	41-23970—41-24003	34
	41-11629—41-11638	10		41-24007—41-24026	20
	41-11643—41-11654	12		41-24030—41-24099	70
	41-11658—41-11673	16	B-24D-20	41-24100—41-24138	39
	41-11677—41-11703	27		41-24142—41-24157	16
	41-11710—41-11727	18		41-24164—41-24171	8
	41-11734—41-11741	8		41-24175—41-24219	45
	41-11748—41-11753	6	B-24D-25	41-24220—41-24311	92
	41-11757—41-11787	31		41-24339	1
	41-11790—41-11799	10	B-24D-30	42-40058—42-40137	80
	41-11801—41-11836	36	B-24D-35	42-40138—42-40217	80
	41-11839—41-11863	25	B-24D-40	42-40218—42-40257	40
	41-11865—41-11906	42	B-24D-45	42-40258—42-40322	65

Charlot the Harlot, *42-40339, a B-24D-50-CO. She began her war with the 480th Antisubmarine Group and ended it as a trainer at Peterson Field, Colorado, in 1944.* (*Bill Zoerb*)

Model	Serial Numbers	Quantity
B-24D-50	42-40323—42-40344	22
B-24D-53	42-40345—43-40392	48
B-24D-55	42-40393—42-40432	40
B-24D-60	42-40433—42-40482	50
B-24D-65	42-40483—42-40527	45
B-24D-70	42-40528—42-40567	40
B-24D-75	42-40568—42-40612	45
B-24D-80	42-40613—42-40652	40
B-24D-85	42-40653—42-40697	45
B-24D-90	42-40698—42-40742	45
B-24D-95	42-40743—42-40787	45
B-24D-100	42-40788—42-40822	35
B-24D-105	42-40823—42-40867	45
B-24D-110	42-40868—42-40917	50
B-24D-115	42-40918—42-40962	45
B-24D-120	42-40963—42-41002	40
B-24D-125	42-41003—42-41047	45
B-24D-130	42-41048—42-41092	45
B-24D-135	42-41093—42-41137	45
B-24D-140	42-41138—42-41172	35
B-24D-145	42-41173—42-41217	45
B-24D-150	42-41218—42-41257	40
B-24D-155	42-72765—42-72814	50
B-24D-160	42-72815—42-72864	50

Model	Serial Numbers	Quantity
B-24D-165	42-72865—42-72914	50
B-24D-170	42-72915—42-72963	49
B-24J-1	42-72964—42-73014	51
B-24J-5	42-73015—42-73064	50
B-24J-10	42-73065—42-73114	50
B-24J-15	42-73115—42-73164	50
B-24J-20	42-73165—42-73214	50
B-24J-25	42-73215—42-73264	50
B-24J-30	42-73265—42-73314	50
B-24J-35	42-73315—42-73364	50
B-24J-40	42-73365—42-73414	50
B-24J-45	42-73415—42-73464	50
B-24J-50	42-73465—42-73514	50
B-24J-55	42-99936—42-99985	50
B-24J-60	42-99986—42-100035	50
B-24J-65	42-100036—42-100085	50
B-24J-70	42-100086—42-100135	50
B-24J-75	42-100136—42-100185	50
B-24J-80	42-100186—42-100235	50
B-24J-85	42-100236—42-100285	50
B-24J-90	42-100286—42-100335	50
B-24J-95	42-100336—42-100385	50
B-24J-100	42-100386—42-100435	50
B-24J-105	42-109789—42-109838	50
B-24J-110	42-109839—42-109888	50
B-24J-115	42-109889—42-109938	50
B-24J-120	42-109939—42-109988	50
B-24J-125	42-109989—42-110038	50
B-24J-130	42-110039—42-110088	50
B-24J-135	42-110089—42-110138	50
B-24J-140	42-110139—42-110188	50
B-24J-145	44-40049—44-40148	100
B-24J-150	44-40149—44-40248	100
B-24J-155	44-40249—44-40348	100
B-24J-160	44-40349—44-40448	100
B-24J-165	44-40449—44-40548	100
B-24J-170	44-40549—44-40648	100
B-24J-175	44-40649—44-40748	100
B-24J-180	44-40749—44-40848	100
B-24J-185	44-40849—44-40948	100
B-24J-190	44-40949—44-41048	100
B-24J-195	44-41049—44-41148	100
B-24J-200	44-41149—44-41248	100
B-24J-205	44-41249—44-41348	100

Weather Witch, *a B-24L-11-FO specially modified for the 55th Recon Squadron (long Range Weather) and based on Guam.*

Ramp Champ, *44-41996, a B-24M-10-CO. This black-bellied ship flew with the 3rd Photo Recon Squadron from the Marianas in June 1945, as a part of XXI Bomber Command.* (Barry Gilkes)

Model	Serial Numbers	Quantity	Model	Serial Numbers	Quantity
B-24J-210	44-41349—44-41389	41	B-24M-10	44-41949—44-42048	100
B-24L-1	44-41390—44-41448	59	B-24M-15	44-42049—44-42148	100
B-24L-5	44-41449—44-41548	100	B-24M-20	44-42149—44-42248	100
B-24L-10	44-41549—44-41648	100	B-24M-25	44-42249—44-42348	100
B-24L-15	44-41649—44-41748	100	B-24M-30	44-42349—44-42448	100
B-24L-20	44-41749—44-41806	58	B-24M-35	44-42449—44-42548	100
B-24M-1	44-41807—44-41848	42	B-24M-40	44-42549—44-42648	100
B-24M-5	44-41849—44-41948	100	B-24M-45	44-42649—44-42722	74

DOUGLAS, TULSA

Model	Serial Numbers	Quantity	Model	Serial Numbers	Quantity
B-24D	41-11754—41-11756	3	B-24J-1	42-51226—42-51292	67
B-24D	41-11864	1	B-24J-5	42-51293—42-51395	103
B-24D-1	41-23725—41-23727	3	B-24J-10	42-51396—42-51430	35
B-24D-5	41-23756—41-23758	3	B-24H-5	41-28640—41-28668	29
B-24E	41-29007—41-29008	2	B-24H-10	41-28669—41-28752	84
B-24E-1	41-28409—41-28416	8	B-24H-15	41-28753—41-28941	189
B-24E-10	41-28417—41-28444	28	B-24H-20	41-28942—41-29006	65
B-24E-15	41-28445—41-28476	32	B-24H-20	42-51077—42-51103	
B-24E-20	41-28477—41-28500	24	B-24H-25	42-51104—42-51181	73
B-24E-25	41-28501—41-28573	73	B-24H-30	42-51182—42-51225	44
B-24H-1	41-28574—41-28639	66			

NORTH AMERICAN, DALLAS

Model	Serial Numbers	Quantity	Model	Serial Numbers	Quantity
B-24G	42-78045—42-78069	25	B-24G-16	42-78353—42-78474	122
B-24G-1	42-78070—42-78074	5	B-24J-1	42-78476—42-78794	319
B-24G-5	42-78075—42-78154	80	B-24J-2	42-78475	1
B-24G-10	42-78155—42-78314	160	B-24J-5	44-28061—44-28276	216
B-24G-15	42-78315—42-78352	38			

FORD, WILLOW RUN

Model	Serial Numbers	Quantity	Model	Serial Numbers	Quantity
B-24E	42-7770	1	B-24J-10	42-51611—42-51825	215
B-24E-1	42-6976—42-7005	30	B-24J-15	42-51826—42-52075	250
B-24E-5	42-7006—42-7065	60	B-24J-20	42-52076	1
B-24E-10	42-7066—42-7122	57		44-48754—44-49001	248
B-24E-15	42-7123—42-7171	49	B-24L-1	44-49002—44-49251	250
B-24E-20	42-7172—42-7229	58	B-24L-5	44-49252—44-49501	250
B-24E-25	42-7230—42-7464	235	B-24L-10	44-49502—44-49751	250
B-24H-1	42-7465—42-7717	253	B-24L-15	44-49752—44-50001	250
B-24H-5	42-7718—42-7769	52	B-24L-20	44-50002—44-50251	250
	42-52077—42-52113	37	B-24M-1	44-50252—44-50451	200
B-24H-10	42-52114—42-52302	189	B-24M-5	44-50452—44-50651	200
B-24H-15	42-52303—42-52776	474	B-24M-10	44-50652—44-50851	200
	42-94729—42-94794	66	B-24M-15	44-50852—44-51051	200
B-24H-20	42-94795—42-95022	228	B-24M-20	44-51052—44-51251	200
B-24H-25	42-95023—42-95288	266	B-24M-25	44-51252—44-51451	200
B-24H-30	42-95289—42-95503	215	B-24M-30	44-51452—44-51928	477
B-24J-1	42-95504—42-95628	125	XB-24N	44-48753	1
	42-50509—42-50759	251	YB-24N-1	44-52053—44-52059	7
B-24J-5	42-50760—42-51076	317			
	42-51431—42-51610	180			

CONSOLIDATED, FORT WORTH

Model	Serial Numbers	Quantity	Model	Serial Numbers	Quantity
B-24D	41-11588—41-11589	2	B-24H-1	41-29116—41-29187	72
	41-11604—41-11605	2		42-64432—42-64440	9
	41-11607	1	B-24H-5	41-29188—41-29258	71
	41-11627—41-11628	2		42-64441—42-64451	11
	41-11705	1	B-24H-10	41-29259—41-29335	77
B-24D-1	42-63752—42-63796	45		42-64452—42-64501	50
B-24D-5	42-63797—42-63836	40	B-24H-15	41-29336—41-29606	271
B-24D-10	42-63837—42-63896	60	B-24H-20	41-29607—41-29608	2
B-24D-15	42-63897—42-63971	75		42-50277—42-50354	78
B-24D-20	42-63972—42-64046	75	B-24H-25	42-50355—42-50410	56
B-24E-10	41-29009—41-29023	15	B-24H-30	42-50411—42-50451	41
B-24E-15	41-29024—41-29042	19	B-24J-1	42-64047—42-64141	95
B-24E-20	41-29043—41-29061	19	B-24J-5	42-64142—42-64236	95
B-24E-25	41-29062—41-29115	54	B-24J-10	42-64237—42-64328	92
	42-64395—42-64431	37		42-64330—42-64346	17

Cherokee Strip, *an F-7B from the 20th Combat Mapping Squadron; this model differed from the F-7A by having all its six cameras located in the bomb bay. (E. P. Stevens)*

Leo, *41-29605, a B-24H-15-FO from the Zodiacs, the 834th Squadron of the 486th Bomb Group. The other eleven planes in the unit were decorated with equally liberal interpretations of the stars. (Gerald Maddux)*

Model	Serial Numbers	Quantity
B-24J-12	42-64329	1
B-24J-15	42-64347—42-64394	48
	42-99736—42-99805	70
B-24J-20	42-99806—42-99871	66
B-24J-25	42-99872—42-99935	64
B-24J-30	44-10253—44-10302	50
B-24J-35	44-10303—44-10352	50
B-24J-40	42-50452—42-50508	57
	44-10353—44-10374	22
B-24J-45	44-10375—44-10402	28
B-24J-50	44-10403—44-10452	50
B-24J-55	44-10453—44-10502	50
B-24J-60	44-10503—44-10552	50
B-24J-65	44-10553—44-10602	50
B-24J-70	44-10603—44-10652	50
B-24J-75	44-10653—44-10702	50

Model	Serial Numbers	Quantity
B-24J-80	44-10703—44-10752	50
B-24J-85	44-44049—44-44148	100
B-24J-90	44-44149—44-44248	100
B-24J-95	44-44249—44-44348	100
B-24J-100	44-44349—44-44448	100
B-24J-105	44-44449—44-44501	53
C-87	41-11608	1
	41-11639—41-11642	4
	41-11655—41-11657	3
	41-11674—41-11676	3
	41-11704	1
	41-11706—41-11709	4
	41-11728—41-11733	6
	41-11742—41-11747	6
	41-11788—41-11789	2
	41-11800	1

Model	Serial Numbers	Quantity	Model	Serial Numbers	Quantity
	41-11837—41-11838	2	C-87A	41-24174	1
	41-11907—41-11908	2	C-87	42-107249—42-107265	17
	41-23669—41-23670	2	AT-22	42-107266	1
	41-23694—41-23696	3	C-87	42-107267—42-107275	9
	41-23791—41-23793	3		43-30548	1
	41-23850—41-23852	3	AT-22	43-30549	1
	41-23859—41-23862	4*	C-87	43-30550—43-30560	11
C-87A	41-23863	1	AT-22	43-30561	1
C-87	41-23903—41-23905	3	C-87	43-30562—43-30568	7
	41-23959	1	C-87A	43-30569—43-30571	3
	41-24004—41-24006	3	C-87	43-30572—43-30573	2
	41-24027—41-24029	3	AT-22	43-30574	1
	41-24139—41-24141	3	C-87	43-30575—43-30583	9
	41-24158	1	AT-22	43-30584	1
C-87A	41-24159	1	C-87	43-30585—43-30627	43
C-87	41-24160—41-24163	4		44-39198—44-39298	101
	41-24172—41-24173	2		44-52978—44-52987	10

*41-23860 was one of the C-87s which were armed for the Hump operation. Two .50 caliber guns were fitted beneath the nose cargo door and on either side of the nose. This particular aircraft arrived at Chabua in April 1943 and was lost the same month.

LIBERATOR SPECIFICATIONS

	B-24D	B-24J	B-24M	C-87	PB4Y-1
LENGTH	66'4"	67'2"	67'2"	66'4"	67'3"
WINGSPAN	110'	110'	110'	110'	110'
HEIGHT	17'11"	18'	18'	18'	17'11"
WING AREA	1048 sq ft	1048 sq ft	1048 sq ft	1048 sq ft	1048 sq ft
EMPTY WEIGHT	32,605 lbs	36,500 lbs	36,000 lbs	31,935 lbs	36,950 lbs
GROSS WEIGHT	60,000 lbs	65,000 lbs	64,500 lbs	56,000 lbs	60,000 lbs
POWER PLANT	R-1830-43	R-1830-65	R1830-65	R-1830-43	R-1830-43/65
ARMAMENT	10 x .50-cal	10 x .50-cal	10 x .50-cal		10 x .50-cal
BOMB/CARGO					
LOAD	8800 lbs	8800 lbs	8800 lbs	8800 lbs	8800 lbs
MAXIMUM SPEED	303 mph	290 mph	300 mph	306 mph	279 mph
CRUISING SPEED	200 mph	215 mph	215 mph	200 mph	200 mph
SERVICE CEILING	32,000 ft	28,000 ft	28,000 ft	31,000 ft	31,800 ft
RANGE	2,850 miles	2,100 miles	2,100 miles	2,900 miles	2,960 miles

The above table of Liberator specifications has been compiled from standard references on the subject, but can only be applied generally.

THE HALVERSON DETACHMENT

Plane No.	Serial	Name	Original Pilot, Co-Pilot and Navigator/Bombardier
1	41-11595	Ole Faithful	Capt. Alfred Kalberer, Lt. Richard Rhoades, Lt. Francis Rang
2	41-11596	Brooklyn Rambler	Lt. Nathan Brown, Jr.
3	41-11625	Yank	Capt Paul Davis, Lt. Ted Crouchley, Lt. William Joyner
4	41-11618	Ole Rock	Lt. George Uhrich, Lt. Ferdinand Schmidt, Lt. Allen Hopkins
5	41-11622	Town Hall	Lt. Fred Nesbitt, Jr., Lt. Wilbur West, Lt. Lyman Smith
6	41-11609	Little Eva	Lt. Howard Walker
7	41-11600	Eager Beaver	Lt. Charles Brown, Lt. John Taylor, Lt. Malcolm Anderson
9	41-11591	Queen B	Lt. James Sibert
10	41-11613	Florine Jo Jo	Lt. Kenneth Butler, Lt. Herbert Kysar, Lt. Robert Humphreys
11	41-11624	Ball of Fire	Lt. Walter Clark, Lt. Jackson Clayton, Lt. Robert Helms
12	41-11617	Old King Solomon	Lt. James Solomon
14	41-11616	Arkansas Traveller	Lt. Homer Adams, Lt. Lin Parker, Lt. Robert Kirkaldy
15	41-11614	Ripper the First	Lt. Robert Paullin, Lt. Charles Peek, Lt. Tom Shumaker
16	41-11620	Edna Elizabeth	Lt. Sam Oglesby, Jr., Lt. John Kidd, Lt. Ernest Duckworth
17	41-11592	Draggin Lady	Lt. Therman Brown, Lt. William Dwyer, Lt. Norman Davis
18	41-11593	Black Mariah	Capt. John Payne, Lt. Cecil Patterson, Jr., Lt. Olen Bryant
19	41-11597	Blue Goose	Lt. Andrew Moore, Lt. George Whitlock, Lt. Douglas Welfare
20	41-11615	Mona the Lame Duck	Lt. Francis Nestor, Lt. Charles Shaw, Lt. Marshall Phillips
21	41-11602	Babe the Big Blue Ox	Lt. John Wilkinson, Lt. John Wilcox, Lt. Walter Shea
22	41-11603	Malicious	Capt. Richard "Candy" Sanders, Lt. Louis Prchall, Lt. Francis Smith
23	41-11601	Hellsapoppin	Lt. Edward Cave, Jr., Lt. Virgil Anderson, Lt. Charles Davis
24	41-11636	Wash's Tub	Lt. Martin Walsh, Jr., Lt. Meech Tahsequah, Lt. Alfred Schwanebeck
25	41-11629	Jap Trap	Lt. Mark Mooty, Lt. James Yelvington, Lt. Theodore Bennett

NOTES: The fates of the various Halpro aircraft are not fully recorded; *Brooklyn Rambler,* *Town Hall, Little Eva,* and *Blue Goose* were all interned in Turkey after the first Ploesti mission. *Ole Faithful* was still flying, but not on operations, at the end of July 1943, with thirty-two missions and the new Liberandos' nose number, 25. *Yank* was still flying, with twelve missions and number 27 up front. *Ole Rock* was shot down above Benghazi with Lt. Charles Brown, and *Eager Beaver* went down over Mersa Matruh with Lt. Kenneth Butler. *Queen B* was renumbered 45 and was still serving with the Liberandos. *Florine Jo Jo* assumed the number 71 and a new name, *Blue Streak,* and came home to sell war bonds in 1944, after flying one hundred and ten missions. *Ball of Fire* was shot down over the Delta with Lt. Francis Nestor, *Old King Solomon* was renumbered 50 and was still flying in August 1943. *Arkansas Traveller* had become number 95, was flying, but non-operational. *Ripper the First* was still around as the Liberandos' 82. *Edna Elizabeth* had stood on her nose, and when they lowered her with a bump a shell in a nose gun fired, narrowly missing Sam Nero; Scott Royce repaired her with a nose wheel from a wreck, but it collapsed after a couple of missions, so he renumbered the crumpled nose 15⅞ and she went to be scrapped. *Draggin Lady* was landed wheels-up in the desert by Lt. John Wilcox, *Black Mariah* was shot down over Naples Harbor with John Payne. *Mona the Lame Duck* was abandoned over Lydda airport, and *Babe the Big Blue Ox* went down over Naples. *Malicious* was ditched in the Mediterranean, and *Hellsapoppin* crashed on landing, after wiping out a Palestinian police blockhouse and breaking herself into many usable spare parts, such as the nose wheel for *Edna Elizabeth. Wash's Tub* became the Liberandos' number 63 and returned to the States with the Pyramiders' plane *The Squaw.* And *Jap Trap* had been landed wheels-up in the desert after Ploesti in June 1942.

Acknowledgments

I set out to write a book about the Liberator which would be an acceptable history of the type, but more a kind of diary and photo album for those who were associated with it.

To accomplish this I had to locate the official records, then locate those who made them. In doing this I was cheerfully and patiently assisted at every turn by people who went far out of their way to provide the material I needed. Miss Bettie Sprigg of the Magazine and Book Branch in the Pentagon has tirelessly processed request after request for most of the pictures in this book, most of which were blandly submitted as "final." Mrs. Virginia Fincik of the Aeronautical Chart and Information Center always pointed me in the right direction, and when I failed to locate a particular photo of a particular plane among the thousands of file prints always seemed uncannily able to put her finger right on what I needed.

At the Air Force Museum in Ohio, home of the *Strawberry Bitch,* my old friend Royal Frey welcomed me warmly, as always, and arranged a visit with the lady for me. Charles G. Worman, his historian and assistant, escorted me through her ovenlike fuselage after the museum's restoration chief, Charlie Gebhardt, broke in. Both Royal Frey and Chuck Worman have continued to help as the project progressed.

Al Blue, a true expert on the Liberator, has helped me over many stumbling blocks, particularly concerning B-24 production; I shall not forget his impeccable files on the B-24, his good humor, or his hospitality.

When historians are mentioned, other names come to mind. Ken Crothers of the 11th Bomb Group Association led me through the voluminous collection in the group's archives; when my time in the area was up he researched many copies of *Brief,* the Seventh Air Force magazine, on my behalf, swallowing his pride and including material on the 30th and 494th Groups as well. Roger Freeman in England gave me an insight into Eighth Air Force history which I doubt I could have gained elsewhere, and his friendship has always been something I value highly. His book, *The Mighty Eighth,* is without equal and was my reference in Eighth matters. Merlon Bailey, historian for the 464th Bomb Group's association, delved deep into his files to complete the story of Black Nan and one of the most famous photos of the war, and Brian Garfield graciously let me lean on his unparalleled research into the war in the miserable Aleutians.

David R. Davis cordially discussed his trials and tribulations, Dave Ecoff and Lucky Stevens shed new light on the operations of the 20th Combat Mapping Squadron and their F-7s, Cliff Stocking and Leo Stoutsenberger shared the stories behind several of the most dramatic combat photos of World War II.

Scott Royce, patiently and with much humor, detailed the early days of Halpro, and in so doing produced a remarkable record of an almost forgotten unit. While only a small portion of the hours of tape could be used here, the background was invaluable to me.

Bill cameron, one of the few survivors of the original 67th Bomb Squadron of the Eight Balls, spent many valuable hours digging through his memories for me. The large collection of personal letters, orders, pictures, and notes which he so generously supplied enabled me to understand something of the feeling of those days, and I have tried to impart it here.

Barney Hutain, now an Eastern Air Lines pilot with one Havana mission to his credit, again came to my aid with details and photos of the 446th Bomb Group, as did Steve Gajan. Bob Carlin, artist and raconteur, helped me out once more on the Fifteenth Air Force and the 456th Bomb Group . . . as always with many laughs along the way. Another old ally, Barry Gilkes, sent along an enviable collection of photographs at the mere mention of the word "Liberator." Whit Wright of the Buccaneers sent letter after letter, gradually imparting an awareness of the Navy's role with Liberators to me, as well as voluntarily doing a lot of my work regarding the other Pacific squadrons. Bill Robertie became so enthused with the project that he set about writing a history of his own group, the 44th, but all the while I've had first call on his growing stack of material.

Lieutenant Don Bishop, who called in here on R&R from another war, has devoted much spare time to locating details I could not otherwise have obtained. His ability to track down elusive information is unquestionable, and this book has benefited from it.

Veterans from nearly every bomb group of the Army Air Forces contributed to this book, and the thousands of pages of letters and hundreds of photos have all added something to the story. I would like to add that this material was sent without reservation, the donors trusting completely in my judgment. I have tried to follow their own words as closely as possible where quotations were not used, but any errors or distortions must be my responsibility. I found an alphabetical listing of names and units the best way to say thank you to all of them, and that list follows; it has been a memorable experience and a very great pleasure to work with these generous people.

I also wish to record my gratitude to Edward Hine at the Imperial War Museum, himself a Liberator man from the Royal Air Force's 356 Squadron, Owen Clark of the San Diego Aero Space Museum, W. R. Lancaster of the Australian War Memorial, the RAAF Directorate of Public Relations, Colonel Al Lynn of CINCPAC who has helped with enthusiasm on projects ranging from the Douglas Skyraider to Colonel Isaac Haviland's lost Liberator, Larry Reineke who told me so much about the Eleventh Air Force, Ben Donahue who led me to the story of Black Nan, still indelible in his memory, Gerald Maddux, George Gosney, d'E. C. Darby, Dick Bueschel, Adrian O. Van Wyen and Clarke Van Fleet of the Navy's Aviation History Unit, H. R. Kennedy of Convair, and Paul Vercammen of *Air Combat,* Kenn Rust of *Aero Album,* and Colonel John Frisbee of *Air Force/Space Digest.*

John Preston not only painted the outstanding illustrations here, but also did more of the research into them than I wish to admit. John is an old and good friend who has helped me in many ways over the years . . . in New York I have used his home as a base several times, and my bizarre hours never seemed to bother John or his family. Although I do note he has moved to Dallas. Naturally John wishes to thank his group of contributors . . . Al Blue, Ernie McDowell, Jay Dial, and Dick Hill, and I add my gratitude to those people.

My editor, Harold Kuebler, has an affection for the Liberator which may well have something to do with this book's existence. After teaching him how to assemble a B-24, then for good measure making him fly in it, the Air Force in its wisdom sent him to a P-47 unit . . . but the seed had been sown.

Finally, I must resort to that haggard cliché about people without whose help this book would not have been possible. Bob McGuire and Tom Shumaker, founders of the San Diego based Liberator Club, put their membership and other files completely at my disposal, as well as letting me make liberal use of their magazine, the *Briefing,* in my quest for specific material. Bob McGuire and I launched this project on a quantity of tequila, and it is my fond hope we'll christen it that way soon. And Len Morgan, who will know why his name is here.

My wife Sandra knows relatively little about the Liberator. She knows

Strawberry Bitch, that the B-24 had four engines, and other isolated facts. I would not blame her if she thought her main contribution to the work was emptying ashtrays, retyping drafts, stopping Casper and Tara, our Maltese, barking, or making tea and bolstering my confidence. Her contribution has in fact included all those things, but there has been much, much more, not the least of which was her faith that this was worth doing, and that I could do it well.

Steve Birdsall, Sydney, Australia

Bibliography

Arnold, Henry H. *Global Mission,* New York, Harper & Brothers, 1949

Birdsall, Steve, *The B-24 Liberator,* New York, Arco, 1968

Blue, Allan G., *The Fortunes of War,* Fallbrook, Aero Publishers, 1967

Brereton, Lewis H., *The Brereton Diaries,* New York, William Morrow, 1946

Camerer, David M., *The Damned Wear Wings,* New York, Doubleday, 1958

Craven, W. F., and Cate, J. L., *The Army Air Forces in World War II,* Vol I–VII, Chicago, University of Chicago Press, 1948

Dugan, James, and Stewart, Carroll, *Ploesti,* London, Jonathan Cape, 1963

Dmitri, Ivan, *Flight to Everywhere,* New York, Whittlesey House, 1944

Fain, James E., *The Flying Circus,* New York, Commanday-Roth, 1946

Freeman, Roger A., *The Mighty Eighth,* New York, Doubleday, 1970

Gann, Ernest K., *Fate Is the Hunter,* London, Hodder & Stoughton, 1961

Garfield, Brian, *The Thousand Mile War,* New York, Doubleday, 1969

Gordon, Arthur, *Target: Germany,* London, His Majesty's Stationery Office, 1944

Green, William, *Famous Bombers of the Second World War,* London, Macdonald, 1959

Healy, Allan, *The 467th Bombardment Group,* Brattleboro, E. L. Hildreth, 1947

Howard, Clive, and Whitley, Joe, *One Damned Island After Another,* Chapel Hill, University of North Carolina Press, 1946

MacCloskey, Monro, *Secret Air Missions,* New York, Richards Rosen Press, 1966

Mander, Alexander J., *The Story of the Fifth Bombardment Group,* Raleigh, Hillsborough House, 1946

Markham, Floyd A., *The Black Pirates,* Sydney, John Sands, 1944

Maurer, Maurer, *Air Force Combat Units of World War II,* New York, Franklin Watts, 1963

————, *Combat Squadrons of the Air Forces World War II,* Washington, U. S. Government Printing Office, 1969

McClendon, Dennis E., *Lady Be Good,* New York, John Day, 1962

Miller, Norman M., *I Took the Skyroad,* New York, Dodd, Mead, 1945

Moyes, Philip R., *Bomber Squadrons of the RAF and Their Aircraft*, London, Macdonald, 1964

Odgers, George, *Air War Against Japan*, Canberra, Australian War Memorial, 1957

Redding, John M., and Leyshon, Harold I., *Skyways to Berlin*, New York, Bobbs-Merrill, 1943

Richards, Denis, and Saunders, Hilary St. George, *Royal Air Force 1939–1945*, Vols I–III, Her Majesty's Stationery Office, 1953

Wolff, Leon, *Low Level Mission*, New York, Doubleday, 1957

Author's Note: This bibliography is brief, and represents only a portion of the material used as a foundation for this book. There are a score more unofficial histories of Liberator groups and squadrons which served with the Army Air Forces, the best collection of these being at the New York Public Library. Hundreds of magazine pieces about the Liberator have appeared, and it would be impossible to list them all here. One which should be noted however is *Ringmasters*, by Allan G. Blue, a history of the 491st Bomb Group which appeared in the American Aviation Historical Society's *Journal*, Summer and Fall, 1964. Other documents were found in the collections of Liberator veterans and the several government repositories throughout the United States, England and Australia.

Contributing Liberator Veterans

Sam E. Asquith, 454th Bomb Group, Fifteenth Air Force
Merlon W. Bailey, 464th Bomb Group, Fifteenth Air Force
Raymond J. Bailey, 178 Squadron, Royal Air Force
W. Don Baker, 464th Bomb Group, Fifteenth Air Force
Michael H. Bartow, 30th Bomb Group, Seventh Air Force
Al Bibee, VMD-154, United States Marine Corps
F. M. Blackwell, Jr., 467th Bomb Group, Eighth Air Force
Dayt Blanchard, 43rd Bomb Group, Fifth Air Force
Merle L. Bolen, 98th Bomb Group, Ninth Air Force
Norman J. Borchman, VPB-116, United States Navy
Austin Boyle, 446th Bomb Group, Eighth Air Force
Samuel S. Britt, Jr., 307th Bomb Group, Thirteenth Air Force
William P. Brown, 448th Bomb Group, Eighth Air Force
Walter L. Bruesch, 484th Bomb Group, Fifteenth Air Force
William R. Cameron, 44th Bomb Group, Eighth Air Force
Robert E. Carlin, 456th Bomb Group, Fifteenth Air Force
Paul S. Cash, 454th Bomb Group, Fifteenth Air Force
Richard T. Clark, 449th Bomb Group, Fifteenth Air Force
Jim Clover, 11th & 30th Bomb Groups, Seventh Air Force
Ken Crothers, 11th Bomb Group, Seventh Air Force
Ben Donahue, 465th Bomb Group, Fifteenth Air Force
David W. Ecoff, 20th Combat Mapping Squadron, Fifth Air Force
Charlie Ehemann, VB-104, United States Navy
David W. Ferguson, Consairway
Pat Fleck, 55th Recon Squadron, (LRW), Twentieth Air Force
Alfred E. Flocke, 11th Bomb Group, Seventh Air Force
Don Forke, 307th Bomb Group, Thirteenth Air Force
Al Fowler, 10 Squadron, Royal Canadian Air Force

A. V. Freeman, Jr., 98th Bomb Group, Ninth Air Force
Stephen A. Gajan, 446th Bomb Group, Eighth Air Force
Vern Goettler, 90th Bomb Group, Fifth Air Force
Corwin C. Grimes, 454th Bomb Group, Fifteenth Air Force
Ken C. Gutheil, 5th Bomb Group, Thirteenth Air Force
William R. Hall, 98th Bomb Group, Ninth Air Force
Bernard L. Hutain, 446th Bomb Group, Eighth Air Force
C. G. Jones, 23 Squadron, Royal Australian Air Force
William B. Keese, 484th Bomb Group, Fifteenth Air Force
Sandy Harbin, Second Air Force
Benjamin Kislin, 446th Bomb Group, Eighth Air Force
John T. Hayward, VB-106, United States Navy
George Kubiskie, 90th Bomb Group, Fifth Air Force
Adolph P. Leirer, 22nd Bomb Group, Fifth Air Force
Max J. Leon, India-China Wing, Air Transport Command
Leonard L. Little, 485th Bomb Group, Fifteenth Air Force
Ray Lucas, 484th Bomb Group, Fifteenth Air Force
Ben Marshall, 458th Bomb Group, Eighth Air Force
Gabriel Martin, Jr., 30th Bomb Group, Seventh Air Force
Robert E. McGuire, VD-3, United States Navy
Carl McKinnon, 459th Bomb Group, Fifteenth Air Force
Justin Miller, VPB-101, United States Navy
LeRoy B. Morgan, 98th Bomb Group, Ninth Air Force
Boyd O'Donnell, Consairway
Roy Parker, 22nd Bomb Group, Fifth Air Force
Lawrence Reineke, 28th Composite Group, Eleventh Air Force
Fred J. Replenski, 307th Bomb Group, Thirteenth Air Force
William G. Robertie, 44th Bomb Group, Eighth Air Force
James H. Rothrock, Air Corps Ferrying Command, 480th Antisumbarine Group
Scott Royce, Halpro
Thomas C. Schiebel, 7th Bomb Group, Tenth Air Force
Max Schuette, 450th Bomb Group, Fifteenth Air Force
Ken C. Scroggins, 98th Bomb Group, Fifteenth Air Force
Harry E. Sears, VB-104, United States Navy
Benjamin M. Sheldon, 494th Bomb Group, Seventh Air Force
David Sieber, 24 Squadron, RAAF
Tom Shumaker, Halpro
Irving Smirnoff, 450th Bomb Group, Fifteenth Air Force
Stan Staples, 461st Bomb Group, Fifteenth Air Force
E. P. Stevens, 43rd Bomb Group, 6th Photo Group, 22nd Bomb Group, Fifth Air
    Force
Paul F. Stevens, VPB-104, United States Navy
Cliff Stocking, 493rd Bomb Group, Eighth Air Force
William E. Stone, 451st Bomb Group, Fifteenth Air Force

Leo Stoutsenberger, 451st Bomb Group, Fifteenth Air Force
Robert J. Stroh, VD-3, United States Navy
Robert L. Strong, 11th Bomb Group, Seventh Air Force
Charles B. Taylor, 380th Bomb Group, Fifth Air Force
Donald B. Trudeau, 43rd Bomb Group, Fifth Air Force
Jerre Vliet, 466th Bomb Group, Eighth Air Force
John White, 308th Bomb Group, Fourteenth Air Force
Malcolm E. Wiley, 30th Bomb Group, Seventh Air Force
Stan Winchester, 30th & 11th Bomb Groups, Seventh Air Force
Gomer A. Wolf, 98th Bomb Group, Ninth Air Force
Whitney Wright, VB-104, VPB-104, United States Navy
Robert T. Young, 446th Bomb Group, Eighth Air Force
William J. Zoerb, 459th Bomb Group, Fifteenth Air Force

Index

Jan 28, 74

John Glenn

Around the World in 90 Minutes

by Paul Westman

Illustrated by Cliff Moen

DILLON PRESS, INC. MINNEAPOLIS, MINNESOTA

To Jim Westman

Library of Congress Cataloging in Publication Data

Westman, Paul.
  John Glenn: around the world in 90 minutes.

  (Taking Part; 4)
  SUMMARY: A biography of the first American to orbit the earth who
is now a United States Senator from his native Ohio.
  1. Glenn, John Herschel, 1921- —Juvenile literature.
  2. Astronauts—United States—Biography—Juvenile literature.
  [1. Glenn, John Herschel, 1921- 2. Astronauts. 3. Legislators] I. Series.
  TL789.85.G6W47   629.45'092'4 [B] [92]   79-19515

  ISBN 0-87518-186-4

Dillon Press, Inc., 500 South Third Street
Minneapolis, Minnesota 55415

Printed in the United States of America

JOHN GLENN

John Glenn has come a long way since his
boyhood days in New Concord, Ohio. He was
hailed as a war hero for his daring actions as a
marine fighter pilot in Korea. As an astronaut
he became the first American to orbit the earth.
Later he was elected to the U.S. Senate from Ohio.
In all these ways he has served his country well.

A century ago Jules Verne wrote an exciting
adventure story called *Around the World in 80
Days.* On *Friendship 7* John Glenn circled the
earth in little more than 90 minutes. The boy who
gazed at the sky is a man who has explored the
heavens.

"Wheee! Johnny called into the wind. He leaned out of the open car window. In his outstretched hand was a toy airplane. The summer air rushed by, twirling the plane's propeller.

In the front seat Mr. and Mrs. Glenn smiled. They knew how much Johnny liked airplanes and flying. Often he zoomed around the back yard, acting like a pilot. At other times he lay on his back in the cool grass and stared at the sky. Then he would pretend he was a bird in flight. From high above the earth, he would look down at the trees and fields and tiny houses.

John Herschel Glenn, Jr., was born on July 18, 1921, in Cambridge, Ohio. His father, John Herschel Glenn, Sr., was a conductor on the railroad.

When Johnny was two, his family moved to New

Concord. New Concord was a little town eight miles from Cambridge. Mr. Glenn quit his railroad job and opened a plumbing shop there. In New Concord the Glenns lived on Bloomfield Road in a pretty house with a big yard.

The Glenns were a religious family. Every Sunday they went to church. They were also very loyal to their country. Such holidays as Memorial Day and the Fourth of July were important times for them.

Mr. Glenn had been a soldier in World War I. He had fought in the trenches in France. In one battle he was badly injured and lost part of his hearing.

Johnny came from a long line of pioneers. Often Mrs. Glenn would tell him tales about one of his ancestors named Colonel Sproat. Colonel Sproat had served in the American Revolution under General George Washington. He had settled in Ohio when it was still a wilderness. The Indians had named him "Buckeye." Some people said that Ohio was called the Buckeye state because of him.

Johnny had red hair, a quick grin, and plenty of freckles. He made friends easily. One of his friends was a little girl named Annie Castor. Like Johnny, she lived on Bloomfield Road.

In the summer Johnny played football and base-ball in the neighborhood. When he and his friends got hot, they went for a swim in Crooked Creek. Johnny cleaned cars to make money.

In the winter he went to school. The town grade
school was made of brick and had big windows. A
large bell hung in the belfry. In the yard tall shade
trees grew. Johnny liked it there.

One winter scarlet fever hit New Concord. Many
people became ill. Johnny had to stay in the house

for several weeks to keep from getting sick. To pass the time, he began building model airplanes out of balsa wood and glue. He modeled them after planes he had seen in books. Soon Johnny had so many models that they filled his room. Later he took them outside to fly them in his yard.

Johnny wanted to learn more about real airplanes, too. Columbus was one of Ohio's largest cities. When the Glenns visited Columbus, they stopped at the airport. There Johnny watched planes take off and land. He was amazed at how big the planes were.

Johnny wanted to be a Boy Scout. But there was no scout troop in New Concord. That didn't stop Johnny. He and his friends formed a group of their own. They called themselves the Ohio Rangers. The Rangers did many things together. Every summer they went camping, hunted rabbits, and fished in Crooked Creek. For Johnny being a Ranger was almost as much fun as being a Boy Scout.

Most people in New Concord were Republicans. "You could put all the Democrats in New Concord in our living room," Mr. Glenn would joke, "and still have room to spare." Mr. and Mrs. Glenn were Democrats.

Johnny liked politics, too. Once his class was assigned a paper. Most of the boys wrote about subjects like sports. But Johnny did his paper on the U.S. Senate.

In high school Johnny took part in many things. He won letters in football, basketball, and tennis. He wrote for the school paper, played in the band, and sang in the choir. His classmates thought so highly of him that they chose him as class president.

After high school Johnny entered Muskingum College. Muskingum was right in town. That meant he did not have to move away from home. In college Johnny studied chemistry and played football. Annie Castor was a student there, too. She and Johnny were often together.

While in college Johnny learned how to fly. He took lessons in a government training program. The government wanted to make sure that many men knew how to fly. Then, if war came, the country would have pilots to fight in it.

At first Mr. and Mrs. Glenn did not want Johnny to fly. They knew that flying could be dangerous. But at last they said it was all right. Johnny worked hard at becoming a pilot. He was the first in his group to solo, or fly alone. His grades in the course were very high.

In 1941 the Japanese attacked Pearl Harbor. This forced the United States to go to war. Since Johnny wanted to fight for his country, he joined the navy as an airman. Later he transferred to the marines.

Johnny was sent to three states—Iowa, Kansas, and Texas—for flight training. In training he learned how to fly war planes. Johnny worked harder than most of the flyers. He wanted to be more than just a good pilot. He wanted to be the best.

In 1943 John Glenn became a marine airman with the rank of lieutenant. As soon as his training was over, he flew back to New Concord to get married. For a long time he had known that the woman would be Annie Castor. John and Annie didn't have much time to spend together. Soon John had to leave to fight in the war.

The marines sent Glenn to the Marshall Islands in the Pacific. There he flew an F-4U Corsair. The Corsair was a long, black, propeller-driven plane. It had room for just one pilot. And it was one of the fastest planes around.

The Marshalls were made up of many small islands. At this time most were held by the Japanese. The marines had to take back the islands one by one.

Flying in the Marshalls was dangerous. Often Glenn had to fly at treetop level. Sometimes he

bombed Japanese outposts. At other times he swooped down out of the sky and fired his machine gun. The Japanese fired back at the American planes. Many were hit and crashed into the sea.

The weather in the Marshalls changed without warning. All of a sudden, a storm would move in. Rain and wind lashed at the huts and trees. In such weather pilots could lose their way.

John Glenn flew 59 missions in the Marshalls. This was more than any other pilot in his squadron.

Glenn's most important mission was an attack on Jabor Town. Jabor Town was the center of Japanese strength in the Marshalls. It had been bombed many times. But the Japanese always came back.

Glenn was made a leader of the mission. He and his men roared down out of the clouds. Lower and lower they flew. Glenn saw palm leaves fluttering in the wind and the curve of the island beach.

The bombs fell. With a loud whoosh, Jabor Town burst into flame. It burned long into the night. The Japanese stronghold had been destroyed. Glenn won a medal for this mission. In all, he won two Distinguished Flying Crosses and ten Air Medals during World War II.

In 1949 John Glenn returned to the United States. He became a flying teacher at a marine base in Texas. At this base he saw jets being widely used. Glenn thought that jets were the planes of the future. During vacations he learned how to fly them.

Just a year after Glenn had come home, the Korean War broke out. He and many other pilots were sent to fight in the war. Glenn was a major now.

He was glad he had learned to fly jets. In Korea there were none of the older planes that he had flown in World War II.

Major Glenn flew 90 missions in Korea. At first he flew Panther jets. His plane was hit many times and came close to crashing. Once Glenn returned to his base with 203 holes in his plane.

One day Glenn was on a mission. From the ground a communist gunner spotted him. The gun was hidden in some brush at the bottom of a long valley. Glenn decided to attack it.

Glenn guided his jet in just above the treetops. He flew straight at the gunner. Suddenly his plane was hit by a second gunner hidden in some trees across the valley.

Glenn was over a rice paddy now. The shock from the shell caused the nose of his plane to drop. Quickly Glenn jerked back on the control stick. The jet screamed over the paddy at 460 miles per hour, just above the rice shoots. It was the closest John Glenn had ever come to crashing in his life.

Next Glenn was transferred to a Sabre jet squad-

ron based near the Yalu River. Here his job was to shoot down enemy jets.

Once a pilot in Glenn's squadron was struck by an enemy shell. Before his plane crashed, the pilot jumped to safety. Major Glenn circled the spot where the man landed. He tried to keep enemy troops from seizing the pilot. But it was no use. At last Glenn climbed straight into the air. Then he ran out of fuel. He glided all the way back to his base, more than 100 miles away.

Another time Glenn was flying high above the Yalu River. Suddenly he saw an enemy jet far below him. He went after it but lost sight of the jet in the clouds.

Then he spotted a second jet. At once he swooped down on it and opened fire. A stream of black smoke shot out from the rear of the enemy jet.

Glenn followed the plane down. Just above the ground, he pulled up sharply. His Sabre jet screamed skyward. Looking back, Glenn saw the other plane explode in a sheet of flame.

A week later Glenn was leading a flight of four

Sabre jets. They were flying over a place called Imsan-dong. Suddenly he spotted four enemy planes. Just as Glenn's group attacked, twelve more enemy planes appeared. Before long four American jets joined the battle in the sky. Twenty-four twisting, diving jets fought a life and death struggle. Then an American plane was hit. Glenn left the fight to protect the plane as it flew to safety.

The two planes moved slowly through the air. Six enemy pilots spotted them. Seven times the enemy planes attacked. Seven times Glenn drove them off. His bullets caught one plane by surprise. Trailing smoke, it smashed into a green Korean hillside.

In all, Glenn shot down three planes in nine days. He needed only two more to become an ace. But the war ended before he made it.

After the war John Glenn became a test pilot. He flew new planes and performed tests to see that they worked properly. A test pilot's job was both important and dangerous. Glenn had several close calls. Once a large part of his wingtip broke off. Instead of bailing out, he remained calm. He ran tests to see how well the plane performed with a broken wing. A test pilot had to stay cool under pressure.

While working as a test pilot, Glenn became interested in space. He read everything he could on the subject. He also learned about American space programs.

Glenn worked with many new planes such as the Crusader jet. The Crusader was a very advanced plane. It was sleek, fast, and tough. Every time it had passed with flying colors.

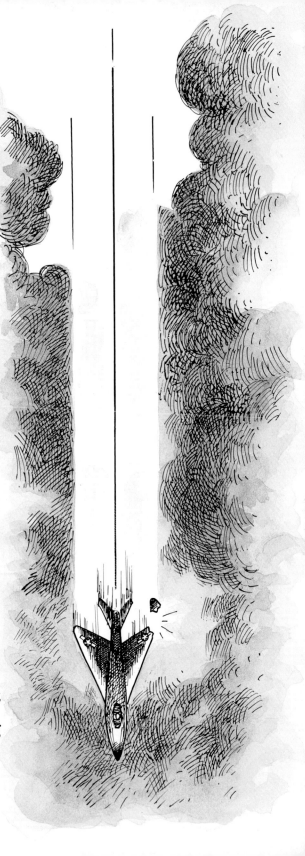

One major test remained. The Crusader had not been flown at top speed over a long distance. Such a test was needed before the plane could gain final approval. A pilot was needed to fly the plane from coast to coast. And the pilot chosen was John Glenn.

Glenn took off from California on July 16, 1957. He flew at a speed of 726 miles per hour. When he reached Ohio, he passed over his hometown of New Concord. He was flying so fast that he created a sonic boom. A sonic boom is a noise as loud as a thunderclap. It happens when a jet flies faster than the speed of sound. Townspeople even saw the white ribbon of smoke Glenn left across the sky.

Less than three and one-half hours after takeoff, Glenn landed in New York. He had set a new coast-to-coast speed record. In fact, he had traveled faster than a bullet. New Concord held parades, banquets, and ceremonies to honor its hometown hero.

In 1958 the National Aeronautics and Space Administration (NASA) set up a program called Project Mercury. The purpose of Project Mercury was to send Americans into space. This was some-

thing that had never been done before.

Project Mercury was a huge program. Thousands of people worked for it, and the whole nation

23

united behind it. Hundreds of pilots wanted to become astronauts. But NASA needed only seven.

John Glenn wanted to be an astronaut, too. He met most of NASA's tough standards. He had a fine record, and he was a leading test pilot. Only two things worried him. He did not have a college degree. And, at 37, he was almost too old to be an astronaut. Still, he was hopeful.

Slowly NASA sifted through long lists of names. Records were studied. More and more names were crossed off. At last only 32 names were left. These 32 men were screened even further. On April 9, 1959, the names of the seven winners were announced. Among them was Colonel John H. Glenn, Jr.

Soon the astronauts began their training. They flew jets, did class work, and trained outdoors. Among the subjects they studied were space flight, stars, and the weather. The astronauts learned how to survive on the ocean and in the desert. They also helped design the Mercury capsule that they would fly in space.

John Glenn (third from left) was one of the first group of seven U.S. astronauts.

At one time Glenn had wanted to be the best pilot in the marines. Now he wanted to be the best astronaut in Project Mercury. Every day he worked hard on his own. He exercised and pored over books, charts, and maps. And he spent many more hours than required in flight practice.

Each of the astronauts hoped to be the first American in space. Glenn, too, wanted to have this honor. But it was not to be. Alan Shepard was picked instead. Glenn was named as backup. If something happened to Shepard, Glenn would make the flight in his place.

In May 1961, Alan Shepard became the first American in space. He did not circle the earth. His capsule rose briefly into space and dropped back again. A few months later, NASA announced its third manned Mercury flight. John Glenn would pilot it. He would be the first American to orbit, or circle, the earth. In fact, his flight would take him three times around the world.

Glenn's tiny space capsule would be mounted on top of a huge Atlas rocket. Before the capsule went into orbit, the rocket would drop away. Then Glenn would be on his own in the capsule.

Each Mercury astronaut named his own capsule. John Glenn wanted his family to choose the name. His two teenage children, John and Carolyn, spent a lot of time finding out about names. At last they

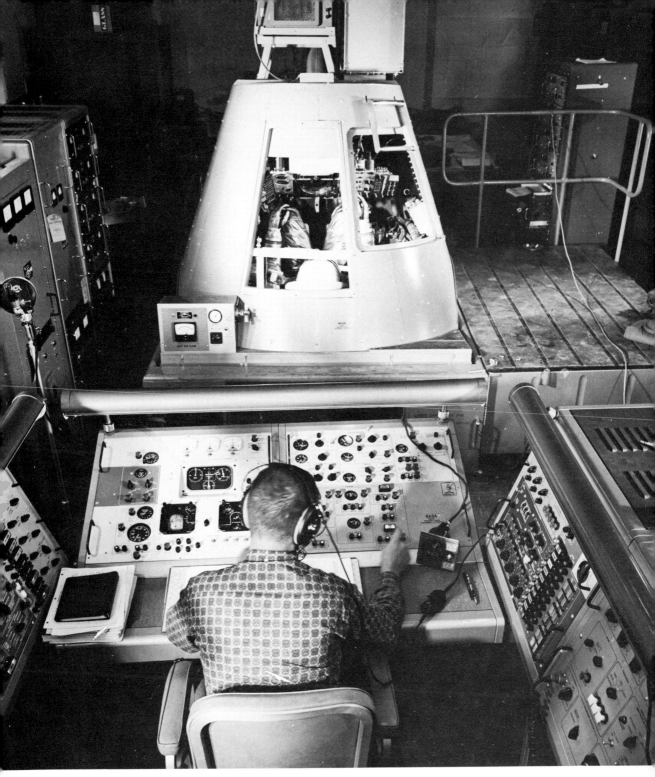

Glenn trained long and hard to prepare for his space flight.

narrowed down the list to a few choices. Then the Glenn family met together to make a final decision.

The name they chose was *Friendship 7*. "Friendship" was what the Glenns wanted the United States to stand for. In space there are no borders between nations. *Friendship 7* would fly over many nations of the world. And to all of them it would carry a message of peace and goodwill. The "7" stood for the seven astronauts.

Americans waited eagerly for the day of the launch. But they were disappointed. Something went wrong, and the launch was called off. A new date was set. Again something went wrong. After that, bad weather set in. In all, the launch was delayed ten times. Once Glenn had to wait five hours in the rocket before a flight was called off.

Finally, on February 20, 1962, everything was ready. Glenn rose at two o'clock in the morning. He ate a big breakfast of scrambled eggs, steak, toast, and juice.

Bright lights lit up the launch pad as an elevator lifted Glenn to the top of the rocket. The astronaut

On the day of the launch, Glenn squeezed through the small hatch of Friendship 7.

squeezed into his tiny capsule. The hatch was bolted shut behind him. Alone, high atop the rocket, Glenn waited.

The sun rose. A brisk wind scattered the clouds and caused the huge rocket to sway gently. Through

The rocket's loud roar shattered the morning stillness.

the window Glenn could see the Atlantic Ocean.

Thousands of people crowded the nearby beaches. Millions more tuned in on radio and TV. When the final countdown began, a hush fell over the entire nation.

Suddenly a loud roar shattered the morning stillness. Billows of smoke and flame shot out of the rocket. Slowly it began to rise. Faster and faster it climbed. Before long the rocket was nothing more than a dot of fire against the sky. Then it was gone.

Soon Glenn was 100 miles above the earth. The rocket dropped away, leaving him alone in *Friendship 7*. He looked out the window. From space the view was stunning. Glenn could see for hundreds of miles. He saw the sun shining on white clouds far below. Here and there among the clouds he saw patches of blue ocean. The state of Florida was laid out like a drawing on a map.

Within minutes Glenn was over Africa. The Atlas Mountains came into view first, and then the Sahara Desert. Huge dust storms were blowing across the desert. Brush fires burned along its edge. Clouds of

In space Glenn watched a plastic tube of food float in front of him.

smoke from the fires showed clearly through the window.

In space Glenn did not weigh anything. He was weightless because in space there is no gravity. He would remain that way for five hours. Doctors had wondered how this would affect him. Glenn found that he enjoyed being weightless. And it was fun to watch an object float in the air without anything to hold it up.

The Indian Ocean passed below. Glenn was now in darkness, for it was nighttime in this part of the world. The moon shone brightly on clouds over the ocean. By watching the clouds, Glenn could judge his flight path.

Bright stars filled the clear sky. They looked as they would on a clear night in the desert. Glenn had a map of the stars outside his window. Looking at their place in the sky helped guide him on his course.

Over Australia Glenn spotted some large patches of light. These were towns along the coast. The people in the towns had turned on their lights for him. Some had even spread white sheets outside their windows to reflect the light upward.

Now *Friendship 7* passed into daylight again. Glenn glanced out the window. He was startled by what he saw. Thousands of specks of light were all around him, floating past like a shower of fireflies.

At first Glenn thought they might be stars.

Perhaps his ship had somehow rolled over. Then he
could be staring upward into the sky. He checked to
see if this was the case. It was not. His capsule was

34

still right side up. As daylight grew brighter, the strange lights vanished.

Two more times Glenn spotted the strange lights. Each time he was coming out of darkness into daylight. Once he turned his capsule around to get a better look at them. The strange sight was never explained. Scientists named it the Glenn effect.

42

From space Glenn could see the state of Florida laid out like a map.

After a full orbit *Friendship 7* passed over Florida again. From the window Glenn could see all the way from the Florida coast to the Mississippi River. He could see north to the Carolinas and south to Cuba. Once more he watched the deep blue Atlantic come into view.

John Glenn circled the earth in a little more than 1½ hours. It was a feat that not even the famous writer Jules Verne had dreamed of 100 years ago. Verne wrote a book about a record-breaking trip called *Around the World in 80 Days.* Today, 90 minutes is more like it!

In orbit Glenn performed many tests. He took pictures, did exercises, and ate food from plastic tubes. From such tests NASA learned much that would be useful to future astronauts.

At last it was time to return to earth. Glenn made one final pass over the United States. He had traveled around the world three times in five hours. Now he fired the rockets that pointed *Friendship 7* back toward home.

On the ground NASA officials were worried

about Glenn's safety. Earlier, in the mission control center, a light had begun to flash. The light showed that the capsule's heat shield had come loose. If this were true, Glenn could be in grave danger when *Friendship 7* returned to earth.

38

The capsule began its downward flight. As it went faster and faster, its shield grew very hot. This happened because of the friction between the capsule and the air. If the heat shield came off now, John Glenn would be burned alive.

Glenn looked out the window. All he could see was a bright orange glow. This came from the great heat around the capsule. He was riding inside a fireball as hot as the surface of the sun.

Luckily, the heat shield remained in place. Near the ocean the capsule's parachute unrolled like a long ribbon. Then it burst open in bright orange and white folds. Slowly the capsule dropped toward the sea.

At last *Friendship 7* landed in the ocean with a loud splash. A huge cloud of steam rose into the air. The capsule sank into the green sea water. Then it bobbed to the surface, where it floated on the waves. The air inside the capsule was very hot. Still, Glenn had to stay there until a ship arrived.

Finally one did. The capsule was hoisted out of the water and onto the deck. There astronaut Glenn

Friendship 7 *bobbed in the ocean until a ship came to hoist it out of the water.*

stepped out of the hot capsule into a nice cool breeze.

After his flight John Glenn became a hero. He spoke before Congress. He visited President Kennedy at the White House. Huge parades were held in his honor.

In New York City 4 million people turned out to

President Kennedy gave John Glenn the NASA Distinguished Service Award.

see him. They stood on rooftops, leaned from windows, and jammed the streets. Tons of confetti rained down from tall buildings. Bands played, bells rang, and people cheered.

Glenn's hometown of New Concord also held a parade. Again thousands of people lined the streets. Many of the people were old friends and neighbors. John Glenn waved and smiled. Their joyful welcome made him very happy. He was even more pleased when the town named its new school John Glenn High School.

In 1964 Glenn left NASA. He was proud of the role he had played in the space program. But he was growing older. He wanted to make way for younger people.

Glenn had always enjoyed politics. But he knew that many people did not. The public liked space heroes, football players, and movie stars. Yet often they would not even bother to vote for their mayor, governor, or U.S. representative. This made Glenn sad. He believed that all citizens should use their right to vote.

John Glenn went back to Ohio to campaign for a seat in the U.S. Senate.

Glenn knew that he was popular. People admired him and looked up to him. Perhaps he could help change such thoughtless ways. He felt it was his duty to try.

Glenn decided to run for the office of U.S. senator from Ohio. But his campaign had barely started when he was injured in a fall. The injury forced him to withdraw from the race.

Later that year Glenn joined the Royal Crown Cola Company. He became vice-president of the company. In 1968 he hosted a number of TV shows. The shows told the stories of great explorers in history. Glenn also remained active in politics. He made speeches and went to dinners. He campaigned for Robert Kennedy when Kennedy ran for president.

In 1970 Glenn ran for the Senate again. He ran against a millionaire lawyer who spent five times as much money as Glenn did. Glenn lost the election. But he did not give up. Four years later he made a third try. This time he won. In fact, he won by one of the largest margins in Ohio history.

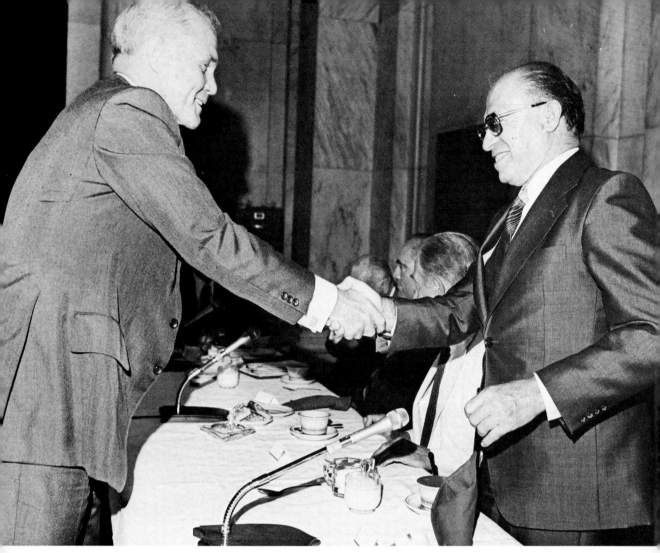

As a senator Glenn worked to halt the spread of nuclear weapons.

As a senator, Glenn had many important tasks. He worked for election and tax reform. He tried to help consumers and people without jobs. He sponsored laws to improve health care and schools. And he worked to halt the spread of nuclear weapons.

46

Soon Glenn was known as one of the best senators in Congress. People began urging him to run for president. In 1976 Jimmy Carter thought of choosing him for vice-president. Glenn was pleased, but he kept right on working.

"I just want to be the best senator Ohio ever had," he said.

Senator, astronaut, war hero—John Glenn has come a long way since his boyhood days in New Concord, Ohio. The boy who gazed at the sky is a man who has explored the heavens. People who meet this famous man today are surprised at how open and friendly he is. John Glenn has not changed so much as grown. His quick grin is still the same.

The Author

Paul Westman is a regular contributor to *Current Biography* and
has written many books for young people, including several for the
Taking Part series. Of the series, Westman says, "Young readers
will learn something about well-known contemporary men and
women in many challenging fields and at the same time begin to
discover some of the joys of reading."

A recent graduate of the University of Minnesota, Westman
lives in Minneapolis.

The Illustrator

Clifford Moen is a self-employed artist who has worked as an
instructor at the Art Instruction Schools in Minneapolis. In 1970
his montage of the life of Abraham Lincoln appeared in *American
History Illustrated.* Moen is a graduate of the Minneapolis School
of Art and has studied art history at the University of Minnesota.

*Photographs reproduced through the courtesy of John Glenn and
the National Aeronautics and Space Administration.*